BASICS MADE EASY

READING REVIEW

Revised 2005 Edition

**Word Meaning
Comprehension
Analyzing Literature
Reference Sources
Maps, Charts, Graphs**

DR. FRANK PINTOZZI
DEVIN PINTOZZI

AMERICAN BOOK COMPANY
P O BOX 2638
WOODSTOCK, GEORGIA 30188-1383
Toll Free: 1 (888) 264-5877   Phone: 770-928-2834   Fax: 770-928-7483
Web site: www.americanbookcompany.com

ACKNOWLEDGEMENTS

Editors: Colleen Pintozzi
             Devin Pintozzi
             Rachel Wall
             Joe Wood

Printed in the United States of America

f0905

TABLE OF CONTENTS

Basics Made Easy: Reading Review

Preface

Basics Made Easy Reading Review is one of several books in the **Basics Made Easy** series. This book will help students who need additional practice to achieve mastery of word meaning, reading comprehension, analysis of literature, graphic aids, dictionary skills, and reference sources. The materials in this book are based on the objectives covered on the *Iowa Test of Basic Skills* (Levels 12, 13, & 14) and the *Stanford 9 Achievement Test* (Level Intermediate 2 through Advanced 2). In addition, **Basics Made Easy Reading Review** teaches the concepts and skills emphasized on end-of-grade tests and on high school exit exams. Each chapter contains concise lessons and frequent practice exercises. Students can begin this book by taking the Diagnostic Test to determine their strengths and areas in which they need to improve their reading. Each chapter ends with an open-ended chapter review followed by a multiple-choice chapter test in a standardized test format.

We welcome comments and suggestions about the book. Please contact the authors at:

American Book Company
PO Box 2638
Woodstock, GA 30188-1383

Toll Free: 1 (888) 264-5877
Phone (770) 928-2834
Fax (770) 928-7483
Web Site: www.americanbookcompany.com

ABOUT THE AUTHORS

Dr. Frank Pintozzi is an adjunct Professor of Reading and English as a Second Language at Kennesaw State University, Kennesaw, Georgia. For over 27 years, he has taught English and reading at the high school and college levels. He holds a doctorate in education from North Carolina State University in Raleigh, North Carolina. He is the author of eight textbooks on grammar, reading, writing strategies, and social studies. He is currently working on a book that helps students improve their writing.

Devin Pintozzi is a graduate of Oglethorpe University in Atlanta, Georgia and recently earned his MBA at Georgia State University. He is an author of the best-selling book, *California Language Arts Review*, and has co-authored reading and writing textbooks. Clear and concise communication of the written word is his goal.

BASICS MADE EASY READING REVIEW
DIAGNOSTIC TEST

> **The English Language Arts Diagnostic Test consists of reading selections and 40 multiple-choice questions. Choose the best answer for each question. You will be given as much time as you need for the test.**

Basics Made Easy Reading Review Diagnostic Test

Green algae become **dormant** until rains revive them.

1. In this sentence, **dormant** means

    A. larger.
    B. dead.
    C. flat.
    D. inactive.

Many people believe that **extraterrestrial** creatures exist on other planets.

2. In this sentence, **extraterrestrial** means

    A. beyond the earth.
    B. tall.
    C. scary.
    D. friendly.

No amount of **coaxing** could get the crowd to move.

3. In this sentence, **coaxing** means

    A. sleeping.
    B. persuading.
    C. hiding.
    D. singing.

Not every **unsatisfactory** mail **transaction** is fraudulent. The inspection Service will try to resolve **legitimate** complaints to the satisfaction of all parties involved.

4. In this statement, which word means **lawful**?

    A. unsatisfactory
    B. fraudulent
    C. transaction
    D. legitimate

Buffalo Soldiers

After the Civil War, many blacks moved to the West to find a better life for themselves. Some became cowhands, ranchers, or shopkeepers. Some farmed the land in a harsh environment with few resources. Several African-American Army regiments served on the frontier and became skilled fighters.

These special soldiers lived among the Indians, but others worked to control and contain the Native American population. In their role as soldiers in the military, African-American men were instrumental in patrolling the Great Plains, the Rio Grande, and areas of New Mexico, Arizona, Colorado, and the Dakotas. Under acts of Congress, four segregated regiments were established in 1866 to use the services of African-American soldiers. Two were cavalry regiments and two were infantry units. Black cavalry regiments consisted of the 9th and 10th Cavalry, and the infantry units included the 24th and 25th Infantry divisions.

The exploits and experiences of the Buffalo Soldiers, a term used by the Native Americans to describe the black troops, are described in a comprehensive account by William H. Lick, *The Buffalo Soldiers: A Narrative of the Negro Cavalry in the West*. (Norman: University of Oklahoma Press, 1963)

5. What is the main idea of the passage above?

    A. African American regiments served on the Frontier with distinction.
    B. The Buffalo Soldiers lived among the Native Americans.
    C. The United States selected four regiments to patrol the West.
    D. African American soldiers became fighters in the American West.

2

6. Which of the following events is in the right order?

   A. Buffalo Soldiers was a name Indians gave African-American soldiers before the Civil War.
   B. African-American soldiers were patrolling the Great Plains before 1866.
   C. The 9th and 10th Infantry units were working to contain American Indian populations before the Civil War.
   D. The 24th and 25th Infantry divisions were established after the Civil War.

7. From the passage, one can infer that the writer

   A. admired the African-American soldiers.
   B. thought that African-Americans should not live with Native Americans.
   C. thought that African-Americans should not move to the West.
   D. was neutral toward the African-American soldiers.

8. Which passage contains propaganda?

   A. The political race for president in the nation of Erewon has been very tight. Emilio Adonaldo, the incumbent president, leads the political party that has remained in power for fifty years. His opponent, Enrique Hernandez, leads the opposition party at a time when a growing number of citizens have been voicing criticism of current presidential policies. Both sides seem equally ready for the coming campaign season.

   B. Through all the recent charges of government mismanagement, only Gene Buxton has kept himself above reproach. He is flawlessly dedicated to the needs of his constituents. He remains popular with the vast majority of voters. Vote for Gene Buxton. Integrity is his middle name.

   C. Protesters on both sides of this emotional Supreme Court decision were on the verge of violence today as the verdict was read. Those wanting tougher restrictions on prisoner's rights were appalled, while those supporting prisoner's rights were pleased by today's verdict.

   D. Kelly Sharp and Vicky Hutchinson are the opposing candidates for the new congressional district carved out of a portion of two other districts. Both candidates have been successful entrepreneurs. Their campaign spending has come out of their own pockets. Because two successful businesswomen are candidates, representing a growing trend in the nation, this race will be closely watched around the country.

He was quick and alert in the things in life, but only in the things, and not in the significant things. Fifty degrees below zero meant eighty degrees of frost. Such fact impressed him as being cold and uncomfortable, and that was all. It did not lead him to meditate upon his frailty as a creature of temperature, and upon man's frailty in general, able only to live within certain narrow limits of heat and cold; and from there on it did not lead him to the conjectural field of immorality and man's place in the universe. Fifty degrees below zero was to him just precisely fifty degrees below. That there should be anything more to it than that was a thought that never entered his head.

As he turned to go on, he spat speculatively. There was a sharp explosive crackle that startled him. He spat again. And again, in the air, before it could fall to the snow, the spittle crackled. He knew that at fifty below spittle crackled on the snow, but this spittle had crackled in the air. Undoubtedly it was colder than fifty below - how much colder he did not know. But the temperature did not matter. He was bound for the old claim on the left fork of Henderson Creek, where the boys were already. They had come over across the divide from the Indian Creek country, while he had come the roundabout way to take a look at the possibilities of getting out logs in the spring from the islands in the Yukon. He would be in to camp by six o'clock; a bit after dark, it was true, but the boys would be there, a fire would be going, and a hot supper would be ready. As for lunch, he pressed his hand against the protruding bundle under his jacket. It was also under his shirt, wrapped up in a handkerchief and lying against the naked skin. It was the only way to keep the biscuits from freezing. He smiled agreeably to himself as he thought of those biscuits, each cut open and sopped in bacon grease, and each enclosing a generous slice of fried bacon.

He plunged in among the big spruce trees. The trail was faint. A foot of snow had fallen since the last sled had passed over, and he was glad he was without a sled, traveling light. In fact, he carried nothing but the lunch wrapped in the handkerchief. He was surprised, however, at the cold. It certainly was cold, he concluded, as he rubbed his numb nose and cheekbones with his mittened hand. He was a warm-whiskered man, but the hair on his face did not protect the high cheek-bones and the eager nose that thrust itself aggressively into the frosty air.

- Jack London

9.   What is the conflict in this story?

A.   the campers against the loners   C.   fire against ice
B.   man against nature   D.   man against mountain

10.   Where does this story take place?

A.   the tundra   C.   the rain forest
B.   the desert   D.   the mountains

11.   What type of literature is this passage?

A.   poetry   C.   autobiography
B.   fiction   D.   mythology

12.   What is the pattern of events in this passage?

A.   A man is lost in the snow and is unsure where he is going.
B.   A man is on his way to a campsite and is traveling through the bitter cold.
C.   A man is trying to find a way to move logs through the Yukon.
D.   A man is on his way to the warmth of the southern United States.

4

After the Blast

At first glance, the beach at Bikini Atoll, a small island in the Pacific Ocean, looks like a tropical paradise. In truth, the land and water share a poisoned past, from the era when 23 atomic tests were conducted at Bikini Atoll.

In 1946, all 167 Bikini residents were relocated. Then 42,000 people and 90 vessels used the island for target practice. This was to be the first peace time testing of nuclear weapons.

Testing continued until November 1958. The most damaging explosion came on March 1, 1954, when a 15 megaton hydrogen bomb, code-named Bravo, was exploded on the island. This bomb was the most powerful ever exploded by the United States. It was a thousand times more powerful than the bomb dropped on Hiroshima. Not only did it open a mile-wide crater on Bikini Atoll, but it also vaporized one small island and part of another.

To this day, the soil on Bikini contains too much radioactive cesium to permit the Bikinians, now numbering 2,025, to return from their exile.

13. Why was an atomic bomb exploded on Bikini Island in 1954?

    A. Few people lived on the island, so they moved to a new location.
    B. Nuclear bombs were being tested for use as weapons.
    C. The soil was already radioactive from earlier blasts.
    D. The United States was preparing to drop a bomb on Hiroshima.

14. Which of the following statements is an opinion?

    A. In 1946, all 167 Bikini residents were relocated.
    B. This bomb was the most powerful ever exploded by the United States.
    C. Bikini Atoll should not be used for nuclear testing.
    D. 42,000 people and 90 vessels used the island for target practice.

15. The author's purpose for writing this passage is

    A. to create suspense.
    C. to inform.
    B. to introduce a character.
    D. to persuade.

16. Based on the passage, the damage to Bikini Atoll suggests that

    A. no more nuclear bombs will be dropped on the island.
    B. more powerful bombs will be dropped on the island in the future.
    C. the island will remain uninhabited for some time to come.
    D. people will be able to return to the island.

17. Which statement best express the main idea of this passage?

    A. Nuclear testing on Bikini Atoll damaged the island and displaced its residents.
    B. Bikini Atoll looked like a tropical paradise, but no one lives there.
    C. The soil on Bikini Atoll is contaminated with radioactive cesium.
    D. On March 1, 1954, the United States dropped a powerful atomic bomb on Bikini Atoll.

Stop the Spraying!

Don't let the Metropolitan Mosquito Control District spray your land! They continue to spew toxic chemicals across the landscape, claiming to protect our children. They say they are killing the mosquitoes that carry La Crosse encephalitis. Encephalitis is a terrible disease that affects the brain and central nervous system, usually of children, and in rare cases can cause death. However, the State Department of Health reported only 66 cases of encephalitis in the state from 1985 to 1996. Last year, there were only five cases.

As a county commissioner, I served on the advisory board for the Control District from 1993 to 1997. During that time, I saw very little change in the number of cases of encephalitis. In fact, the difference from before the spray and after the spray in number of cases was like the difference between six and half a dozen! For this small risk, it is not worth spending $8.5 million each year to spray 200,000 acres of the metro region with chemicals. These chemicals may be harmful to fish or bees and, if improperly used, can cause skin and eye irritation to humans.

I love my children, and I don't want them to get sick, but I also want them to grow up in a clean, chemical-free environment. We don't know the long-term effects of this spraying. Is it worth the risk? I don't think so. Call the District today, and formally request not to have your property sprayed. It's your right as a property owner and tax payer. It's your responsibility to the community and to our children.

- Bill Sutherland, Minneapolis

18. Why is the author upset by the proposed spraying?

    A. Private industries refuse to pay for the spraying.
    B. The author believes that the "cure" for La Crosse encephalitis is a bigger health risk to the community than the disease itself.
    C. The money could be better spent by spraying backyards individually.
    D. Mr. Sutherland is angry because that the government is doing nothing about the encephalitis problem.

19. What connection does Bill Sutherland cite as a source for his information in this passage?

    A. the Metropolitan Mosquito Control District
    B. his previous work as county commissioner
    C. the economic and statistical data from the Centers for Disease Control (CDC)
    D. the State Department of Health

20. How does the author's point of view affect his argument?

    A. As a father, his love for his children is irrelevant to the argument.
    B. As an environmentalist, he shows neglect for children and weakens his argument.
    C. As a former county commissioner, he strengthens his argument by speaking with authority.
    D. As a property owner and taxpayer, he can force others to agree with him.

21. How can you tell that this selection is an editorial?

    A. The passage teaches a moral.
    B. The passage describes the writer's opinion on an event.
    C. The passage includes facts and is free of bias.
    D. The passage has characters and dialogue.

22. In the passage, "In fact, the difference from before the spray and after the spray in number of cases was like the difference between six and half a dozen!" is an example of

    A. alliteration.
    B. irony.
    C. imagery.
    D. hyperbole.

The New Colossus

1   Not like the brazen giant of Greek fame,
2   With conquering limbs astride from land to land;
3   Here at our sea-washed, sunset gates shall stand
4   A mighty woman with a torch whose flame
5   is the imprisoned lightning, and her name
6   Mother of Exiles. From her beacon-hand
7   Glows world-wide welcome; her mild eyes command
8   The air-bridged harbor that twin cities frame
9   "Keep, ancient lands, your storied pomp!" cries she
10   With silent lips. "Give me your tired, your poor
11   Your huddled masses yearning to breathe free,
12   The wretched refuse of your teeming shore
13   Send these, the homeless, tempest-tost to me,
14   I lift my lamp beside the golden door!"

    - Emma Lazarus, 1883, a poem about the Statue of Liberty

23. How does the imagery in lines 13-14 affect the message of this poem?

    A. It inspires the belief that the United States is a land where gold is plentiful.
    B. The contrasted ending with an uplifted light and golden passage leaves the reader with hope.
    C. It leaves the reader to understand that the ships will not crash in the harbor.
    D. The ending creates unfounded fears of death and an afterlife in America.

24. The phrase "the wretched refuse of your teeming shore" means

    A. the garbage from your beaches.
    B. people who desperately search for a better life.
    C. the excess seafood that is spoiled and left on the beach.
    D. the toxic waste that flows from the rivers into the sea.

25. What aspect of this poem reflects a common assumption in contemporary culture in the United States?

    A. The poem suggests that the United States is a land of opportunity for the oppressed of other nations.
    B. The poem explores the common belief that the United States culture encourages other nations to keep their traditions if they favor the rich.
    C. The poem describes how the United States uses a statue to symbolize itself as a country which guards itself from outsiders.
    D. The poem explores the strong belief in the United States to destroy any established order and create a truly classless society.

26. According to the poem, what is the most significant difference between the "new Colossus" and the old one?

    A. One is bigger than the other.
    B. One is Greek, and the other is French.
    C. One symbolizes oppression and the other freedom.
    D. One is of ancient times, and the other is of modern times.

The Tortoise and the Eagle

It was not often that the tortoise and the eagle met, for the one spent his days in the clouds and the other under a bush. However, when the eagle heard what a warm-hearted little fellow the tortoise was, he went to pay a call on him. The tortoise family showed such pleasure in his company and fed him so lavishly that the eagle returned again and again, while every time as he flew away he laughed, "Ha, ha! I can enjoy the hospitality of the tortoise on the ground, but he can never reach my eyrie in the tree-top!"

The eagle's frequent visits, his selfishness, and ingratitude became the talk of the forest animals. The eagle and the frog were never on speaking terms, for the eagle was accustomed to swooping down to carry a frog home for supper. So the frog called from the stream bank, "Friend tortoise, give me beans, and I will give you wisdom." After enjoying the bowl of beans, the frog said, "Friend tortoise, the eagle is abusing your kindness, for after every visit he flies away laughing, 'Ha ha! I can enjoy the hospitality of the tortoise on the ground but he can never enjoy mine, for my eyrie is in the tree-tops!' Next time the eagle visits you, say, 'Give me a gourd, and I will send food to your wife and children too'."

The eagle did as the tortoise suggested. He brought a gourd, enjoyed a feast, and as he left he called back, "I will call later for the present for my wife."

The eagle flew away laughing to himself as usual, "Ha ha! I have enjoyed the tortoise's food, but he can never come to my eyrie to taste of mine."

The frog arrived and said, "Now, tortoise, get into the gourd. Your wife will cover you over with fresh food, and the eagle will carry you to his home in the treetops." Presently the eagle returned.

The tortoise's wife told him, "My husband is away but he left this gourd filled with food for your family."

The eagle flew away with the gourd, little suspecting that the tortoise was inside. The tortoise could hear every word as the eagle laughed, "Ha! ha! I share the tortoise's food but he can never visit my eyrie to share mine."

As the gourd was emptied out onto the eagle's eyrie, the tortoise crawled from it and said, "Friend eagle, you have so often visited my home that I thought it would be nice to enjoy the hospitality of yours."

The eagle was furious. "I will peck the flesh from your bones," he said. But he only hurt his beak against the tortoise's hard back.

"I see what sort of friendship you offer me," said the tortoise, "when you threaten to tear me limb from limb." He continued, "Under the circumstances, please take me home, for our pact of friendship is at an end."

"Take you home, indeed!" shrieked the eagle. "I will fling you to the ground and you will be smashed to bits in your fall."

The tortoise bit hold of the eagle's leg. "Let me go, let go of my leg, let go of my leg," groaned the great bird.

8

"I will gladly do so when you set me down at my own home," mumbled the tortoise through feathers, and he tightened his hold on the eagle's leg.

The eagle flew high into the clouds and darted down with the speed of an arrow. He shook his leg. He turned and twirled, but it was to no use. He could not rid himself of the tortoise until he set him down safely in his own home. As the eagle flew away the tortoise called after him, "Friendship requires the contribution of two parties. For example, I welcome you and you welcome me. Since, however, you have chosen to make a mockery of it, laughing at me for my hospitality, you need not call again."

The End

-Courtesy of the *AFRO-American Almanac*

27. The traditional African American folktale often has a trickster. Who is the trickster in this story and how does his use of the gourd make the trick effective?

    A. The tortoise is the trickster, and using the gourd symbolized the shell on his back, both hard and camouflaging.
    B. The frog is the trickster, and since the gourd is a traditional symbol of hospitality and plenty, the eagle is completely fooled and humiliated.
    C. The tortoise is the trickster, and since everything he has given the eagle has been good, the gourd looks good too, fooling the eagle.
    D. The frog is the trickster, and since he has the tortoise's wife give the gourd to the eagle, the eagle is fooled by a female, and that really humiliates him.

28. How can you tell that this passage is a folktale and not a legend or a myth?

    A. The passage uses superhuman characters to explain seemingly impossible deeds.
    B. The story is full of supernatural characters and events and attempts to explain a natural event.
    C. The passage describes a hero who changes the course of an historical event.
    D. The simple story uses animal characters which take on human qualities.

29. Describe the overall theme of the story.

    A. Hospitality should be respected and returned when possible.
    B. Violence is not an appropriate way to solve problems.
    C. An eagle takes advantage of a tortoise's friendship.
    D. Friends can give you wise advice if you pay them.

30. Why does the eagle in this story repeat himself on three different occasions?

    A. The eagle has a limited vocabulary.
    B. The teller of the folktale wants to emphasize the eagle's selfishness.
    C. The eagle needs to clarify his words to his audience.
    D. The teller of the folktale wants to make sure the story is easy to memorize.

31. Which of the following sentences from the selection represents an <u>opinion</u> rather than a fact?

    A. "The eagle flew high into the clouds and darted down with the speed of an arrow."
    B. "The eagle brought a gourd, enjoyed a feast, and as he left, he called back, 'I will call later for the present for my wife'."
    C. "It was not often that the tortoise and the eagle met, for the one spent his days in the clouds and the other under a bush."
    D. "The eagle's frequent visits, his selfishness, and his ingratitude became the talk of the forest animals."

An Unwelcomed Surprise

Sharice closed her locker and ran to her next class. "I hope I make it in time!" she thought as she ran into the classroom and took her seat. Her mind was already agitated as Cory took a seat behind her. As usual, Cory began telling gross stories to his friends before class started. Sharice had had enough. She turned around and said, "Cory, I am already motion sick from the bus ride to school. Your conversation is making me sicker. Please stop!" She gave Cory a very mean look. Cory didn't care. He just laughed at Sharice and continued on with his gross story. Sharice began looking paler and shouted, "I need to go to the bathroom!" As she began walking, Cory thought it would be fun to trip Sharice. When Sharice tripped, she tried to balance herself by grabbing Cory's desk, but instead, she fell on Cory. Unfortunately for Cory, that surprise was the last straw for Sharice's stomach. When Sharice got up, Cory was wearing her sausage and egg breakfast. Cory ran to the bathroom in disgust and embarrassment while Sharice calmly asked the teacher if she could call her mother.

32. What is the main idea of this story?

    A. Bad deeds rarely go unpunished.
    B. Cory made Sharice's stomach upset.
    C. Sharice got sick on the way to school.
    D. Cory ran to the bathroom to wash his shirt.

33. The author's main purpose in writing this passage is to

    A. create suspense.
    B. persuade students to stay home when they're sick.
    C. criticize.
    D. tell a story.

34. What is the climax of this story?

    A. Cory begins telling gross stories in the back of the classroom.
    B. Sharice vomits on Cory.
    C. Sharice tells Cory to stop telling gross stories.
    D. Cory runs to the bathroom.

35. In what section of the newspaper would you find an opinion on a current news event?

    A. Editorial section   C. Entertainment section
    B. Front page   D. Sports section

36. Which part of the book would you use to find a list of page references of the names, places, and subjects in a book?

    A. index
    B. title page
    C. preface
    D. glossary

37. Where would you look for a book on speed reading?

    A. an electronic card catalog
    B. a telephone book
    C. Reader's Guide to Periodical Literature
    D. glossary

The Experiment

"Before you drink, my respectable old friends," said he, "it would be well that, with the experience of a lifetime to direct you, you should draw up a few general rules for your guidance, in passing a second time through the perils of youth. Think what a sin and shame it would be if, with your peculiar advantages, you should not become patterns of virtue and wisdom to all the young people of the age!"

The doctor's four venerable friends made him no answer, except by a feeble and tremulous laugh; so very ridiculous was the idea that, knowing how closely repentance treads behind the steps of error, they should ever go astray again.

"Drink, then," said the doctor, bowing. "I rejoice that I have so well selected the subjects of my experiment."

With palsied hands, they raised the glasses to their lips. The liquor, if it really possessed such virtues as Dr. Heidegger imputed to it, could not have been bestowed on four human beings who needed it more woefully. They looked as if they had never known what youth or pleasure was, but had been the offspring of nature's old age and always the gray decrepit, sapless, miserable creatures, who now sat stooping around the doctor's table, without life enough in their souls or bodies to be animated even by the prospect of growing young again. They drank off the water and replaced their glasses on the table.

- Nathaniel Hawthorne
"Dr. Heidegger's Experiment"

38. Based on the passage, we can infer that the doctor believes the drinking of the liquor will probably

    A.   make the four persons old and gray.
    B.   make the four persons drunk.
    C.   restore the youth of the four persons.
    D.   make the four persons sick.

39. What is the setting of the passage?

    A.   in the middle of Dr. Heidegger's hospital
    B.   at the dinner table of one of the four elderly people
    C.   at a restaurant
    D.   in Dr. Heidegger's home at the dinner table

Dr. Dunk

When Dominique Wilkins moved to Washington, North Carolina with his mother and seven brothers and sisters, his favorite game was marbles. "I was the Larry Bird of marbles," he said, but he soon discovered basketball. By the time he was fifteen, he was challenging older players in the schoolyard for a dollar per game.

While he played basketball at Washington High School, sportswriters started calling him "Dr. Dunk" because of his crowd-pleasing dunks on the court. By then, Dominique was six feet seven inches and led his basketball team to two Triple-A state championships. At the University of Georgia, Wilkins continued his astonishing success. The Georgia Bulldogs were able to appear twice in the National Invitation Tournament (NIT). The National Basketball Association's (NBA) coaches selected Wilkins for the All-American squad. After 78 games for Georgia, Wilkins averaged 21.6 points and 7.5 rebounds.

The rest of Wilkins' story is history. He went to play for the Atlanta Hawks for twelve seasons. During this time, he developed into one of the most prolific scorers in NBA history. His flying above the rim style challenged Michael Jordan's status as the NBA's greatest scorer and performer. In fact, in the 1983-84 season, Wilkins won the Gatorade Slam Dunk Contest at the all-star festivities, even beating out rookie Michael Jordan of the Chicago Bulls. Dr. Dunk would continue to be a box-office draw for many years to come.

40. Based on this passage, we can conclude that Wilkins' success in basketball primarily resulted from

    A.   luck.   C.   crowd-pleasing dunks.
    B.   size and height.   D.   size, hard work, and playing ability.

EVALUATION CHART
DIAGNOSTIC TEST FOR BASICS MADE EASY
READING

Directions: On the following chart, circle the question numbers that you answered incorrectly, and evaluate the results. Then turn to the appropriate topics (listed by chapters), read the explanations, and complete the exercises. Review the other chapters as needed.

		QUESTIONS	PAGES
Chapter 1:	Word Meaning	1-4	14-37
Chapter 2:	Finding the Main Idea	5,12,17,32	45-54
Chapter 3:	Reading for Details, Sequence, and Cause - Effect Relationships	6,10,18	68-75
Chapter 4:	Inferences, Generalizations, Conclusions, Predictions, and Summary	7-8,13,16, 38,40	87-101
Chapter 5:	Fact and Opinion	21-25,14,31	115-118
Chapter 6:	Reading Graphic Aids	26-30	128-140
Chapter 7:	Dictionary Skills		
Chapter 8:	Using and Choosing Reference Sources	35-37	162-181
Chapter 9:	Analysis of Literature	9,11,15,19-30, 33-34,39	189-219

Chapter 1

WORD MEANING

Anything you read requires that you understand the meaning of words in sentences. Otherwise, written material would not make sense to you. Ultimately, the more words you know, the better you'll be able to comprehend written information.

In this chapter, you will practice the following vocabulary strategies:

1. **Context Clues**
2. **Prefixes, Suffixes, and Roots**
3. **Definition Recall**
4. **Words from Daily Life**
5. **Dialect, Idioms, and Slang**
6. **Abbreviations and Symbols**
7. **Synonyms and Antonyms**
8. **Word Classification**
9. **Analogies**

The list of strategies above are the most effective for understanding words.

Now let's choose the best response to the following sentences.

> **Green algae become <u>dormant</u> until rains revive them.**

1. In this sentence, **dormant** means

   A. larger.   C. smaller.
   B. dead.   D. inactive.

> **<u>Aerobic</u> conditioning is low impact exercise that requires oxygen and is sustained for long periods of time.**

2. In this sentence, **aerobic** means

   A. hair.   C. light.
   B. skin.   D. diabetic.

> **Many people believe that <u>extraterrestrial</u> creatures exist on other planets.**

3. In this sentence, **extraterrestrial** means

   A. beyond the earth.   C. scary.
   B. tall.   D. friendly.

CONTEXT CLUES

Using **context clues** is the most common strategy for unlocking the meaning of words you don't know. For example, if you chose D for question 1, you made use of the clause, "until rains revive them." This group of words suggests that dormant is not a "dead" state but an **inactive** one since the rains bring the algae back from a state of rest. In addition, the signal word, "until" tells us that **dormant** is the opposite of **revive**. Consequently, you use a **contrast clue** to determine the meaning.

In question 2, the answer should be C, light. In this example, you used a **definition clue**. The meaning of **aerobic** is explained in the phrase following "is," which becomes the signal word leading us into the definition. Low impact suggests light exercise.

Therefore, context clues help us determine the meaning of words from the way they are used in a sentence. By analyzing the phrases and signal words that come before or after the underlined word, you can often figure out its meaning.

Here are three main types of **context clues** with their signal words:

CONTEXT CLUES	SIGNAL WORDS
Comparison	also, likewise, resembling, too, both
Contrast	but, however, until, instead of, yet, while
Definition or Restatement	is, or, that is, in other words, which
Example	for example, for instance, such as, a dash or a colon used in punctuation

PRACTICE 1: CONTEXT CLUES

Using context strategies, write the meaning above the boldfaced word from these sentences.

1. Pre-trial release is hard for those who cannot afford **bail**.
2. Strong **herbicides** are needed to eliminate weeds from the garden.
3. Henri said the ocean was very **tranquil**. I also thought the ocean was peaceful.
4. When a car **accumulates** weight, it will burn more gas.
5. At the sound of Lancelot's **clattering** footsteps, the hermit turned with a start.
6. **Residues** such as ammonia even show up in grain sprayed with **pesticides**.
7. While Greenland is labeled an island, Antarctica's larger size makes it a **continent**.
8. You could smell the freshly caught catfish **sizzling** over the fire.
9. **Mulch,** which is composed of grass clippings and leaves, keeps soil moist around trees and shrubs.
10. Instead of **incarcerating** youthful offenders, let's educate them so that they can hold well-paying jobs in the workplace.

PRACTICE 2: CONTEXT QUESTIONS

Choose the best meaning for the bold words in the following examples.

> Recently, Loganville celebrated the **centennial** of its founding in 1898.

1. In this sentence, **centennial** means

    A. victory.
    B. 100 years.
    C. place.
    D. time.

> Mr. Carver does not **tolerate** or permit talking during class.

2. In this sentence, **tolerate** means

    A. prevent.
    B. restrict.
    C. hear.
    D. accept.

> We were able to **apprehend** the thief.

3. In this sentence, **apprehend** means

    A. capture.
    B. chase.
    C. see.
    D. help.

> Sam is now **eligible** to play on the team. Vin is able to play too.

4. In this sentence, **eligible** means

    A. reluctant.
    B. qualified.
    C. irritated.
    D. pleased.

> The teacher **intervened** to prevent a fight between the girls.

5. In this sentence, **intervened** means

    A. yelled.
    B. came between.
    C. laughed.
    D. withdrew.

> Most mammals have strong **maternal** instincts to protect their young.

6. In this sentence, **maternal** means

    A. nesting.
    B. fighting.
    C. fatherly.
    D. motherly.

> Don't **distract** me when I'm studying. In other words, keep quiet.

7. In this sentence, **distract** means

    A. phone.
    B. criticize.
    C. disturb.
    D. ask.

> The **finale** of the concert was the best part of the show.

8. In this sentence, **finale** means

    A. beginning.
    B. middle.
    C. end.
    D. singing.

> Can you **visualize** the day you will graduate from high school?

9. In this sentence, **visualize** means

    A. picture.
    B. place.
    C. remember.
    D. plan.

> Someone gave an **anonymous** gift to the homeless shelter.

10. In this sentence, **anonymous** means

    A. amazing.
    B. enormous.
    C. urgent.
    D. unnamed.

Choose the best meaning for the bold words in the following phrases.

11. The **black** doorway

    A. clear
    B. ebony
    C. hard
    D. translucent

12. Her **thrifty** habits

    A. dangerous
    B. many
    C. obvious
    D. economical

13. A **foggy** day

    A. misty
    B. silvery
    C. tired
    D. clear

14. A familiar **rhythm**

    A. spacing
    B. harmony
    C. beat
    D. melody

15. The little **twerp**

    A. thief
    B. brave person
    C. nerd
    D. silly person

16. **Evade** the dentist.

    A. avoid
    B. entertain
    C. jump on
    D. bite into

17. A **sarcastic** wit

    A. sincere
    B. snide
    C. sordid
    D. gracious

18. **Creeping** through

    A. running
    B. foraging
    C. skipping
    D. crawling

19. Have good **posture**

    A. memory
    B. ability
    C. stance
    D. growth

20. The **gracious** host

    A. thankful
    B. unhappy
    C. polite
    D. unremarkable

21. **Scrumptious** pie

    A. rotten
    B. delicious
    C. beautiful
    D. smelly

22. **Reiterate** your idea.

    A. repeat
    B. explain
    C. change
    D. create

23. He looks **relaxed**.

    A. formal
    B. casual
    C. uptight
    D. weird

24. A **raucous** sound

    A. loud
    B. soft
    C. melodious
    D. hoarse

25. Ed is **arrogant**.

    A. humble
    B. conservative
    C. proud
    D. narcissistic

26. Her **tendency** is

    A. work
    B. plan
    C. belief
    D. habit

27. My dog **salivates**.

    A. drools
    B. barks
    C. howls
    D. sits

28. Terri **procrastinates**.

    A. cries
    B. delays
    C. hasten
    D. debates

PRACTICE 3: WORDS FROM PASSAGES

Read some passages from a newspaper or magazine. Underline words you don't know, and try to figure out their meanings from context. Write the sentence in which the word appears on a 3 × 5 card with the meaning on the back. With other students, form quiz panels to test each other on the words.

17

PREFIXES, SUFFIXES, AND ROOTS

Recognizing **prefixes, suffixes,** and **roots** is another useful way to identify word meaning. Prefixes, suffixes, and roots refer to the use of word parts to figure out definitions. For example, the answer to question 3 on page 1 is A, beyond the earth. "**Extra**" is a prefix that means outside or beyond, and "**terra**" is the Latin root for earth. Therefore, by dividing **extraterrestrial** into its word parts, you can define it easily.

Actually, you could also apply word parts to the answers for questions 1 and 2 on page 1 as well. **Dormant** comes from the Latin root for sleep, and **aerobic** is derived from **aer** and **bio,** the Greek words for "air" and "life." Word parts consist of **prefixes** (the beginning of words), **roots** (the main part of the word), and **suffixes** (the end part of a word). Learning these word parts will unlock the meaning of countless words in your reading. Here is a list of some common word parts you will encounter in your reading.

Review these **prefixes, suffixes,** and **roots** to increase your understanding of word meanings. Check the ones you do not know, and then learn their meanings.

PREFIXES

Prefix	Meaning	Example	Prefix	Meaning	Example
ab	from	absent	il, in	not	insecure
ad	to	adhere	inter	between	interstate
anti	against	antigravity	intra	within	intramural
be	by	bemuse	post	after	postnatal
com	with	communion	pre	before	premix
de	reverse, remove	deregulate	pro	in front of	proclaim
dis	not	dishonest	re	to do again	review
en	in	enkindle	sub	under	submarine

ROOTS

Root	Meaning	Example	Root	Meaning	Example
annum	year	annual	multi	many	multiply
aqua	water	aquarium	pathos	feeling	sympathy
bio	life	biography	phon	sound	telephone
centum	hundred	century	portare	carry	transport
chronos	time	chronological	rad	ray	radiation
dicere	to speak	dictator	scope	see	microscope
genus	race, kind	genetic	scrib	to write	scripture
hetero	different	heterogeneous	tele	distance	television
ject	throw	injection	venire	to come, go	convene
medius	middle	median	viv, vit	life	vital

18

SUFFIXES

Suffix	Meaning	Examples	Suffix	Meaning	Examples
able	capable of being	adorable lovable	ly	in like manner	easily quietly
age	related to	marriage	less	without	thoughtless groundless
al, ial	of, like	industrial	logy	study of	psychology
ance	act or process of	transmittance insurance	ment	result of action or process	contentment assortment
er, or	one who performs a specific action	employer actor	ness	quality, condition	business neatness
ful	full of	cheerful plentiful	ous	full of	nervous
hood	state of	manhood	ship	state of	relationship
ish	like	foolish	tion	action, process	construction education
itis	inflammation	arthritis	ure	process of	venture
ive	having the nature of	talkative inquisitive	ward	in a specified direction	forward homeward

PRACTICE 4

Directions: In a group or on your own, find an example of a word derived from any of the prefixes, suffixes, and roots on this page and the previous page. Consult a dictionary, a newspaper, or an English book if needed. Then share your findings with the class or your instructor.

PRACTICE 5

Directions: Choose the best answer for each question.

1. What should you add to the word <u>legible</u> to make it mean "not legible"?
    A. un
    B. dis
    C. il
    D. pro

2. The "ness" in <u>kindness</u> means
    A. type.
    B. full of.
    C. capable of.
    D. condition.

3. What should you add to the word <u>stated</u> to make it mean "stated again"?
    A. pre   C. post
    B. re   D. de

4. The "able" in <u>washable</u> means
    A. capable of being.   C. opposite of.
    B. similar to.   D. a way of.

5. What root added to <u>logy</u> would mean the study of life?
    A. chronos   C. bio
    B. viv   D. post

6. The "cent" in <u>centennial</u> means
    A. ten.   C. thousand.
    B. hundred.   D. ten thousand.

Matching Prefixes

_____	1. sub	A.	reverse
_____	2. ad	B.	again
_____	3. in	C.	outside
_____	4. com	D.	under
_____	5. ex	E.	by
_____	6. pro	F.	not
_____	7. ab	G.	to
_____	8. pre	H.	with
_____	9. be	I.	in front of
_____	10. re	J.	before
_____	11. en	K.	from
_____	12. de	L.	in

Matching Roots

_____	13. ject	A.	year
_____	14. chronos	B.	kind
_____	15. scrib	C.	ray
_____	16. genus	D.	feeling
_____	17. tele	E.	write
_____	18. annum	F.	come
_____	19. portare	G.	throw
_____	20. rad	H.	sound
_____	21. pathos	I.	different
_____	22. venire	J.	distance
_____	23. hetero	K.	time
_____	24. phon	L.	to carry

Matching Suffixes

_____ 25. ment	_____ 31. less	A.	inflammation	G.	upward
_____ 26. ful	_____ 32. er	B.	capable of	H.	related to
_____ 27. tion	_____ 33. ward	C.	one who	I.	full of
_____ 28. ly	_____ 34. itis	D.	state of	J.	action, process
_____ 29. able	_____ 35. age	E.	result of action	K.	without
_____ 30. ness	_____ 36. ship	F.	quality, condition	L.	like, in manner

DEFINITION RECALL

Another possible strategy for defining a word is **definition recall.** With this strategy you simply remember the meaning of the underlined word because you have heard it, or you have seen it before in class, in your reading or on television.

In many cases, you will easily spot the right answer from among your choices. However, in some cases, the word to be identified may have multiple definitions. You would then have to examine the context in which the word is used before choosing your answer. For example, the word **fix** has several meanings. These sentences illustrate this point:

The driver **fixed** her flat tire. (to repair)

He **fixed** his eyes on the painting. (to stare)

I'm **fixing** a salad for dinner. (to prepare)

Without the money, we'll be in a real **fix.** (tough position)

Reviewing the context in which **fix** is used would directly affect the definition you would choose for an answer. Consequently, definition-recall may still involve reading the sentences carefully for specific meanings.

Tips for Answering Questions on Word Meaning

1. **Use context clues and signal words.**

2. **Use your knowledge of prefixes, roots, and suffixes.**

3. **Use your knowledge of words you already learned.**

PRACTICE 6: DEFINITION RECALL

MULTIPLE DEFINITIONS

Try to recall as many meanings as you can from the following words with multiple definitions. If you don't know all the definitions, look them up in a dictionary. Then use the words in sentences that reflect their various meanings: **access, band, bore, class, desert, eye, fall, flood, floor, lift, mix, open, present, run, set, smooth, turn, wind.**

PRACTICE 7: WORD GAMES

A. WORDS AROUND US

Find words you have seen or heard on radio, television, in conversations, newspapers, books, or magazines. State where you found the words. Bring the words to class with the sentences in which they were used. Do the words have prefixes, suffixes, or roots?

Exchange the words with another student or with groups of students. Then have a contest to see which student or groups can define the most words by hearing them based on the sentences in which they appeared. Decide on prizes for winners.

B. WORD BINGO

Make a list of 25-30 words based on this chapter's activities. Then create bingo boards for your group or the class. Each student writes one word in each bingo square in any order. Then the teacher or student leader calls out clues or definitions for each word in any order. After the definition is called, students find and cross out the word on the bingo board. The first student to call "BINGO" is the winner.

C. WORD GAMES

You can also play versions of **Password, Concentration, Word Rummy** or **Pictionary** based on words you develop from this chapter's activities. These games and their rules are available in retail stores.

D. COMPUTER PROGRAMS

Some web sites and computer software programs allow you to create personalized word lists and/or games for learning them. Inquire at your local computer store or on the Internet.

WORDS FROM DAILY LIFE

You will need to recognize words and phrases from daily life situations. You should learn the definitions of these words, so you will use them correctly.

Review the following list of words to know. You will see them frequently in your reading. You will also use them in your writing. Cross off the words that you already know. Then learn the meanings and spellings of the words that you do not know. Review them periodically. Possible learning strategies include 3×5 cards, word bingo, quizzes, games, and using the words in sentences and paragraphs.

ability	conversation	frozen	occur	service
accept	convicted	function	offered	settled
accident	convince	furniture	operation	signature
account	council	garage	opportunity	silent
activities	couple	groceries	options	sincerely
actually	courage	habit-forming	ordinary	situation
address	credit	healthy	organize	social
affect	daily	height	parents	soldier
agree	dangerous	high voltage	peace	spelling
allowed	daughter	hospital	pedestrian	spouse
altogether	decipher	husband	perfect	standard
amber	deductions	identity	personal	stomach
angle	departure	immediately	physical	structure
annual	dependents	improve	physician	students
antidote	depicts	inaudible	place of birth	style
apartment	design	income	planet	success
applicant	details	increase	poisonous	suggested
apply	determined	indicate	police	support
arrange	dictionary	individual	political	surname
arrival	dietetic	industry	popular	swimming
arrived	disappear	influence	position	symbol
article	discuss	insects	potatoes	tax
artificial	disease	instance	prepare	telephone
attached	dividends	instrument	prescription	terminal
audience	dollars	interest	president	terrible
author	dosage	junction	prevent	thank
authorized	dozen	knife	principal	they're
available	education	laugh	program	threw
avenue	emergency	leader	progress	title
avoid	employed	leather	prohibited	tongue
balance	employee	liability	project	traffic
barbecue	employer	library	pronounce	transportation
baseball	enemy	license	punctual	vegetable
belong	entered	local	quality	vehicle
beneath	environment	located	quarter	violations
bicycle	equipment	lose	railroad	voter
bottle	escape	magazine	realize	wages
calories	event	maiden name	receive	warranty
cancel	evidence	marital status	recently	waste
chapter	exactly	married	recognize	whenever
character	excellent	massive	recommend	whisper
charge	excited	medicine	references	worse
citizen	experience	merge	refill	yesterday
citizenship	expiration	message	registration	yield
climate	express	military	remain	
climbed	extra	mistake	repeat	
coffee	factory	model	required	
collect	fare	motor	residence	
college	fatigue	muscles	restriction	
combine	favorite	narcotic	resume	
combustible	feather	neighbor	review	
concern	fifty	newspaper	rhythm	
condition	fight	no admittance	rough	
connect	flammable	no trespassing	round trip	
consider	foreign	nobody	rubber	
construction	forget	notarized	salary	
contaminated	fragile	observe	schedule	
continue	frequently	occupation	secret	
contributions	frighten	occupied	serious	

PRACTICE 8: MATCHING WORDS AND DEFINITIONS

Directions: For this exercise, match the word from daily life on the left with its definition on the right.

_____	1. tax	A.	an addictive drug
_____	2. license	B.	a person who applies for a job
_____	3. employee	C.	certified
_____	4. balance	D.	act of enrolling
_____	5. registration	E.	percentage of income required to support the government
_____	6. narcotic	F.	capable of burning
_____	7. interest	G.	the difference between the debits and credits in an account
_____	8. applicant	H.	a person hired by another
_____	9. notarized	I	a charge for a loan
_____	10. combustible	J.	a formal permission to do something

Directions: Match the word from daily life on the left with the definition on the right.

_____	11. spouse	A.	a partner in marriage
_____	12. pedestrian	B.	a brief record of personal history and experience
_____	13. income	C.	amounts subtracted from your gross pay
_____	14. address	D.	limiting food intake
_____	15. resume	E.	one that hires one or more persons to work for wages or salary
_____	16. maiden name	F.	one who relies on another person or thing for help
_____	17. dietetic	G.	a woman's surname before marriage
_____	18. deductions	H.	destination for delivered items
_____	19. employer	I.	money for labor, goods, or financial investments
_____	20. dependent	J.	a person who travels by foot

PRACTICE 9: MULTIPLE CHOICE QUIZ

Directions: Choose the correct meaning for each underlined word.

1. The word <u>flammable</u> means

    A. hot.
    B. bright.
    C. unable to burn.
    D. easily burned.

2. The word <u>occupation</u> refers to your

    A. job.
    B. income.
    C. age.
    D. social status.

3. The word <u>antidote</u> means

    A. poison.
    B. against medicine.
    C. remedy against poison.
    D. ant poison.

4. Leaving a place is called a

    A. return.
    B. departure.
    C. stadium.
    D. conference.

5. Drinking coffee every day can become

    A. habit-forming.
    B. violent.
    C. painful.
    D. hilarious.

6. The word <u>annual</u> means

    A. renewal.
    B. final.
    C. yearly.
    D. monthly.

7. The word <u>signature</u> means your

    A. symbol.
    B. printed name.
    C. written name.
    D. last name followed by your first name.

8. The word <u>residence</u> means the

    A. place you work.
    B. school you attend.
    C. old part of town.
    D. place you live.

9. The word <u>expiration</u> means

    A. a special date.
    B. coming to a close.
    C. an authority.
    D. exhaling.

10. The word <u>contributions</u> refers to

    A. acting as one group.
    B. gifts to a common fund.
    C. items bought at a store.
    D. earning weekly salaries.

11. The word <u>yield</u> means to

    A. salute.
    B. impress.
    C. concede.
    D. ask.

12. The phrase <u>place of birth</u> means

    A. your neighborhood.
    B. your present address.
    C. your family's address.
    D. where you were born.

DIALECT, IDIOMS, AND SLANG

   Dialect is a form of spoken language peculiar to a particular region, community, or social group. Have you ever heard the expressions, "Down yonder" or "y'all"? These phrases are part of southern dialect. In the northern part of the United States, you'd be more likely to hear "pop" or "soda" whereas in the South you'd be offered a "coke" or a "soft drink." All of these expressions are examples of dialects spoken in the United States.

PRACTICE 10: DIALECT

Directions: Dialect often varies from standard English, but it is sometimes used in informal settings. For clearer understanding, rewrite the following sentences in standard English.

1. We ain't got no money. _____

2. I be in Texas tomorrow. _____

3. Gimme five, man! _____

4. Shona and me talks all the time. _____

5. They was dissin' yo mamma! _____

6. Wa' you say? _____

7. My bad. _____

8. Set a spell, and then cross the crick up the road a piece. _____

    _____

9. Hang a right at Dawson Place. _____

    _____

10. Steve got hooked up with a job in car manufacturing. _____

    _____

11. Carissa, why you trippin'? _____

12. Chill out, man. Everything's gonna' be fine. _____

    _____

PRACTICE 11: DIALECT

Directions: Make a list of dialect words or phrases you have heard. Translate them into standard English. Then quiz your classmates on their meanings.

BONUS ACTIVITY: Perform a short play or skit using dialect.

Idioms are phrases or expressions in which the real meaning is different from the literal or stated meaning. For example, the literal meaning of "It's raining cats and dogs." indicates that cats and dogs are falling out of the sky with the rain. However, the real meaning is that the rain is falling heavily from the sky. Another example of an idiom is "The apple does not fall far from the tree." The stated meaning is clear, but the actual meaning is quite different. This expression really says that a child is very similar mentally or physically to a parent.

PRACTICE 12: IDIOMS

Directions: Match the underlined idiom on the left with the actual meaning on the right.

_____ 1. Her life is <u>an open book</u>.

_____ 2. You're <u>driving me up the wall</u>.

_____ 3. <u>Take up</u> your complaint with Tito.

_____ 4. You want your meal for <u>here or to go</u>.

_____ 5. Don't <u>make waves</u> when you're in this class.

_____ 6. <u>Knock it off</u>, or I'll tell Dad!

_____ 7. Today we're going to <u>have it out</u> with Vinny.

_____ 8. Mr. Sanchez <u>picked up the tab</u> for our class party.

_____ 9. Bethany will <u>catch cold</u> near the window.

_____ 10. <u>Off the top of my head</u>, I'd like to go to El Paso.

_____ 11. <u>Cut off</u> the lights, please.

_____ 12. She <u>caught my eye</u>.

a. pay for expenses

b. create a disturbance

c. without thinking

d. stop doing something

e. turn off

f. making crazy

g. eat here to take home

h. got my attention

i. confront

j. get sick

k. not a secret

l. talk about

PRACTICE 13

Directions: Make a list of your favorite idiomatic expressions. Translate them into standard English. Then quiz your classmates on their meaning.

PRACTICE 14

Directions: On your own or in a group, write down all the idioms you can make from the following words: get, put, take, turn, pick, look, make, dog, cat. Examples: get up, get over, etc. Translate them into standard English. Then quiz your classmates on their meaning.

BONUS ACTIVITY: Give some reasons why we use idioms.

Slang is informal language that is popular with certain groups of people. Slang becomes obsolete over time, but it can also become a permanent part of the English language. In the 1960s and 1970s, young people talking to each other would say, "Can you <u>dig</u> my new <u>threads</u>?" or "<u>Groovy, man</u>!" Most of these "cool" terms from the 70s have disappeared, but today's young people have created their own slang terms. "Geek" and "nerd" may offend some students, but "tight" and "awesome" are compliments.

PRACTICE 15

Directions: Review the following slang expressions. Then rewrite them in standard English.

1. Hey, that's awesome! _____

2. Don't wig, Jessica! _____

3. You want to go to my crib this weekend?_____

4. Jeb's a real preppy guy. _____

5. They freaked on me. _____

6. You're the man! _____

7. Get a life! _____

8. That was a trip! _____

9. Her story is bogus. _____

10. Stacy's chillin' out today. _____

PRACTICE 16

On your own or in a group, make a list of slang words you've heard from friends, relatives, music, or television. Define these words and then quiz other class members about their meanings.

PRACTICE 17

Using slang words from Practice 16, write a short play or skit in which these words are used. Perform this skit for the class.

PRACTICE 18

Many words that were once considered slang or foreign words have become part of the English language. Look up the following words in a dictionary or English book, and tell where they came from: **jazz, square, chigger, banjo, cola, bagel, glitch, schmaltz, phooey, hoodlum, fink, balcony, plaza, hooligan, gringos, mustang, alligator, depot, squash, skunk, teepee, rodeo.**

COMMON ABBREVIATIONS AND SYMBOLS

Review these common abbreviations and symbols. Check (✓) the ones you do not know. Then learn them as you prepare for the practice tests that follow.

a.m.	time between midnight and noon	No.	number
Apr.	April	Nov.	November
apt.	apartment	Oct.	October
Aug.	August	oz.	ounce
Ave.	Avenue	p.m.	time between noon and midnight
Blvd.	Boulevard	P.O.	Post Office
cm	centimeter	pt.	Pint
c/o	care of	qt.	Quart
Dec.	December	Rd.	Road
Dept.	Department	R_x	take/prescription
Dr.	Doctor/Drive	S or S.	South
E or E.	East	Sat.	Saturday
etc.	and so on	sec.	Secretary
Feb.	February	Sept.	September
Fri.	Friday	Soc. Sec.	Social Security
ft.	foot	St.	Street
g	gram	Sun.	Sunday
gal.	gallon	Thurs.	Thursday
in.	inch	tbs., tbsp., T.	tablespoon
Jan.	January	tsp.	teaspoon
Jr.	Junior	Tues.	Tuesday
km	kilometer	U.S.	United States
L	liter	W or W.	West
lb.	pound	Wed.	Wednesday
m	meter	yd.	yard
Mar.	March	&	and
M.D.	Doctor of Medicine	?	cent
mph	miles per hour	$	dollar
mo.	month	@	at
Mon.	Monday	©	copyright
Mr.	Mister	"	inches
Mrs.	a married woman	'	foot
Ms.	a female	#	number
mtn.	mountain	%	percent
N or N.	North, NE, NW (or any combination of E, W, N and S)		

In letters and on envelopes, use the United States Postal Service abbreviations for names of states. Examples: AL - Alabama, CA - California, FL - Florida, GA - Georgia, TX - Texas.

PRACTICE 19

Directions: Match the abbreviations from the left column with their meanings in the right column.

MATCHING TEST

_____	1.	M.D.	A.	miles per hour
_____	2.	km	B.	gram
_____	3.	etc.	C.	Social Security
_____	4.	tsp.	D.	ounce
_____	5.	@	E.	care of
_____	6.	R$_x$	F.	Junior
_____	7.	P.O.	G.	Boulevard
_____	8.	?	H.	quart
_____	9.	yd.	I.	liter
_____	10.	qt.	J.	Avenue
_____	11.	mph	K.	secretary
_____	12.	oz.	L.	Post Office
_____	13.	sec.	M.	take / prescription
_____	14.	g	N.	yard
_____	15.	Soc. Sec.	O.	cent
_____	16.	Jr.	P.	teaspoon
_____	17.	Ave.	Q.	kilometer
_____	18.	L	R.	at
_____	19.	Blvd.	S.	and so on
_____	20.	c/o	T.	Doctor of Medicine

PRACTICE 20

Directions: Write the abbreviations or symbols for the following words.

1. Thursday   _____

2. March   _____

3. United States   _____

4. apartment   _____

5. dollar   _____

6. time between midnight and noon   _____

7. mountain   _____

8. meter   _____

9. street   _____

10. a married woman   _____

PRACTICE 21

Directions: Write the word or phrase for the following abbreviations and symbols.

1. gal. _____

2. Sun. _____

3. cm _____

4. Rd. _____

5. & _____

6. Dr. _____

7. W _____

8. p.m. _____

9. mo. _____

10. Apr. _____

11. Wed. _____

12. ft. _____

13. S _____

14. Ms. _____

15. c/o _____

16. # _____

SYNONYMS AND ANTONYMS

Synonyms - words that have **similar** or the **same** meanings. Synonyms can help you increase your word knowledge. A <u>thesaurus</u> can help you expand your word power. It is a mini-dictionary which contains synonyms.

Examples: <u>Height</u> is a synonym for <u>elevation</u>. <u>Increase</u> is a synonym for <u>intensify</u>.

Antonyms - words that mean the **opposite** of other words. The words <u>hot</u> and <u>cold</u> have opposite meanings, so they are antonyms. Use a thesaurus to expand your knowledge of antonyms.

Examples: <u>Apart</u> is an antonym for <u>together</u>. <u>Increase</u> is an antonym for <u>decrease</u>.

PRACTICE 22: SYNONYM MATCHING

Directions: Match the terms in the left column with a similar meaning from the right column.

_____	1. courageous	A.	silhouette
_____	2. currency	B.	quiet
_____	3. direction	C.	awful
_____	4. freedom	D.	money
_____	5. outline	E.	stable
_____	6. permanent	F.	fearless
_____	7. praise	G.	know
_____	8. silence	H.	congratulate
_____	9. tragic	I.	way
_____	10. understand	J.	independence

PRACTICE 23: ANTONYM MATCHING

Directions: Match the following terms in the left column with the opposite meaning from the right column.

_____	1. democracy	A.	trivial
_____	2. disgusting	B.	crooked
_____	3. easy	C.	lose
_____	4. fight	D.	withhold
_____	5. give	E.	dictatorship
_____	6. important	F.	evening
_____	7. locate	G.	difficult
_____	8. morning	H.	beautiful
_____	9. straight	I.	demand
_____	10. supply	J.	cooperate

WORD CLASSIFICATION

Many words in the English language have very broad meanings. As a result, many other concepts and ideas can be organized under these words. When words are classified, words that have meanings that come from the same source are grouped together.

Example: The word **science** can be grouped into different categories, such as **biology, physics,** and **astronomy. Astronomy** can be further broken down into the study of **stars, planets,** and **black holes.**

Below are two semantic maps of word classifications and the categories in which they can be divided:

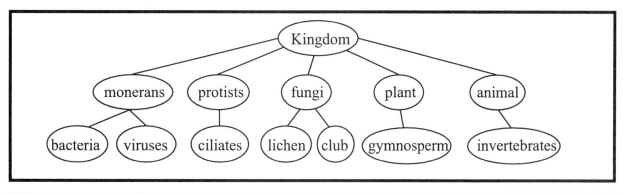

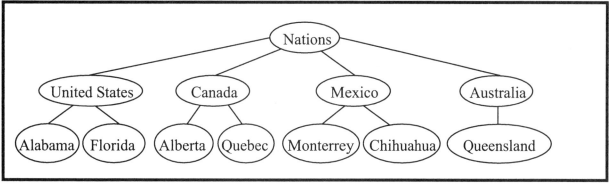

PRACTICE 24: WORD CLASSIFICATION DIAGRAM

Directions: Review each set of words, and draw a semantic map showing how the words should be classified together. Use the maps above as guides.

1. books, newspapers, television, internet, video, print, electronic media, magazines, information

2. Chinese, pizza, Mexican, won ton soup, fajitas, Italian, fried rice, tacos, foods, spaghetti

PRACTICE 25

Match the items below with the correct classification title.

		Items		**Classification Title**
_____	1.	Monopoly, Risk, Life	a.	elements
_____	2.	broom, dust pan, mop	b.	body fluids
_____	3.	azaleas, tulips, daisies	c.	transportation
_____	4.	measles, flu, cold	d.	spices
_____	5.	blood, water, mucus, phlegm	e.	board games
_____	6.	oxygen, silicon, nickel, sulfur	f.	flowers
_____	7.	Cherokee, Navajo, Apache	g.	poisons
_____	8.	boat, car, airplane	h.	floor cleaning
_____	9.	cloves, curry, pepper, nutmeg	i.	diseases
_____	10.	arsenic, cyanide, strychnine	j.	Native American Tribes

PRACTICE 26

Match the word on the right with the word group to which it belongs.

		Word Group		**Word**
_____	1.	North America, Europe, Asia	a.	purple
_____	2.	history, mathematics, grammar, literature	b.	science
_____	3.	dogs, cats, mice	c.	Alaska
_____	4.	yellow, green, red	d.	German
_____	5.	Alabama, Georgia, Mississippi	e.	Arctic
_____	6.	New York, Los Angeles, Houston	f.	whole numbers
_____	7.	French, English, Spanish	g.	Antarctica
_____	8.	Atlantic, Pacific, Indian	h.	dolphins
_____	9.	North, East, South	i.	Birmingham
_____	10.	fractions, decimals, integers	j.	West

ANALOGIES

An **analogy** is a partial or limited similarity between groups of words or ideas. Two things, essentially different in nature, that possess something in common can make an analogy. We can express the relationship between the words with the symbol : which means "is to." The double symbol :: between the two sets of words means "as." Thus, the analogy **man : boy :: woman : girl** can be stated: **man is to boy as woman is to girl.** There are several ways that sets of words can have something in common. In fact, there are at least ten ways.

1. **cause - effect** - One word (cause) has an effect on the second word.
   Example: **cut : pain**

2. **size** - One word object is drastically different in size than another.
   Example: **elephant : hamster**

3. **shape** - Two word objects share the same shape in common.
   Example: **chessboard : square**

4. **time** - Two words measure increments of time.
   Example: **Thursday : Friday**

5. **similarities** - Two words have a similar meaning (synonyms).
   Example: **icy : freezing**

6. **opposites** - Two words have an opposite meaning (antonyms).
   Example: **darkness : light**

7. **part to whole** - One word is a category of the other word.
   Example: **leaves : branch**

8. **purpose or use** - Both words are used together in some action.
   Example: **needle : thread**

9. **object to action** - A word is <u>paired</u> with an action.
   Example: **basketball : dribble**

10. **worker and tool** - A type of worker is paired with a tool of his or her trade.
    Example: **doctor : stethoscope**

PRACTICE 27: ANALOGY QUESTIONS

Directions: Read the following statements and fill in the blanks with the appropriate analogies.

1.   Bubble is to sphere as can is to _____.

      A. will   C. cylinder
      B. jar   D. peanut butter

2. Studying is to school as singing is to _____.

    A. playing   C. clapping
    B. chorus   D. birds

3. Spoke is to wheel as bone is to _____.

    A. body   C. cartilage
    B. muscle   D. hard

4. Car is to driving as book is to _____.

    A. worm   C. talking
    B. opening   D. reading

5. Island is to ocean as mountain is to _____.

    A. river   C. cave
    B. valley   D. continent

6. Day is to month as month is to _____.

    A. week   C. hour
    B. year   D. century

7. Dragonfly is to eagle as minnow is to _____.

    A. tadpole   C. algae
    B. shark   D. goldfish

8. Bible is to preacher as scissors is to _____.

    A. tailor   C. cutting
    B. doctor   D. miner

9. Burn is to scar as pierce is to _____.

    A. ear   C. hole
    B. through   D. nail

10. Pen is to paper as brush is to _____.

    A. tangle   C. away
    B. push   D. canvas

11. Finger is to hand as tooth is to _____.

    A. brush   C. mouth
    B. tiger   D. tongue

36   Copyright © American Book Company

12. Birth is to death as fire is to _____.

    A. walking   C. burning
    B. ice   D. melting

13. Fork is to knife as canoe is to _____.

    A. oar   C. water
    B. fish   D. jet ski

14. Marble is to bowling ball as CD is to _____.

    A. baseball   C. Frisbee
    B. cassette   D. light bulb

15. Minute is to second as day is to _____.

    A. minute   C. night
    B. hour   D. week

16. Prism is to triangular as lens is to _____.

    A. square   C. triangle
    B. elliptical   D. concave

17. Lens is to camera as wheel is to _____.

    A. oven   C. computer
    B. motorcycle   D. table

18. Sun is to moon as computer is to _____.

    A. calculator   C. pencil
    B. microchip   D. chaos

19. Brewing is to coffee as baking is to _____.

    A. oven   C. gas
    B. hot   D. cookie

20. Spinning is to dizzy as relaxing is to _____.

    A. excited   C. sleepy
    B. ready   D. confused

CHAPTER 1 REVIEW

Write a synonym for each underlined word.

1. A long <u>surname</u> _____

2. A large <u>fraction</u> _____

Write a definition for each underlined word.

3. United States <u>citizen</u> _____

4. The young man's <u>charisma</u> _____

Write a synonym for each underlined word in the sentences below.

5. More <u>options</u> are possible with a high school diploma. _____

6. We are covered by a full manufacturer's <u>warranty</u>. _____

7. Be <u>punctual</u> for your job interview tomorrow. _____

Write the best meaning for each prefix, root, or suffix.

8. The "ance" in <u>insurance</u> makes the word mean _____.

9. What should you add to the word <u>smooth</u> to make it mean "like" or "in manner"? _____

10. The "pre" in <u>pretrial</u> means _____.

Write the best meaning for the underlined examples of dialect, idioms, and usage.

11. <u>Look over</u> this story, and tell me what you think. _____

12. <u>Drop me a line</u> when you visit Disney World in Florida. _____

Write the correct meaning for the underlined symbol or abbreviation.

13. The symbol <u>c/o</u> means _____.

14. The symbol <u>R_x</u> means _____.

15. The correct abbreviation for <u>South</u> is _____.

Write the word that means the opposite of the underlined word.

16. The United States <u>exports</u> many products to Mexico and Canada. _____

17. Brett's injury resulted in a <u>temporary</u> leave for the basketball team. _____

Write the correct classification.

18. Lichen, molds, and mushrooms would be classified as _____.

19. Richard Nixon, Gerald Ford, Jimmy Carter, and Ronald Reagan can all be classified as _____.

20. <u>Men</u> <u>Women</u> <u>Children</u> _____

Solve the following analogies.

21. <u>Danger</u> is to <u>security</u> as <u>peace</u> is to _____.

22. <u>Bee</u> is to <u>hive</u> as <u>bird</u> is to _____.

23. <u>Cheetah</u> is to <u>mammal</u> as <u>iguana</u> is to _____.

24. <u>Justice</u> is to <u>unbiased</u> as <u>injustice</u> is to _____.

25. <u>Social studies</u> is to <u>education</u> as <u>baseball</u> is to _____.

CHAPTER 1 TEST

Circle the answer that has the same or almost the same meaning as the underlined word.

1. Protect against <u>liability</u>

    A. freedom   C. popularity
    B. obligation   D. viewpoint

2. An adult's <u>marital status</u>

    A. single   C. divorced
    B. married   D. single, married, or divorced

3. The <u>opaque</u> surface

    A. invisible   C. smooth
    B. translucent   D. non-transparent

4. <u>Prescription</u> for a sore throat

    A. an order for military duty
    B. the thought process before you write
    C. a physician's instruction for preparing and administering medicine
    D. written instructions for billing and receiving a magazine

5. Good <u>credit</u>

    A. ability to borrow and repay money
    B. relationship with your employer
    C. knowledge about various types of information
    D. experience with people in your community

6. A <u>round trip</u> plane fare

    A. the cost for a ticket to a destination
    B. the cost of a ticket from a destination
    C. the cost of a ticket around the world
    D. the cost of a ticket to and from a destination

Select the word or phrase that matches the meaning of the underlined word.

7. Just a few years ago, computers were <u>massive</u> machines.

    A. complex   C. large
    B. rare   D. small

8. I felt so <u>inadequate</u>; I almost wanted to leave.

   A. strong   C. cool
   B. helpless   D. ridiculous

9. The video <u>depicts</u> a real volcanic eruption.

   A. releases   C. avoids
   B. ignites   D. shows

10. <u>Fatigue</u> is more common in adults than in children.

   A. weariness   C. joy
   B. energy   D. disease

11. Headache, nausea, and fever are <u>symptoms</u> of the flu.

   A. principles   C. purposes
   B. causes   D. signs

12. Studies of volcanoes provide unique opportunities to <u>decipher</u> how the earth was formed.

   A. feel sorry for   C. figure out
   B. disapprove   D. exaggerate

13. Her whispers were <u>inaudible</u> in the crowded mall.

   A. heard   C. unheard
   B. spoken   D. loud

Choose the best meaning for each prefix, root, or suffix.

14. What do you add to the word <u>appear</u> to make it mean "to do again"?

   A. re   C. dis
   B. in   D. un

15. What does the "scope" in <u>telescope</u> mean?

   A. hear   C. expand
   B. see   D. shrink

16. The "inter" in <u>interstate</u> makes the word mean

   A. out of state.   C. between states.
   B. within the state. D. understate.

17. The "tele" in <u>telescope</u> means

    A.   star.   C.   phone.
    B.   distance.   D.   communicate.

18. What does the "ject" in <u>ejection</u> mean?

    A.   pop   C.   throw
    B.   shift   D.   slip

Choose the best meaning for the underlined examples of dialect, idioms, and slang.

19. Anton <u>be</u> mean when I tells him 'bout Talisha.

    A.   walks   C.   was
    B.   talks   D.   is

20. She's <u>a trip</u> when she bowls.

    A.   funny   C.   happy
    B.   mean   D.   sad

21. <u>In a nutshell</u>, Vu got all B's on his report card.

    A.   Sadly   C.   Finally
    B.   In a short time   D.   In summary

Choose the meaning for the underlined symbol or abbreviation.

22. The symbol <u>&</u> means

    A.   and.   C.   dollar.
    B.   percent.   D.   only.

23. The correct abbreviation for time between noon and midnight is _____.

    A.   a.m.   C.   p.m.
    B.   P.O.   D.   pt.

24. The correct abbreviation for <u>pound</u> is _____.

    A.   &   C.   lb.
    B.   pd.   D.   *

25. The correct abbreviation for <u>mountain</u> is _____.

    A.   mtn.   C.   mo.
    B.   mph   D.   m

26. The symbol @ means

    A. percent.
    B. afternoon.
    C. Avenue.
    D. at.

Select the word that means the <u>opposite</u> of the underlined word.

27. To <u>recruit</u> high school graduates, the United States Army offers good pay and benefits.

    A. enlist
    B. discourage
    C. contact
    D. discharge

28. A <u>majority</u> of people in this state like baseball.

    A. population
    B. minority
    C. large number
    D. variety

29. The musicians gave an <u>impressive</u> performance.

    A. amazing
    B. interesting
    C. lively
    D. inferior

Select the correct classification.

30. <u>Georgia</u> <u>Alabama</u> <u>Mississippi</u>

    A. countries
    B. rivers
    C. states
    D. regions

31. Langston Hughes, Zora Neale Hurston, William Faulkner, and Flannery O'Connor would be classified as

    A. diplomats.
    B. singers.
    C. athletes.
    D. writers.

32. <u>Biology</u> <u>Geology</u> <u>Chemistry</u>

    A. living things
    B. social sciences
    C. glossaries
    D. natural sciences

33. <u>surprise</u> <u>sadness</u> <u>anger</u>

    A. degrees
    B. emotions
    C. interests
    D. synonyms

34. What do the following items share most in common? Truck, car, van, sedan.

    A. transportation
    B. size
    C. color
    D. cost

Solve the following analogies.

35. <u>Salt</u> is to <u>pepper</u> as <u>sugar</u> is to _____.

    A.   cinnamon   C.   milk
    B.   chocolate   D.   jelly

36. A <u>clock</u> is to <u>time</u> as a <u>liter</u> is to _____.

    A.   volume   C.   length
    B.   coke   D.   quart

37. <u>Computer</u> is to <u>monitor</u> as <u>VCR</u> is to _____.

    A.   television   C.   movie theater
    B.   CD player   D.   remote control

38. <u>Actor</u> is to <u>entertainment</u> as <u>engineer</u> is to _____.

    A.   college   C.   biology
    B.   calculator   D.   construction

39. <u>Tunnel</u> is to <u>skyscraper</u> as <u>cave</u> is to _____.

    A.   river   C.   boulder
    B.   mountain   D.   gold

40. <u>Anger</u> is to <u>calmness</u> as <u>mental illness</u> is to _____.

    A.   sickness   C.   exercise
    B.   sanity   D.   intelligence

<table>
<tr><td>

Chapter

2

</td><td>

FINDING THE MAIN IDEA

</td></tr>
</table>

The **main idea** is the central point or controlling idea of a passage. Many times it is stated directly in the title, the beginning, or at the end of a passage. Sometimes, however, the main idea may only be implied rather than stated directly. You need to identify two kinds of main idea statements about a reading selection. They are the following:

1) **A Statement or Paraphrase of a Directly Stated Main Idea**

2) **A Summary Statement of an Implied Main Idea**

A DIRECTLY STATED MAIN IDEA IN A PARAGRAPH

When you read a paragraph where the **main idea is directly stated,** you will usually find some or all of the main idea in the title, beginning, or ending sentences. Consequently, the main idea will be a statement or restatement (paraphrase) of those sentences. Look at the following examples.

The Comeback of Rabies

Rabies, a deadly disease to both animals and humans, is on the increase in many areas of Florida. In fact, the number of reported human exposures to rabies has not been as high since the 1940s. This particular strain of rabies was brought to Florida by Texas coyotes. Truckloads of these coyotes are imported into the state by hunting clubs and are used in fox hunts. The disease has always been found among wild animals, but the real problem is that fewer than half of all dogs, cats, and farm animals have been vaccinated against it. In 1994, twenty cats, ten dogs, and three horses contracted rabies, an increase of 500% in the last five years. Domestic animals must be vaccinated, for they are the ones most likely to have contact with humans.

Based on this passage, what is the main idea of the paragraph?

A. Rabies is a very contagious and dangerous disease.
B. Brought to Florida by coyotes, rabies is quickly spreading among domestic animals.
C. Few domestic animals have been vaccinated against rabies.
D. Domestic animals have more contact with humans than do wild animals.

Because the title, first sentence, and last sentence contain the main points of the paragraph, the best choice is B. **Florida, rabies, quickly spreading,** and **domestic animals** are the key words in the answer that state or paraphrase the main ideas in the first and last sentences.

Choices A, C, and D contain only parts of the main idea. While they each refer to key topics like rabies, disease, and domestic animals, they do not mention that rabies is **spreading** or **on the increase in Florida.**

A DIRECTLY STATED MAIN IDEA IN A PASSAGE OF SEVERAL PARAGRAPHS

At times you need to locate the **directly stated main idea in a passage of several paragraphs.** In this situation, you need to skim the title, the first, and last sentences of all the paragraphs before choosing the best statement or restatement of the main idea in the passage below.

East Meets West

It is amazing how the Japanese have retained their cultural heritage while simultaneously integrating many parts of Western culture. One of the most popular adaptations is the style of dress. Many Japanese today wear "western" style clothing such as business suits, active wear, jeans and T-shirts. Traditional clothing is often reserved for special occasions.

Many Japanese also have adopted western furnishings into their homes. It is not unusual to have a completely westernized home with only one traditional Japanese room. Western influences can be seen throughout Japanese popular culture, such as fast-food restaurants, music, and the movies.

The Japanese also have more time to devote to leisure. Surveys show that spending time with family, friends, home improvement, shopping, and gardening form the mainstream of leisure, together with sports and travel. The number of Japanese making overseas trips has increased notably in recent years. Domestic travel, picnics, hiking and cultural events rank high among favorite activities.

Japan is a land with a vibrant and fascinating history, varied culture, traditions, and customs that are hundreds of years old, yet segments of its society and economy are as new as the microchips in a personal computer.

The best statement of the main idea is that

A. in Japan, you will find evidence of both traditional customs and culture as well as examples of Western-style adaptations.
B. in Japan, jeans, fast-food, picnics, and personal computers are very popular.
C. in Japan, people always enjoy traveling overseas and shopping.
D. Japanese and American culture are so similar that you really cannot tell the difference between them.

As you review this paragraph again, you will use the same strategies for this multiple-paragraph passage as you did for a single paragraph. Once again, the title, the first sentences of each paragraph, and the last sentence of the passage contain the key words **Japan, culture, customs, traditions, Western-style,** and **adaptation.** Since choice A contains all of these key ideas, it would be the best restatement of the main idea of the passage.

Choices B and C focus only on a few details in the passage. Choice D is incorrect because the facts in the passage indicate that the Japanese still maintain some of their traditions. Therefore, Japanese and American cultures are not identical.

Tips for Finding a Stated Main Idea

1. **Read the title.** The main topic for the paragraph or passage is often mentioned in the title.

2. **Read the entire paragraph or passage.** You'll get an overview of who or what the selection is about.

3. **Read the first and last sentence of each paragraph.** Most of the key words and ideas will be stated in these places.

4. **Choose the answer that is the best statement or restatement of the paragraph or passage.** Your choice should contain the key words mentioned in the title, the first sentence or the last sentences of the paragraph or passage.

AN IMPLIED MAIN IDEA IN A PARAGRAPH

First, let's look at the meaning of the word implied. Consider the following sentence.

> Outside, the wind was bitterly cold, and the snow was falling fast.

What season of the year is it? It is winter, of course. Does the sentence state that it is winter? The answer is no, but you can tell it is winter because of the description. If the word "winter" were in the sentence, the season would be **directly stated.** Because the season is described without using the word "winter," the season of the year is **implied or inferred.**

You may read a paragraph where the **main idea is implied** rather than directly stated. Then you must develop a different set of strategies to identify the main idea. You are still looking for the central point of the paragraph, but the author includes only details and facts in the selection. No one sentence summarizes the entire paragraph, but together these sentences revolve around a main idea that is not directly stated. The reader must infer what that idea is.

A good approach for determining an implied main idea could be learned by reviewing the paragraph below. Read this paragraph, and answer the question that follows.

Putting Energy Back Into Your Life

Are you getting enough water? Think of your houseplants. When they are short on water, they droop. The same thing happens to you! Our bodies are made up of millions of cells, the principal part of these cells is water. If the cells are low on water, you will function at less than full efficiency. Strive for six to eight glasses of water each day.

What is the main idea of this paragraph?

A. Houseplants need water to live.
B. The body's cells are composed of a high percentage of water.
C. Our bodies are made up of millions of cells.
D. Drink water because your body needs it to be efficient.

As you reread this paragraph and its question about the main idea, you would learn from the title that the topic is **regaining energy.** However, this paragraph does not deal specifically with regaining energy. Only by examining the whole passage is this topic fully discussed. So the main idea of this paragraph is about the importance of water but not about regaining lost energy.

In a paragraph with a directly stated main idea, you would usually find the main idea by reading the first or last sentence of the paragraph. The first sentence asks the question, "Are you getting enough water?" Though the middle sentences make other assertions about the importance of drinking water, they do not really discuss how to replace the body's energy. The last sentence commands the reader to drink six to eight glasses of water per day, but again ignores discussion on replacing lost energy in the body.

Since the title, first, and last sentences do not provide a complete main idea statement, the only other choices are the middle sentences. However, they mainly relate facts about how all living cells are mostly composed water and need water to be efficient.

On the other hand, **if you combine all of these factual sentences together,** you can arrive at a main idea about the paragraph. That statement, of course, is D in your choice of answers. Even though D is not directly stated, it is a broad enough summary of all the other sentences in the paragraph. Therefore, it is the **main idea**. The other choices (A, B, or C) are specific facts mentioned in the paragraph, but they are not broad enough to be the main point.

AN IMPLIED MAIN IDEA IN A PASSAGE OF SEVERAL PARAGRAPHS

At times, you may need to determine the implied main idea in a passage of several paragraphs. The main idea will summarize all of the facts and ideas in the passage. The title would help you decide on the topic, but you would need to combine the various ideas in the paragraphs to come up with a main idea statement for the passage.

Read the entire passage about the **Scourge of the South**, and determine the main idea.

Scourge of the South is Heading North

Look out Yankees. The plant that ate Dixie may be coming your way. Kudzu, a vine with lush green leaves and beautiful purple flowers, originated in Japan. It first appeared in the U. S. at the 1876 Centennial Exposition in Philadelphia and became popular in the 1930s when soil conservationists urged farmers to plant it to halt erosion. They succeeded–too well. Kudzu is now a common weed from East Texas to Florida and as far north as Pennsylvania. It can grow a foot a day and covers roadsides, telephone poles, trees, stop signs, and anything else in its way. Kudzu is tough, too: Only repeated doses of strong and expensive herbicide can eradicate it.

Researchers at Duke University have studied the plant and have decided its northward spread is limited by low temperatures. They concluded, however, that just a 3° increase in average temperature could allow kudzu to spread as far as Michigan.

But goat ranchers can rejoice. Research at the University of Georgia has shown that four grazing goats can destroy one acre of kudzu in two years.

The best statement of the main idea is that

A. only powerful herbicides can kill kudzu.
B. kudzu originated in Japan and prevents soil erosion in the United States.
C. some people love kudzu. Others despise it.
D. at one time beneficial, kudzu is now a nuisance which is hard to eliminate.

How did you decide that D was the best choice? You found that D best combines the facts and ideas in each paragraph, even though there is no sentence like D in the passage. It is simply the **broadest statement** of this passage's main idea. Thus, by joining the facts together, you arrive at an implied main idea.

Choice A has only one detail mentioned in paragraph 3. Choice B summarizes only paragraph 2 of the passage, and choice C is not clearly discussed in the passage.

Tips for Determining an Implied Main Idea

1. **Read the title.** The title will help you identify the topic of the selection.

2. **Read the entire paragraph or passage.** You'll get a general understanding of the selection.

3. **Reread the facts and details in each paragraph.** Think of overall ideas that they share in common.

4. **Choose the answer that summarizes all of the facts and ideas in the passage.** Confirm your choice by going back to the passage to check your evidence one more time.

PRACTICE 1: MAIN IDEA IN A PARAGRAPH

Read each of the following paragraphs. Decide whether the main idea is stated or implied. If the main idea is stated, underline it. If the main idea is implied, write it in your own words in the space provided. Discuss your answers with the class or instructor.

1.   A back to the basics movement is shaking up the business of farming agribusiness by getting impressive yields with fewer chemicals. An example of the cycles of a healthy dairy farm includes a farm aerated by earthworms and brimming with fungi and bacteria. Legume roots such as peas, beans, and clover fix nitrogen in the soil. Five year crop rotations on this dairy farm begin with an alfalfa harvest; roots are left for soil enhancement. After corn is harvested, rye is planted for winter cover, a pattern repeated the second year. Oats and alfalfa replace corn and rye in the third year. In years four and five, alfalfa is cut monthly, late in spring to fall. Alfalfa and grasses provide feed for cattle which produce fertilizer as does plant residue. Ladybugs and other insects are introduced to the fields to control pests. With fewer insecticides used and entering the atmosphere to return to earth in rain, the purity of rivers and drinking water improves.

_____

_____

2.    Scientists don't know much about the hagfish swimming the waters of the Gulf of Maine except that it has become a nuisance to New England fishermen. The Shoals Marine Laboratory sent out an underwater laboratory to study the fish, and at first, they could find hardly any. Then they set out some smelly, rotten fish and soon the sub was surrounded by hundreds of hagfish. It was picnic time for the fish, but not the scientists. The hagfish produces large amounts of slime as a defense mechanism: hence the nickname "slime hag." The fishermen have no compliments for these creatures that raid their lobster cages and fishing nets leaving only skin and bones behind. They look similar to an eel. Some fishermen are getting even by selling the skins of the hagfish to Korean tanners who make them into wallets and checkbook covers.

_____

_____

3.   For ship owners, barnacles are a multimillion dollar headache. Workers remove around 15 tons of marine growth–mostly barnacles–from one ship each year. The drag caused by a six month accumulation can force a vessel to burn 40 percent more fuel just to maintain a normal cruising speed. The cost for idle hours in port plus cleanup charges for U.S. shipping interests— military and civilian–comes to several hundred million dollars per year.

_____

_____

4.   Named for Atropos, a Greek goddess who determined the length of one's life, deadly nightshade (*Atropa belladonna*) is a poisonous plant from Europe, Asia, and North Africa. Now Czech researchers have found a new role for nightshade: In their lab, it absorbs and detoxifies PCBs, major pollutants. Martina Mackova and her colleagues at the institute of Chemical Technology in Prague are beginning tests in contaminated soil, planting nightshade infected with a bacterial parasite that whets the plants' appetite.

                        – *National Geographic*, May 1998

5.   Were dogs already "man's best friend" by 6500 B.C.? Did their human masters mourn the loss of human helpers?

      The people who lived in the Illinois River Valley 8,500 years ago certainly cared about their domesticated dogs. A team of scientists has uncovered almost complete skeletons of four dogs, carefully laid on their sides, in specially dug, shallow graves. They are the oldest known dog burials in North America and among the oldest domestic dog remains found anywhere, says Darcy F. Morey of the University of Tennessee.

                        – *National Geographic*, November 1992

PRACTICE 2: MAIN IDEAS IN PASSAGES

Read the following passages. Decide whether the main idea is stated or implied. If the main idea is stated, underline it. If the main idea is implied, write it in your own words in the space provided. Discuss your answers with the class or instructor.

1.   **Volunteering**

      Nothing can be more satisfying in life than taking the opportunity to volunteer. Taking time out of your play and work schedule to spend with others can be very rewarding. For instance, spending time with cancer patients in the children's wing of the hospital is really special. Playing games and reading books to the children just make you feel tingly inside knowing you brought a smile to a little child.

      One volunteer, Dalilah, made a special impression on the children by teaching them to finger paint with their hands and with their feet. She also taught them magic tricks with coins and handkerchiefs! Everyone who volunteers, whether they teach the children something or just listen to them, makes a difference in their lives. That is what volunteering is all about – making a difference!

51

2.   **The House is Burning!**

      I was so mad when my mom came home from work and announced that we all had to plan and practice a fire escape plan. We had to go outside as quick as possible from whatever room we were in when Mom rang the bell. My job was to grab my little brother Josh. We had to meet under the maple tree outside our house. Since there were eleven of us, Mom assigned us numbers in case she would forget our names. I hated practicing these fire drills because we had to do these drills in school, too.

      One day after two years of these monthly drills, my sister, Carolyn, was playing with logs in the fireplace. Sparks jumped out of the fire and started burning up the living room carpet. Eagerly, the flames licked the furniture and the wallpaper. Smoke filled all of the rooms, setting off our twelve smoke detectors. It was our familiarity with the escape plan that saved our lives, valuables, and even our pets, Fluffy and Foofoo. Unlike our neighbors who lost all of their valuables in a fire, we were able to save many important pictures and jewelry that had been in our family for decades.

_____

_____

3.   **The Little Girl That Could**

      Little Zack went outside and walked around the outdoor pool. There was something shiny in the bottom of the waters, and when he looked closer, he fell in the water. His sister, Penny, was making her little brother a peanut butter and jelly sandwich when she heard the splash. Seeing that her brother was nowhere in sight, Penny ran outside toward the pool.

      When Penny arrived at the pool, she saw that her brother was motionless at the bottom of the pool. Quickly, Penny jumped in and brought Zack to the surface. At nine years old, Penny had just taken a CPR course at her school in her gym class. She immediately started doing what she had learned. Zack was not breathing and did not have a pulse. She turned Zack's head upwards and began doing chest compressions and mouth-to-mouth resuscitation. At this moment, Penny's mom came outside looking for her children. "Mom, call 911. Zack fell into the pool," Penny yelled. Penny's mom ran back inside and did what she was told. Penny's CPR had worked. Zack spit out the water quickly. Soon, Zack's pulse returned, and he was breathing on his own.

      By the time the ambulance arrived, Zack's color had returned to his face, and he could talk. The paramedics were amazed that this little girl had saved her brother's life. Instantly, the girl became a celebrity at school, and the school threw a party for her and the firemen that had taught her class CPR.

_____

_____

4. **All the World's a Stage**

Stella and her new friend, Max, were in line for lunch in the cafeteria. Everyone was eating their food without making too much noise. Max had just finished telling Stella about the self-defense class he was taking after school. Stella asked Max, "Why don't you show me one of the special self-defense moves you learned?"

"Sure," Max said. "Just watch this!" Max, full of concentration, tilted his head back and slammed it into his cafeteria tray. Stella and the rest of the lunch room looked up in shock to see that Max had broken the cafeteria tray, and the skin on his forehead was wide open.

"Are you OK?" Stella asked as Max recovered from his display of power.

"Of course I am," Max said as he lost balance and crashed to the floor.

"What does breaking a cafeteria tray have to do with self-defense?" Stella asked. Max could not respond. He could only see stars spinning quickly around his head.

When Max returned from the hospital, he was just fine except for the thin scar he had on his forehead. One day several weeks later, Max was once again in line next to Stella at lunch. He turned to her and said, "That self-defense move turned out badly. Let me show you a new move I learned in gymnastics class!"

"Please," Stella said, "No more special tricks. Just be yourself, and stick to what you do best."

---

5. **The Dish Monster**

Kenny came home one day and checked the list to see what his daily chore was. Today, Kenny had to do the dishes. He went to the kitchen and rinsed the excess food off the dishes and silverware. He then loaded the dishwasher and made sure the plates did not touch each other. "Oh no!" Kenny said. "There is no dishwasher soap!" He kept looking on top of the sink and found a bottle of soap for washing dishes by hand. "Oh great!" Kenny said. "I'll just load this soap into the dishwasher and use it instead." Kenny put the soap in the dishwasher, turned it on, and went into the living room to watch TV.

About thirty minutes later, Kenny's dad walked into the kitchen with two bags full of groceries. He slipped all over the kitchen floor, and two heads of lettuce dropped into the foamy water. "Kenny!" his dad yelled when he regained his balance. "Come in here now!" Kenny ran into the kitchen and straight into a surprise. Suds covered the entire kitchen floor and the dishwasher kept making more.

"Whoa!" Kenny said as he fell down and slid into the kitchen table. "Ouch!" Kenny said, "What's happened here? I loaded the dishwasher and turned it on like the note said."

"Did you use hand dishwashing soap, Kenny?" his dad asked.

"Yes, Dad." Kenny answered.

"So that's what happened!" Kenny's dad chuckled. Soon, they began the biggest foam fight that kitchen had ever seen. Then they cleaned up the mess.

_____

_____

PRACTICE 3: MAIN IDEAS FROM PASSAGES

On your own or in a group, reread other paragraphs from this book starting with Chapter 3. Are the main ideas stated or implied? If they are stated, underline them. If they are implied, write them in your own words. Then share your findings with the class or the instructor. Have them rate the main ideas in four columns labeled **Too Narrow, Too Broad, Unrelated,** and **Appropriate.**

PRACTICE 4: MEDIA SEARCH FOR MAIN IDEAS

A. **IDEA EXCHANGE:** On your own or in a group, find paragraphs and passages on different topics in newspapers, magazines, or books. Write out the stated or implied main ideas you find on a separate sheet of paper. Bring the articles to class.

Exchange only the articles with another student or group members. See if they identify the same main ideas that you did. Then share the results of your efforts with your instructor. Again, rating the main ideas as **Too Narrow, Too Broad, Unrelated,** and **Appropriate** would be helpful.

B. **PHOTO TITLES:** Share photos or pictures with a partner. Then think of titles (main ideas) to go with them.

C. **NEWS STORY TITLES:** Bring news stories to class. Cut out the titles, and keep them separate. Exchange only the articles, and come up with your own titles. Then see how closely they match the original titles.

CHAPTER 2 REVIEW

Read the following passages, and answer the question(s) that follow each passage.

This was the first week of middle school. The classes were so different – we had to change classes and rooms every time the bell rang. The lockers were little cubicles, and unfortunately, mine was on the bottom by the floor. The books for the classes were heavy and ripped my backpack. School was exciting, though, because there were so many new kids to meet and make friends with. The seating was assigned in all my classes, which forced me to talk to kids that were not already my friends. Everyone seemed to laugh and talk the whole class. It was hard for the teachers to keep us under control in the beginning. But somehow, they always knew how to make us behave ourselves and learn something important.

1. What is the main idea of this section? _____

_____

Selling Door-to-Door

Selling door-to-door can be very exciting, but there are important precautions to take when selling. When walking around the neighborhood, be aware of moving cars and stray dogs so you can avoid them. Always remember to be courteous to everyone you talk to. If a child answers the door, be sure to ask for the parents to come to the door. Look at the person you talk to in the eye and remember to smile. Never enter the house even if you are invited. Always thank people for their time when you leave. Most importantly, have a good time!

2. What is the main idea of this paragraph? _____

_____

Mowing the Grass – A Tragedy

One sunny day, Allen went outside to mow the lawn for his parents. Quickly, he started the motor and began mowing. "I bet I can finish this whole lawn in under thirty minutes!" Allen said. Because he was mowing so quickly, Allen did not notice the large rock in the middle of the lawn. He did not think to clear the lawn of sticks and rocks before he started mowing. The rock entered his lawn mower with a *crunch* and broke apart the blade. Rock fragments pelted Allen in his shoes and ankles. Allen cried and spoke aloud, saying, "Ouch. My ankle really hurts. My new shoes are all messed up. Now I can't even mow the grass. I'll never mow the lawn so quickly again."

3. What is the main idea of this paragraph? _____

_____

The men, for their parts, just like the Indians, impose all the work upon the poor women. They make their wives rise out of their beds early in the morning. At the same time, the men lie and snore till the sun has risen one-third of its course and lifted the fog. Then, after stretching and yawning for half an hour, they light their pipes, and under the protection of a cloud of smoke, venture into the open air; though if it were a little cold they return shivering into the chimney corner. When the weather is mild, they stand leaning with both their arms upon the cornfield fence and gravely consider whether they had best go and work a little with the hoe but generally find reasons to put it off until another time.

–Paraphrase from William Byrd, *In the History of the Dividing Line*

4.   What is the main idea of this passage? _____

_____

She was only 20 years old when she passed into eternity, her mummified body wrapped in fine linen and flower garlands. Carbon dating places the burial at 220 B.C. The mummy of a child lay at the foot of the coffin. When the woman lived, religious practices in Egypt were changing, influenced by contact with other Mediterranean peoples. But the inscriptions and the drawings on the mask, breastplate, and coffin reflect beliefs in physical resurrection and a ritual passage to life in the after-world. "Pure old-time Egyptian religion was doing well just before the Christian Era, thank you," states Dr. Griggs, "even here outside the Nile Valley." DNA studies should reveal the relationship between the woman and child and their ethnicity. The mummy will soon have an honored place in Cairo's Egyptian Museum.

– *National Geographic*

5.   What is the main idea of this passage? _____

_____

It's lovely to live on a raft. We had the sky, up there, all speckled with stars, and we used to lay on our backs and look up at them, and discuss about whether they was made, or only just happened – Jim he allowed they was made, but I allowed they happened; I judged it would have took too long to *make* so many. Jim said the moon could a laid them; well, that looked kind of reasonable, so I didn't say nothing against it, because I've seen a frog lay most as many, so of course it could be done. We use to watch the stars that fell, too, and see them streak down.

– Mark Twain *Huckleberry Finn*

6.   The main idea of the passage above is _____

_____

Once there was a beautiful woman who lived in a pleasant valley on the earth. The rest of the world was filled with rocks and mountains. In this valley, summer was the ruling season, and honey and fruit were always available. Her only companions were the beaver and the doe. She was the reigning spirit of this world, and nothing ever grew old or died.

One morning the woman followed a scarlet butterfly to a remote waterfall where the butterfly disappeared. Realizing she was lost, the woman fell asleep from exhaustion. When she woke, a being like herself stooped down and lifted her off the ground. Clothed in a robe of clouds, the man being told her he saw her as he traveled across the sky.

Because he rescued her, the man being had broken the command of the Great Spirit. He would remain on earth and share her companionship. For many moons, they lived happily in the valley. The woman bore a child. Sad because he broke the law, the man sought the guidance and forgiveness of the Great Spirit. The Great Spirit took pity on the man and the woman. He opened up many more valleys and plains for the future inhabitants, but because of the broken command, the Great Spirit caused the man and woman to labor for their food. They would also suffer from cold, grow old, and die when their heads became white as the feathers of swans.

– A Catawba Myth

7.   The main idea of this story is _____

_____

One of the most famous prime ministers in British history was Sir Winston Churchill. When he attended Harrow public school as a teenager, however, he was known for mischief and poor grades. In fact, this man who was so admired for his speaking ability failed his English class at Harrow. If his father had not been so well-known, young Winston would probably have been expelled from school.

After finishing at Harrow school, Winston went on to college. Narrowly escaping death, he served very capably in the military in India and Africa. As a British prime minister during World War II, his moving speeches and strong leadership inspired his people to continue fighting against Germany despite the challenges.

In his last years as a prime minister, Winston Churchill was invited back to Harrow to speak at their graduation ceremony. The students looked forward to hearing the wisdom of this man of many accomplishments. After a long introduction by the headmaster, Sir Winston Churchill came to the podium. He gave a short but stirring speech. "Young men, never give up," he said. "Never give up! Never give up. Never, never, never, never."

8.   What is the main idea of this passage? _____

_____

Poaching the Giant Panda

Deeply in debt and desperately seeking a way out, Wu Hui Chen of Shanghai decided to buy, then resell, a giant panda's pelt. His decision will cost him 12 years in a Chinese prison.

Wu went to Sichuan Province, home of the Giant Panda, and paid two men 30,000 yuan – about $5,500 – for a panda skin. He returned home, had it photographed, and, with the help of his associate Wang Shu He, he lured a buyer to Shanghai's Peace Hotel. When the buyer turned over payment of 200,000 yuan, police swooped in and arrested both Wu and Wang. For his help, Wang will spend eight years in prison.

Giant pandas, which number only 1,000 or so in the wild, are at risk of extinction; Chinese poachers and traffickers face the death penalty if they are caught. Still, more than 200 people have been arrested for illegal dealings in panda skins.

Stuart Parkins of the World Wide Fund for Nature says that demand for the exotic pelts is strongest in Taiwan but exists also in Japan and Hong Kong. The going price is about $10,000.

9.   The main idea is _____

_____

American teen-age girls must find their own husbands, and no one else can do it for them.

This concept is very difficult for teenagers in India to understand as you can tell from the following interview with two Indian teen-age girls.

"Don't you want to be able to choose your own husbands?" I asked.

"No, Never!" the girls answered vehemently. Nisha, a very beautiful girl with wide, almond-shaped eyes went on to say, "I don't want to worry about whether I'll get married or not. I know I'll get married. I know my parents are a better judge of character than I am. I am too young to make such a decision. When my parents choose someone for me, I know it will be someone that will be able to support me, and someone that my family already likes and respects.

"What if I lived in America and I chose a boy my family didn't like? Before it was over, everyone might be against me. There might be bad feelings at home with my parents because of my choice, and if I argued with my husband, who would support me?"

It was Rasheed's turn. "It seems the American system would be very humiliating for me. I would have to spend a lot more time making myself beautiful and attractive and try to figure out ways to get boys to notice me. And if the boy I liked didn't notice me, maybe I would feel like a failure as a person. I would have to compete with other girls to be the prettiest - it seems so demeaning and stressful. And what if I were shy? Would I get married?"

"Possibly not," I answered honestly.

Nisha asked the hardest question, "In America, does the girl get to choose? Isn't it the boy who chooses anyway?" A good question.

10.   The main idea is _____

_____

Lobstergate

An electrifying discovery was made by New Hampshire Fish and Game officers. A worker at the Portsmouth power plant allegedly found his job offered some outstanding employee benefits—a steady supply of lobsters sucked into the plant through a cooling pipe.

"We were in shock, obviously," said state marine biologist Bruce Smith. During peak times, 50 to 80 lobsters were being taken. An officer caught the employee headed home with 28 lobsters for his freezer, which was stuffed with 508 more.

The plant lies four miles from the Atlantic Ocean on the Piscataqua River, salty and rich in lobsters. Sand buildup had raised the bottom of the river allowing lobsters to crawl into an intake pipe. They wound up on a screen that is washed every four hours. The suspect could be fined $30,000 and spend a year in jail.

11.   What is the main idea of this passage? _____

_____

During the terrible Irish famine of 1847-1852, large numbers of Irish people immigrated to the United States. The most common route was Ireland to Liverpool, England and then to North America, usually to New York or Quebec, Canada.

The English and, sad to say, some Americans took great advantage of these poor immigrants, both upon leaving and arriving. Both governments looked the other way while ruthless businessmen brutalized and ripped off the immigrants.

When arriving at Liverpool, England, brokers would gather the starving immigrants and sell tickets at high prices and force them to stay in extremely crowded houses, also at high prices, until the ships were ready to sail. They promised safe and secure passage aboard good ships with plenty of food and water en route. They took the immigrants for as much as they could before letting them leave. There were plenty of laws regulating this traffic, but they were never enforced. The prejudice against the Irish was deeply seated in the culture of the time.

The ships, also called packets, were mostly old and small, a mere 180-250 tons. The immigrants called them "coffin ships" and for good reason. Thousands of people died en route from disease, starvation, and brutal treatment. It was not uncommon for a ship to lose half its passengers during the trip over.

12.   The main idea is _____

_____

CHAPTER 2 TEST

Read the following passages and answer the question that follows each passage.

Dolphins Ride a Wave

The United States Navy wanted to find out how much energy dolphins expend while swimming. The answer: as little as possible.

Terrie Williams and her team of researchers in Hawaii trained a pair of dolphins to swim next to a boat. They attached monitors to the dolphins to record heart and breathing rates and then took them out in a bay for tests.

The pair swam amid ships until the boat doubled its speed. Then they shifted to the stern wake and rode the wave, like bicyclists riding behind a truck. No amount of coaxing could get them to move.

Their average heart and breathing rates while riding the wake of the boat matched the rates at the lower speeds. They were going twice as fast with little change in energy use.

1. The best statement of the main idea is that

    A.   dolphins ride bicycles better than people.
    B.   dolphins can be easily trained to swim next to a boat.
    C.   dolphins conserve energy riding ocean waves.
    D.   the United States Navy studies dolphins to learn how they live in the ocean.

An Odd Bird With a Cow's Stomach

The hoatzin is an odd bird. Not only does it eat leaves, far more than any other bird, but it digests them like a cow or a sheep, grinding the leaves up in a specialized muscular crop. Up close, the hoatzin smells bad and flies poorly.

Scientists have known about the hoatzin for years. Recently, Wildlife Conservation International conducted a long study of this Venezuelan bird, supplying many more details.

About 85% of the hoatzin's diet is made up of green leaves. It prefers young, fresh leaves which are richer in protein and easier to digest. Since the hoatzin, unlike a cow, has no teeth, it "chews" the leaves up by rubbing them against sandpapery ridges in its crop. It keeps food in its gut 20 hours or more; a chicken digests its food in a few hours. Like a cow, the hoatzin produces fatty acids that aid fermentation, giving the hoatzin the nickname, stinkbird.

The hoatzin's digestive system has a price: The large crop results in a small breastbone and undersize muscles that limit its ability to fly. On landing it may crash into branches.

The bird *can* fly, however, enough to avoid predators or researchers.

2. The best statement of the main idea is that

    A.   the hoatzin's unique digestive system makes it different from most other birds.
    B.   scientists have known about the hoatzin for years.
    C.   like a cow, the hoatzin produces fatty acids that aid in fermentation, giving the hoatzin the nickname, stinkbird.
    D.   on landing, the hoatzin may crash into branches.

The Amusement Park

Jan and her friends, Dave and Peggy, saved their money and begged their parents to drive them to the amusement park. Finally, one sunny Saturday in March, they got their wish. Peggy's parents promised to pick them all up at eight o'clock. They ran to the roller coasters first. Dave got sick on the *Slingshot*, while Peggy and Jan screamed their heads off. After this ride, they rode the most thrilling roller coasters. Then they took a tour through the haunted house. All of them were very scared of the creeping things lurking around the corner. Dave promised to protect the girls, but at the first scare, he ran out the front door. Jan and Peggy promised to never let him live it down. With the sun setting, Peggy's parents arrived to pick them up, and they went home full of good memories.

3. The best statement of the main idea is that

    A. three friends decide to ride roller coasters until they are sick.
    B. three friends save their money and beg their parents to drive them to the amusement park.
    C. Dave, Peggy, and Jan are very excited about going to the amusement park.
    D. Dave, Peggy, and Jan spend an exciting day at the amusement park.

Manned Space Flight

For thousands of years, we have dreamed of the day when we would explore the vast universe that surrounds our planet. This aspiration stemmed not only from our curiosity, but also from our fundamental thirst for knowledge and our readiness to accept a challenge.

When Orville Wright made the first powered airplane flight in 1903 at speeds of 50 kilometers (31 miles) per hour, the significance of his achievement was barely recognized. Yet in little more than half a century following that historic event at Kitty Hawk, we succeeded in orbiting the Earth at speeds measured in thousands of miles per hour, and set foot on the moon.

Viewed in terms of time and distance, the challenge of space exploration seems insurmountable. Yet, a review of the technological accomplishments of the 20th century indicated that what appears as "impossible" is merely "difficult."

The exploration of space is following the pattern by which flight within the atmosphere was mastered. Each new development provides a platform from which to take the next step, and each step adds an increment of scientific knowledge, technological skill, and previously undreamed of benefits to mankind.

–NASA

4. The best statement of the main idea is that

    A. the space age began with the first powered airplane flight in 1903 at Kitty Hawk.
    B. the launching of satellites into the universe is one of many accomplishments of the Space Age.
    C. because of the many past achievements in technology, exploration of the universe is now possible.
    D. in the 20th century, advances in technology have provided many benefits to mankind.

WSA

PO Box 147829
Atlanta, GA 30032
1-800-555-1100

April 28, 1997

Ms. Tomika Jones
1234 First Street
Rock Hill, SC 29732

Dear Ms. Jones:

Thank you for your inquiry regarding your WSA water filtration system. The following information is of a general nature. If additional information is needed, please don't hesitate to contact me at our toll free telephone number, 1-800-555-1100.

The water filter is tested and rated to remove chlorine and remain bacteriostatic (inhibit bacteria growth within the unit) for a period of three (3) years. WSA cannot guarantee the unit's effectiveness after this three (3) year period of time. It is for this reason we strongly recommend the unit be replaced or removed after three (3) years. Under the pro-rata warranty, you may purchase a new 100S (under sink) for $180.00 less a 10% customer discount. The total price including shipping and handling charges for a new unit with a three (3) year pro-rata warranty will be $167.00 plus your local sales tax. You may expedite the shipment by calling me at 1-800-347-8525 and using your VISA or Mastercard, or you may send a check to my attention to the above address.

Sincerely,

Margie Walker

Margie Walker

5. The best statement of the main idea is that

   A. the WSA filtration system costs $167.00 plus tax, and it removes water impurities for up to three years.
   B. the WSA water filtration system is the best of its kind on the market today.
   C. the WSA water filtration system should be replaced after a period of three years.
   D. discounts of 10% are provided for customers using a VISA or Mastercard to pay for their WSA Water Filtration System.

Right Pillow For The Right Position

As the saying goes, "Different strokes for different folks." Everyone's got a favorite sleeping position and a favorite kind of pillow. But some pillows and positions are better than others.

Side Sleeping - Whether you've got trouble with your back or breathing, most doctors will tell you that sleeping on your side is best. But this position also creates the widest gap between the neck and mattress, so you'll want the firmest pillow for neck support. Keep in mind that a foam pillow will probably offer you more than a cushy down-filled one.

Thickness counts as well. If your pillow is too thick, the spine will bend up at the neck. If the pillow is too slim, it will bend down. Just right would be a pillow that's as thick as the distance from the ear to the outside of the shoulder. A slight upward curve is O.K. as long as the pillows don't arch your neck too much.

Back Sleeping - It's not quite as good as side sleeping, but it is acceptable, say physicians, if you find it comfortable. Pillow needs for back sleeping are a little different, however. You want to be careful not to have so much pillow under you that your head is bent forward, pressing the chin to the chest and cramping the neck. You may want to try a soft, down-filled pillow that allows your head to sink in but still supports and helps maintain your neck's natural curve.

6. The best statement of the main idea is that

   A. to avoid back pain at night, sleeping on your side is better than sleeping on your back.
   B. whether you sleep on your side or on your back, the firmness and thickness of your pillow is very important.
   C. for side sleeping, make sure your pillow is firm but not too thick.
   D. pillows are not as important as your sleeping position at night.

Antarctica

Antarctica would be the smallest continent if you counted only the actual land. The ice covering it makes it larger than Europe or Australia. The deepest ice is thicker than ten times the height of the Sears Tower in Chicago, the world's tallest building.

Antarctica is a land of breathtaking landscape and life-taking climate. On Antarctica, scientists recorded the world's lowest temperature, $-128°F$, on July 21, 1983. This continent also has one of the driest climates on earth. It receives no rain and hardly any new snow each year.

The ice on Antarctica has trapped the purest air ever found and fossils of tropical plants and animals that were alive 1.5 million years before the last ice age. Scientists believe that Antarctica at one time belonged to a land mass that was part of Africa, Australia, India, and South America, before they drifted apart.

Today, an American travel company will take you to Antarctica for $37,000. You will be in danger of freezing to death at all times, unless you are near enough to Mt. Erebus, a live volcano with bubbling lava. There are no souvenirs to buy. And if your guide is good, you will return alive.

7. The best statement of the main idea is that

   A. Antarctica is a frozen continent filled with beauty and danger.
   B. traveling to Antarctica is expensive and memorable.
   C. Antarctica is bigger than Europe or Australia, and it has the deepest ice in the world.
   D. Antarctica has the coldest temperature and the driest air in the world.

An Unexpected Surprise

Sharice closed her locker and ran to her next class. "I hope I make it in time!" she thought as she ran into the classroom and took her seat. Her mind was already racing as Cory took a seat behind her. As usual, Cory began telling gross stories to his friends before class started. Sharice had had enough. She turned around and said, "Cory, I am already motion sick from the bus ride to school. Your conversation is making me sicker. Please stop." The look in her eyes seemed to bore a hole right through Cory's head. Cory didn't care. He just laughed at Sharice and continued on with his gross story. Sharice began looking paler and shouted, "I need to go to the bathroom!" As she began walking, Cory thought it would be fun to trip Sharice. When Sharice tripped, she tried to balance herself by grabbing Cory's desk, but instead, she fell on Cory. Unfortunately for Cory, that surprise was the last straw for Sharice's stomach. When Sharice got up, Cory was wearing her sausage and egg breakfast. Cory ran to the bathroom in disgust and embarrassment while Sharice calmly asked the teacher if she could call her mother.

8.   What is the main idea of this passage?

   A.   Sharice is very upset with Cory.
   B.   Cory suffers consequences when he does not respect Sharice.
   C.   Cory is a very immature person who needs punishment.
   D.   Sharice should have not gone to class if she knew she was feeling sick.

The Tornado Chasers

Much of what has been learned about tornadoes in recent years has come from scientists at the National Severe Storms Laboratory (NSSL) in the heart of Tornado Alley in Norman, Oklahoma. Every spring since 1972, researchers from the lab, often in cooperation with teams from the University of Oklahoma, have driven vehicles into the teeth of violent thunderstorms to gather information unavailable anywhere else.

From their encounters with tornadoes, NSSL teams have made some important observations. They confirmed that strong tornadoes almost always appear on the rain-free rear sides of severe thunderstorms, which typically move from southwest to northeast. Such tornadoes usually descend from a wall cloud, which hangs like a great horizontal wheel from the flat base of the storm. This wall cloud, half a mile to six miles in diameter, is part of a huge, rotating cylinder of air called a mesocyclone, the true source of the tornado's power.

– National Geographic

9.   The best statement of the main idea is that

   A.   chasing down a tornado takes a great deal of courage.
   B.   observations made by NSSL researchers give us important insight into how tornadoes form.
   C.   tornadoes usually descend from a wall cloud that is part of a larger, rotating cylinder of air.
   D.   every spring, researchers from NSSL drive their vehicles into the path of oncoming tornados.

Predators Purr Excellence

Felix has dethroned Fido as the most popular pet in the United States and in much of Europe. In 20 years, the number of house cats in the United States has doubled, and within each of these beloved companions beats the heart of a hunter. Ironically, the cat's ticket to domestication lies in its very wildness–its remarkable ability to hunt. This was once an asset for controlling rats aboard sailing ships, but with more that a hundred million cats now prowling the United States, what are the consequences for birds and small mammals?

Finding the balance between cats and wildlife sometimes makes people go at it tooth and claw. Nowhere is the debate more intense than in Australia, where cats have colonized the entire continent, putting many native animals at risk. Millions of feral cats roam the country, and they don't read the endangered species list before they pounce...

Many humans love their stealthy and proud felines. Cats, though, have their own notions about affection and what they take to be their just deserts.

– National Geographic, October, 1998

10. The best statement of the main idea is that

A. cats are by far the best pets for humans.
B. cats are very independent and make excellent hunters.
C. cats are becoming a large problem in Australia.
D. cats are very popular, but this may cause imbalances in the ecosystem.

North America

In the sixteenth century, part of North America – the present-day United States and Canada – was home to hundreds of tribes speaking a striking variety of languages and dialects. These groups occupied distinctive habitats, from the Eastern woodlands to the grassy Midwestern plains and southwest, and had strong ties to the land on which they lived. In some areas, the food was fairly limited, but most of the people of these regions of North America derived a sufficient and satisfying diet from fishing, farming, hunting, and gathering.

These tribes of North America domesticated dogs, turkeys, and possibly other animals as well. They took to the ocean, rivers, and streams in dugout or birch bark canoes and traded with one another–sometimes over long distances for products such as buffalo robes, copper, turquoise, shells, paint, pottery, and food. They wore clothes made from animal hides or cotton, spun or beaten bark, woven Spanish moss, or other cloth. The Native Americans lived in houses built of wood and covered with mats, bark, mud, or whitewash, in multilevel dwellings constructed of stone and mud, and in easily transportable shelters made of poles and animal hides. They played games such as lacrosse and chunky. Their spiritual life and religious beliefs tied them to the land, to other living things, and to the spirits that animated and governed the world. The religious differences among tribes helped to define them as distinctive peoples.

11. The best statement of the main idea is that

A. many early North American tribes fought with each other to gain territory and power.
B. hundreds of tribes surviving in many habitats occupied North America in the sixteenth century.
C. the beliefs and practices of early North American tribes were tied to the land.
D. many North American tribes traded with one another in the sixteenth century.

Dr. Bigelow's Magic Potion
A Cure For Chills

10? Per Bottle
Logan County
Square

Potion

Have you ever tried Dr. Bigelow's Cure for Chills? How about Mother Dora's Magic Oil for stomach pain, itchy feet, or headaches? If you were sick in the mid 1800s, your "doctors" would probably be dishonest quacks traveling in medicine shows. Their entertaining routines and persuasive sales pitches would easily convince you to buy their super, magical potions and tonics.

Slick ads on the sides of trees, barns, and stores would boast of proven cures for everything from arthritis to pneumonia. In fact, where the pain was really didn't matter. What mattered was that prominent people had testified that the cures really worked.

When Congress finally investigated the claims of these products, it discovered quite an assortment of strange mixtures in these medicines. One remedy included spider webs or chimney soot to stop bleeding. Fatback was the main ingredient to relieve sore muscles. Some preparations contained so much alcohol that customers often drank them as a substitute for whiskey or gin.

12. The best statement of the main idea is that

    A.   people often bought and used fake medicines in the 19th century.
    B.   pneumonia or headaches could be cured with special tonics in the 1800s.
    C.   people rarely visited quack doctors in the 1800s.
    D.   medicines in the 1800s always contained spider webs, alcohol, and fatback.

The Catawba Nation

The Catawbas were a great and powerful tribe of Native Americans who lived in what is now the states of North and South Carolina. After several contacts with the English, they united to become one of the four main nations of the Southeast in 1736.

Famous as hunters and warriors, they were known for their bravery and skill in battle. As faithful friends of early English and Scotch-Irish settlers, the Catawbas lived in numerous villages throughout the region. At heart, however, they were fighters and rovers who pursued deer, bear, and other wild game in the forest. One of their practices was to drink the liquid from the intestines of newly butchered buffalo. This custom strengthened them for future hunts.

The Catawba roamed primarily through North and South Carolina, but some witnesses observed their hunting parties as far south as Florida and as far north as New York. Several names of places in South Carolina are derived from the Catawba language. For example, the Santee River comes from the Catawba word for flowing or gentle. The town of Socastee gets its name from the word for house. The Pee Dee and Congaree Rivers are named after tribes that were part of the Catawba nation.

13. The best statement of the main idea is that

    A.   the Catawbas hunted for deer, bear, and buffalo in North and South Carolina.
    B.   the Catawbas were a great and powerful nation in the Carolinas.
    C.   names of places in South Carolina come from the Catawba language.
    D.   the Catawbas were a powerful tribe of hunters and warriors in South Carolina, and the names of several towns and rivers come from the Catawba language.

The Cape St. George Lighthouse

In 1831, a unique lighthouse was built on St. George Island in Florida's Apalachicola Bay. For many years, this lighthouse guided ships into and out of this region for the major cotton growers of Alabama and Georgia. Even when a storm cut off the lighthouse from the main part of the island, it remained standing. Though the Cape St. George Lighthouse was moved twice, it has remained in its present location since 1852.

For 164 years, this historic structure served as a beacon of welcome and safety for the many sea-going vessels that passed its way. Now surf from the Gulf of Mexico is eroding its foundation. In addition, the winds of Hurricane Opal tipped the lighthouse at a ten degree angle.

Many citizens of Apalachicola, Florida want to save the Cape St. George Lighthouse. Some local leaders think it should be moved 100 yards further inland, but raising $250,000 for this project would not be easy. Others would like to see the lighthouse remain in its present location. "It's an important part of our history," said one citizen. "Removing the Cape St. George Lighthouse from its historical setting would diminish its significance."

14. The best statement of the main idea is that

   A.   surf erosion and Hurricane Opal have damaged the historic Cape St. George Lighthouse.
   B.   for 164 years, the historic Cape St. George Lighthouse has welcomed ships to Apalachicola Bay.
   C.   the Cape St. George Lighthouse will be moved to a new location.
   D.   citizens of Apalachicola, Florida must decide how to preserve the historically significant Cape St. George Lighthouse.

Walking

I can easily walk ten, fifteen, twenty, any number of miles, starting at my own door, without going by any house, without crossing a road except where the fox and mink do: first along by the river, and then the brook, and then the meadow and the woodside. There are square miles in my vicinity which have no inhabitant. From many a hill I can see civilization and the abodes of man afar. The farmers and their works are scarcely more obvious than woodchucks and their burrows. Man and his affairs, church and state and school, trade and commerce, and manufactures and agriculture, even politics, the most alarming of them all, I am pleased to see how little space they occupy in the landscape. Politics is but a narrow field, and that still narrower highway yonder leads to it. I sometimes direct the traveller there. If you would go into the political world, follow the great road, follow that market-man, keep his dust in your eyes, and it will lead you straight to it. I pass from it as from a beanfield into the forest, and it is forgotten. In one half-hour I can walk off to some portion of the earth's surface where a man does not stand in the same place from one year's end to another, and there, politics do not exist, for they are but as the cigar-smoke of man.

—Thoreau, paraphrase of "Walking"

15. What is the main idea of the passage?

   A.   Politicians smoke cigars to impress people, but the world of nature does not put on airs.
   B.   Politicians can steal the writer's land, so he avoids any contact with civilization.
   C.   Politics removes us from the peace and solitude of the natural world.
   D.   Politics causes businesses and schools to be built on land that belongs to everyone.

Locating details is an essential skill for reading comprehension. Comprehension also includes understanding the **sequence of events** in a story or steps in a set of directions. Finally, you need to understand **cause-effect relationships** in a passage.

LOCATING DETAILS

Locating details is the ability to identify **facts, reasons,** and **examples** that support the main idea in a paragraph or passage. An easy way to understand details is to picture a table. The main idea is like the top of the table, and the details are like its legs. A table without its legs would be useless. Likewise, a main idea would not be understood without details and facts to explain it.

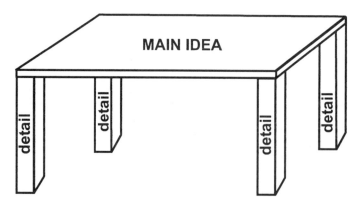

Many passages are organized around details and facts. The details are based on the 5 W's and H (who, what, when, where, why, and how). When you are asked to find a detail or fact, you should scan or look for a specific piece of information by reading the passage again. For example, if you were given a passage on armadillos, you may be asked: What is an armadillo? Where do armadillos live? How big are armadillos? Why are armadillos a nuisance? When you read a question containing one of the 5 W's or H, you will be looking for an answer with a fact or detail.

Tips for Locating Details

1. **Read the passage carefully.**

2. **Scan the passage to answer the questions with the 5 W's or H.**

3. **Match key words in your choice of answers with those in the passage.**

4. **Always confirm your answer by going back to the passage.**

For practice, read this paragraph. Use the <u>Tips for Locating Details</u> to answer the questions that follow.

During the early 1900s, Hollywood and New Jersey were competitors for the movie industry. New Jersey was desirable because so many actors and actresses worked on Broadway, which is near New Jersey. However, all filming had to take place outside where the light was strong enough. As a result, Hollywood, nestled in the hills of sunny southern California, became the better choice for year-round filming. By 1911, fifteen film companies had made their home there.

1.   Where were movies made?

2.   Why was Hollywood a better choice for making movies?

3.   How many companies moved to Hollywood?

4.   What made New Jersey popular for film makers?

Draw a table with six legs and label the main idea, the 5 W's, and H for the selection below. Compare your answers with those of your classmates or instructor.

Geronimo

Geronimo is the most famous of the Apaches. He and his small band of warriors, 12 women, and six children managed to resist 5,000 United States soldiers and perhaps 3,000 Mexican soldiers from 1881-1886.

He was a talker–not an orator of eloquence but a spokesman, a debater, a thrasher-out of ideas. With either revolver or rifle, he was one of the best Chiricahua marksmen.

What made Geronimo such a remarkable leader? His fearlessness in battle, his apparent ability to foretell future events, and his sharp intelligence all gave his advice deep authority. In addition, his refusal to give in when faced with hopeless odds inspired others.

By his family he was named Goyahkla, which is usually taken to mean "one who yawns." It was the Mexicans who started calling him Geronimo, perhaps for St. Jerome. The name came from a battle in which Goyahkla repeatedly ran through a hail of bullets to kill soldiers with his knife. When they saw the Indian warrior coming toward them, they began to yell out in desperation, "Geronimo!"

PRACTICE 1: LOCATING DETAILS

A.   **5 W's and H.** On your own or in a group, read three to four news stories or short stories from your literature book. Make a chart listing the 5 W's and H for each selection. Then create questions based on these details for classmates to answer. See how many details they can recall.

B.   **Creating Questions.** Bring in newspaper or Internet articles. Create questions for your classmates to answer based on the 5 W's and H. See how many details they can answer correctly.

C.   **Pantomime.** Act out an experience that happened to you recently. Other students observe, take notes, and record the 5 W's and H. Then see how many can retell the event accurately.

SEQUENCE OF EVENTS OR DIRECTIONS

Questions dealing with a **sequence of events or directions** require you to make connections between events or instructions in a passage. The subject of these passages may be a historical event, a story, a news report, or directions. The passage will generally follow a **chronological or time order,** starting with the first event, then the second event, third event, and so on.

Questions about events or directions are often worded a certain way. For example, if you were answering questions about the California Gold Rush, you might be asked these kinds of questions. Find the answers in a history book or encyclopedia.

1.   What was California like **before** the gold rush?

_____

2.   **When** and **where** was gold discovered in California?

_____

3.   What was California like **during** the gold rush?

_____

4.   Which important events happened **after** gold was discovered?

_____

Sequence questions usually contain **key words** that will help you locate the answers in a passage. Some examples of these key words are the following:

first	before	next	second	after	until	later	now
third	then	most important	finally	when	last	between	

Tips for Answering Questions About a Sequence of Events or Directions

1.   **Skim the passage.** Look for key words that indicate a sequence of events or directions.
2.   **Read the passage.**
3.   **Read the question and scan the sequences to find the answer.**
4.   **Try to match key words from the question with the events or directions in the passage.**
5.   **Check your answer against the evidence in the selection.**

For practice, read the following two passages. Use the <u>Tips for Answering Questions About Sequence of Events or Directions</u>. Then answer the questions.

When the Pilgrims landed in November of 1620 in what is now Massachusetts, they needed to provide food and shelter if they were to survive. There were no stores and markets for buying things, and no houses for the Pilgrims to move into. They had to meet their own needs, and even the smallest hands contributed to that effort.

The Pilgrims overcame many hardships to establish a colony. The winter was long and cold, and much work had to be done for spring planting. Their hard work that first year was rewarded with a bountiful harvest in the autumn of 1621, and the Pilgrims celebrated the first Thanksgiving as a time of gratitude.

Over the next several years, Plymouth grew into a successful community of 180 colonists. By 1627 more than one-third of them were age 16 or younger. There were no schools, but the children were always learning. They learned by working.

1.   What happened first in this story?_____

2.   What was the last event mentioned in the passage? _____

_____

3.   Where did the pilgrims live before 1620? _____

4.   List the main dates and events in the passage in chronological order. _____

_____

5.   Underline the key words that guide the sequence of events in the passage.

Surviving a Home Fire

If a fire should occur during the night in your home, follow these steps for survival. First, roll out of bed. Next, crawl to the door, and feel the door. If it is hot, do not open the door. Or, if smoke or hot gases rush into the room when you open the door, close it and find another method of escape. If the door is not hot, then brace yourself against it very slowly. Toxic gases or fire may be on the other side. Third, if no smoke enters the room, open the door, covering your nose and mouth with a moist cloth. Then crawl quickly to safety. Most importantly, get out by the quickest, safest route. Finally, use an escape ladder, knotted rope, or a fire escape to leave your home. Or you may be able to climb out a window on the roof and drop to the ground. Then find a phone, and call the fire department.

– Shriners' Burn Institute, Cincinnati, Ohio

1. What should you do before opening the door? _____

2. When should you cover your nose and mouth with a moist cloth? _____

_____

3. What should you do after escaping from a burning house? _____

_____

4. In your own words, list the steps for escaping from a fire in your home. _____

_____

_____

5. Underline the key words that introduce the steps for escaping.

PRACTICE 2

A. **Passage Analysis.** Read the following passage entitled **"Typhoon."** Review the list of key words for sequence on page 54. Then complete the activities.

Typhoon

There was no escape from the severe regimen Ida was compelled to follow. She had work to do; she had rules to observe. First, there was breakfast at seven-thirty sharp because the store had to be opened by her father at eight, which meant rising at seven; next, luncheon at twelve-thirty, so as to satisfy her father and her own noon recess hour which was completely filled in by this; finally, dinner always at six-thirty because there were many things, commercial and social, which fell upon the shoulders of William Zobel at night. And between whiles, from four to six on weekdays and later from seven to ten at night, as well as all day Saturdays, there was store duty in her father's store.

While other girls walked the streets arm in arm, or made pairs with young men of the region or elsewhere and were off to the movies, or to some party – and came in at what hours after – (didn't she hear them laugh and chatter at school and on their way home, afterwards) – she, because of her father's and later her step-mother's attitude, was compelled to adhere to the regimen thought advisable for her. No parties that kept her out later than ten at night at anytime – and then only after due investigation. Those she really liked were always picked to pieces by her step-mother and, of course, this somewhat influenced the opinion of her father.

– Theodore Dreiser

1. Underline the key words that provide clues to the story's sequence of events.

2. Retell the story in your own words with correct sequence of events.

3. In a small group or on your own, scramble the story's events. Work in pairs to put them back in the proper sequence. Then compare your answers with the events in the original passage.

B. Sequence Practice. Review some news stories or short stories from your literature book.

1. Underline the key words that reveal the sequence of events.

2. Retell or rewrite these stories in your own words.

3. Scramble the stories' events and then unscramble them again.

C. Pantomime or act out a personal experience or directions on how to do something. Then see how many can retell the events or directions correctly.

D. Giving Directions. Imagine you are helping someone who is lost find: the principal's office, the cafeteria, the media center, the restroom, etc. Tell and then write the directions. What key words did you use? List two or three questions a person might ask about your directions.

CAUSE-EFFECT RELATIONSHIPS

Authors sometimes explain a topic by including the **causes** or **reasons** for an event and the **effects** or **results** of an event. Passages about **cause-effect relationships** may center on a story, a scientific topic, history, or a news event. Questions often require you to identify causes or effects discussed in a passage. **Review this passage, and then answer the questions that follow.**

The Popularity of New Shoes

Nike designed shoes appealing to joggers and 15-22 year olds. The results of Nike's efforts were an expanded market of 20 million walkers and joggers and 30% of the teenage and young adult buyers in the United States.

1. What **caused** an expanded market for Nike shoes? _____

2. **Why** are Nike shoes so popular? _____

3. What **effect** did Nike's designs have on joggers and 15-22 year olds? _____
   _____

4. What were the **results** of Nike's new shoe designs? _____
   _____

Cause-effect questions often contain **key words** that will guide you in scanning the passage to find the answers. These key words are listed below:

Causes	
why	basis
reason	due to
because	origin
source	cause

Effects	
affect	product
result	aftermath
consequence	therefore
outcome	effect

Tips for Answering Cause-Effect Questions

1. **Read the passage.**

2. **Look for key words that signal that the passage is about causes or effects.**

3. **Note any key words in the questions that suggest a cause or effect would be an answer.**

4. **Scan for the answer, and use the text to confirm your response.**

For practice, read the following passage. Use the **Tips for Answering Cause-Effect Questions** as a guide. Then answer the questions that follow.

Pesticides in Our Food

Many Americans are unaware of how pesticides affect our food supplies. Health risks are the inevitable result. Pesticides can run off into groundwater and run off into nearby streams, where they are carried from their original dispersal site. This is how pesticides end up in drinking water, fish, and game. And because of wind, rain, and evaporation, residues routinely show up in animals in the remotest parts of the world. For example, if grain fields or rough lands are sprayed with pesticides, residues can show up in poultry, eggs, milk, and butter. The end result is that every food we eat carries pesticides as the inevitable consequence of spraying crops with these poisons. And human exposure doesn't even end there; residues are transferred from mother to child through the placenta and mother's milk.

– <u>Citizen Action News</u>, Summer 1995

1. What causes harmful residues in a newborn child? _____

2. Why are residues found in animals in remote parts of the world? _____

_____

3. What effects do pesticides have on streams? _____

    _____

4. What are the results of pesticides sprayed on grain fields? _____

    _____

PRACTICE 3: CAUSE & EFFECT

A. **Passages.** Review 3-4 passages from a newspaper, magazine, or textbook that show cause-effect relationships. Articles on science, history, health, or news editorials might be good examples.

    1. What causes and effects can you identify in the selections?
    2. Underline key words that indicate the selections emphasize causes or effects.
    3. Create questions based on these selections about cause-effect relationships. Exchange your questions with classmates and see how many they can answer correctly.

B. **Personal Choices.** Recall some important decisions you made recently. List 2-4 reasons and 2-4 results of your decisions. Share your lists with a partner, a small group, or your instructor. Do they agree that the reasons are causes and the results are effects of your decisions? Why or why not?

C. **News Event.** Discuss a recent news event about your school, community, or country. On your own or in a group, list all the possible causes and effects of that event. Each group should then decide on which ones they agree. The group shares its causes and effects with the class until the entire class can develop a final list it can agree on.

D. **Graphic Organizer.** Victor's teacher asked him to create a graphic organizer of a successful student. He identified three causes or reasons and three effects of being a successful student.

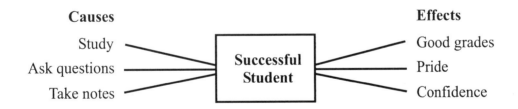

Using the above diagram as a guide, create cause-effect graphic organizers for the following topics:

river pollution   flooding   high school diploma
allergies   meeting a famous athlete   winning athletic team
moving to another town   exercise   prejudice

Share your graphic organizers with your partner or class. Choose your best one and write a paragraph or essay on your topic.

Read the following passages, and answer the questions that follow.

Emily's Birthday

 Emily was sitting with her family and friends in a restaurant when the hostess announced that Emily had a telephone call. Confused by who would be calling her at the restaurant, she left to go to the phone. While she was gone, her sister went to the car and brought in gifts and cards for Emily's birthday including the best gift of all, a toy poodle puppy. After finding out the caller wanted an Emily with a different last name, she returned to the table and was completely surprised. She couldn't believe her parents were going to let her have a puppy after all!

1. Do we know who was calling Emily? _____

2. In the story above, who changed his/her mind? _____

3. After the phone call, who got back to the table first? _____

4. Why was Emily so surprised? _____

> ## Harriet "Moses" Tubman
> ### $40,000 reward!!
> **for capture of Harriet Tubman**
> **Slave Fugitive!**

Slave owners around the South distributed posters like the above example because of one woman's efforts to help slaves escape to freedom. Her name was Harriet Tubman. Between 1844 and 1865, she rescued between 300-400 slaves from farms and plantations.

Using the Underground Railroad, Tubman guided them on the perilous journey to freedom. The Underground Railroad was a secret organization of Whites and Blacks that provided refuge and escape routes to the Northern states where slavery was abolished. Food, blankets, shelter, and transportation were available through this network. Like a real railroad, the "passengers" were the slaves, and the "station" was a house along the way. The "ticket" was a map or letter giving directions to the house, and the "conductor" was any person guiding the slave from one station to another. "Stations" connected the slave states of the South to Northern States and to Canada

Sometimes Tubman and her passengers experienced great hardships. To avoid capture, they hid in snowy woods or rainy fields where they slept in the cold. Once on the journey, this 19th century Moses made sure no person would ever turn back from the challenges. "You must go on or die," she would tell everyone. She carried a pistol as a warning to anyone who would turn back, but she never used it. And no one was ever captured on her many rescue missions.

5. What was the Underground Railroad? _____

_____

Directions for Performing a Magic Trick

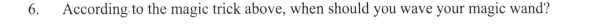

1. Show the audience the rabbit and the inside of the hat.
2. Place the rabbit inside the hat.
3. Wave your magic wand around the hat, and say, "Presto!"
4. Turn the hat upside down to demonstrate that the rabbit disappeared.

6. According to the magic trick above, when should you wave your magic wand?

_____

Directions for a Science Experiment

1. Place a small amount of water in a glass dish.
2. Make a two inch diameter circle of sewing thread.
3. Float the thread on the water.
4. Sprinkle pepper on the water inside the circle.
5. Put one drop of a dish washing detergent in the circle.

7. According to the science experiment above, when should you sprinkle the pepper?

_____

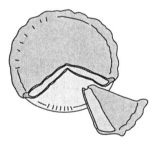

Pumpkin Pie
1   pie crust
2   eggs
$\frac{1}{2}$ cup sugar
$2\frac{1}{2}$ teaspoon cinnamon
1   teaspoon nutmeg
$\frac{3}{4}$ teaspoon salt
1   (16-oz.) can pumpkin
1   (12-oz.) can evaporated milk

Heat oven to 425°. Prepare pie crust according to package directions for filled one-crust pie using 9-inch pie crust. In large bowl, beat eggs slightly. Add remaining ingredients; blend well. Pour into crust-lined pie pan. Bake at 425° for 15 minutes. Reduce oven temperature to 350° and continue baking for 45 minutes or until knife inserted near center comes out clean. Cool. Store in refrigerator.

8. What must be done immediately before the ingredients are placed in the pie pan?

_____

Seahorses Make Great Fathers

From start to finish, a male seahorse does all the parenting. His is indeed a real pregnancy, closely resembling that of mammals, including humans. Just as a woman provides her fetus with oxygen, transfers nutrients, and regulates conditions in the uterus, a seahorse does no less for the babies in his pouch. Remarkably, the hormone prolactin, which stimulates milk production in women, also governs seahorse pregnancy. Perhaps this explains a tantalizing note in the March 1753 issue of *Gentleman's Magazine*: "The ladies make use of them (seahorses) to increase their milk."

Males of the smallest species have fewer than ten offspring. Then there was James from the Caribbean—surely the world record holder for "most young in one pouch." His pouch was only half a tablespoon in volume, but in it were packed 1,573 babies; end to end they would have stretched more than 12 yards.

9. What causes the male seahorse to sustain the babies in his pouch? _____

Sea Adventure

Four men in an open life boat caught glimpses of the steamer sinking into the sea…

A seat in this boat was not unlike a seat on a bucking bronco, and, by the same token, a bronco is not much smaller. The craft pranced and reared and plunged like an animal. As each wave came, and she rose for it, she seemed like a horse leaping a fence outrageously high. A singular disadvantage of the sea lies in the fact that after successfully surmounting one wave, you discover there is another behind it just as important and just as nervously anxious to do something effective in the way of swamping boats.

"Good thing it's an on-shore wind," said the cook. "If not where would we be?"

"That's right," said the correspondent.

The busy engine master nodded his assent.

Then the captain in the bow chuckled in a way that expressed humor, contempt, tragedy, all in one. "Do you think we've got a show, now, boys?" said he.

Whereupon the three went silent, save for a little hemming and hawing. To express any particular optimism at this time they felt to be childish and stupid, but they all doubtless possessed this sense of the situation in their mind. A young man thinks doggedly at such times. On the other hand, the ethics of their condition was decidedly against an open suggestion of hopelessness. So they were silent.

"Oh well," said the captain, soothing his children, "we'll get ashore all right."

But there was that in his tone which made them doubt, so the engine master said, "Yes, if this wind holds!"

The cook was bailing water, "Yes! If we don't break apart in the surf."

– Stephen Crane "Open Boat"

10. What caused the four men to be together? _____

Life is but a Dream

Steve got up one Saturday morning, barely awake. He stumbled into the kitchen and grabbed some orange juice. His roommate, Jeff, came in a little later. Jeff said, "Man, that was a strange dream I had last night."

"What did you dream, Jeff?" Steve said.

"Well," said Jeff, "I dreamed that you and I were at a gas station. We found some fire hoses and were dousing each other with water. Then, you jumped into your pickup truck and wrecked it in the woods."

"That's pretty weird," Steve muttered, "You know, I had a similar dream last night. Only in my dream, I was driving my truck, and it slipped and spun out of control on a patch of ice."

Just then, the phone rang. Jeff picked it up, "Hello." He said.

"Hi, is this Steve?" the woman asked.

"Just a second." Jeff said and handed the phone to Steve.

"Hello?" Steve said.

"Hi, my name is Allison. I work with your girlfriend, Jenny. She just had a small seizure and wants to know if you can pick her up."

"OK," Steve said, "I'm on my way." After he hung up, Steve told Jeff what had happened and jumped in his truck.

"Rats," Steve said, "I'm almost out of gas." Steve pulled into a gas station near his apartment and fueled up. After paying the attendant, he went on the road. It was a four-lane road with no divider lane. It was raining, so he had to drive carefully. Driving in the left lane, Steve suddenly had to slam on his brakes, as the car in front of him was stopping to make a left turn. The truck began to skid forward. Quickly, Steve turned the wheel to the right. Because he was hydroplaning, the truck went to the left instead of the right, directly into oncoming traffic. Steve braced himself as he hit a smaller white sedan in a head-on collision.

Steve opened his eyes in shock at the scene before him. His truck was bashed in past the radiator. Luckily, Steve was wearing his seat belt and was unhurt. The car Steve hit was smashed in to the engine, and the engine was on fire. The driver in this car was also unhurt because his air bag had opened. He got out of his vehicle, the police came, and fire trucks were called in to put out the fire. Totally freaked out, Steve called Jeff back at the apartment from a pay phone. "Jeff," he said, "I think that maybe you were supposed to pick up Jenny today…"

11. The outcome of this story suggests that _____

_____

12. The main reason Steve drove his truck Saturday morning was because _____

_____

13. Who is the main character in this story? _____

_____

14. Based on the lesson learned in this story, how is Steve likely to change? _____

_____

15. What event caused Steve's truck to collide with another car? _____

_____

CHAPTER 3 TEST

Read the following passages, and answer the questions that follow each passage.

The Quest

Traveling at an easy canter through the forest of Esterwild, the human Kitiara was sitting astride her horse, Thunder. Her Dwarf friend, Regis, was riding beside her on a pony called Dancer. "Regis, when are we going to find that glowing herb, Canaris? Every day, the people of our village grow sicker from the Creeping Death," Kitiara remarked. "I know it's here. Drat it anyway. The stuff grew all over the place last year when I was here," muttered Regis. Dusk approached quickly, and the two lit torches to light their path through the all too quiet forest.

"Aha!" cackled Parsnip, "I am very poor troll, but soon I very rich!" He quickly closed his leather pouch, and the area around him grew dark. The troll glanced up and saw the two travelers approaching his way. "mm . . . Dwarf make tasty dinner and woman nice dessert."

The two didn't know what hit them. A large spear quickly dispatched Dancer, throwing Regis to the ground. The large troll pounced on him, clawing away at his armor to expose his back. Weaponless, Kitiara took Parsnip's large leather pouch from his belt. "Yoo Hoo!" she screamed. "I got your money." As she bolted, Parsnip turned around to give chase. Taking the opportunity, Regis threw his war hammer and neatly severed Parsnip's right arm. The troll screamed in agony, and Regis and Kitiara watched in horror as the one troll suddenly became two. Remembering an old nursery rhyme, Kitiara shouted, "Fire!" Both torches were hurled at the newly made trolls, and the forest was lit up with the sight of two trolls, their flesh crackling and popping into the night sky.

Opening Parsnip's pouch, Kitiara smiled with glee. The glow from the pouch bathed the two travelers in a warm light.

1. What happened after Kitiara opened the pouch?

   A. She saw Canaris in the pouch.
   B. She was warmed by the fire that killed the trolls.
   C. She found money to save the village.
   D. She was glad to have the troll's magic potion.

2. Why does Kitiara need the glowing herb, Canaris?

   A. This herb grows plentifully in the forest.
   B. Parsnip stole Canaris, and Kitiara wants it back.
   C. Canaris will heal the villagers suffering from the Creeping Death.
   D. The dwarf, Regis, uses the herb to improve his strength.

3. When does the attack on Kitiara and Regis take place?

   A. at dawn
   B. at midnight
   C. in the afternoon
   D. in the early evening

Who Robbed The Zoo?

Only a rat would think of stealing from a zoo, but that's exactly what happened Tuesday. A thief with a gun robbed the cashier at the Daytonville Zoo just after closing. Over $5,000 in cash was taken.

According to the cashier and two witnesses, a woman in her 40s entered the main ticket booth and demanded all the cash from the zoo's safe. The robber also released two large rats from a bag to scare the cashier. The robber then fled on foot.

"I was never so scared in my life," said the cashier after the incident. Zoo officials were able to capture the rats later and feed them to the pythons.

Police were unable to catch the thief, but they believe that the woman planned the place and time of the robbery. Anyone having any information about the robber is asked to contact police.

4.   What happened before the robbery took place?

    A.   Zoo keepers fed the pythons their daily meal.
    B.   The Daytonville Zoo closed for the day.
    C.   A woman in her 40s robbed the zoo.
    D.   The police arrived to arrest a thief.

5.   Where did the robbery occur?

    A.   at the main ticket booth
    B.   at the python exhibit
    C.   near the zoo's entrance
    D.   behind the zoo's snack bar

6.   How did the two rats affect the cashier during the robbery?

    A.   The cashier ran away.
    B.   The cashier fed the rats to the pythons.
    C.   The cashier was frightened.
    D.   The cashier told the robber to leave.

Star Birth

Stars are believed to originate by the condensation of enormous clouds of cosmic dust and hydrogen gas; the latter is the most plentiful of the elements. There are many such clouds in our universe.

The motivating force behind the birth of a star is gravity. According to Newton's law of gravity, all bodies in the universe attract each other in proportion to their mass and distance apart. The gas and dust particles in these vast interstellar clouds attract each other and gradually grow closer together. Eventually, enough particles coalesce to form a clump which is massive enough that all parts are bound to each other by gravitation. At this point, the edges of the cloud begin to collapse inward, separating it from the remaining gas and dust in the vicinity.

At first, the cloud contracts rapidly, because the heat released by contraction is easily radiated outward. Then the cloud grows smaller and more dense, so that heat created at the center cannot immediately escape to the exterior. This causes a rapidly rising internal temperature, slowing down but not stopping the constant contraction.

At a certain point, the interior of the star becomes so dense and its temperature so high, that thermonuclear fission begins. This is the actual "birth" of the star.

7. What happens after the cloud shrinks and becomes more compact?

    A. Particles gather near the edge of the cloud.
    B. The cloud begins to expand again.
    C. The temperature increases at the center.
    D. The gas and dust move much faster.

8. When does the star birth actually occur?

    A. before the clouds of cosmic dust and hydrogen gas collapse
    B. as thermonuclear fission begins
    C. after gravity clumps gas and dust particles together
    D. when the gas cools to its final temperature

Compost Pile

The home compost pile is an efficient mulch factory, and mulch is very valuable in the garden. Avid gardeners usually have several compost piles "cooking" at various stages of decomposition. Rather than putting grass clippings and leaves in the landfill, they can be composted and recycled back into your garden as mulch. Thus, the garden benefits in many ways; it looks more attractive, weeds are smothered out, moisture is conserved, and soil temperature fluctuations are reduced. Mulch can also be used to disguise unsightly surfaces in the garden.

For a more effective weed barrier, cover the soil with a three-page layer of newspapers, and then apply a layer of mulch. The bottom layer of mulch is constantly decomposing and adding organic matter to your soil. Rough, unattractive mulch can be covered with a more aesthetically pleasing top layer of pine straw. Layer mulch up to four inches deep, but keep it pulled back a few inches from the base of plants to avoid stem and crown rot.

Remember a healthy compost pile attracts worms. The more worms the better. They are very beneficial to your garden. They assist in the decomposition of the vegetable and paper material. Anything added to the compost pile is worm food.

9. According to the passage, what should be done before applying a layer of mulch to the soil?

    A. The bottom layer of mulch should be covered with pine straw.
    B. Newspaper should be placed down on the soil.
    C. Several bins of mulch should be placed in the garden.
    D. Grass clippings should be placed on top of the soil.

10. Which of the following processes of mulch creation is best supported by the passage?

    A. The newspaper clippings are put down to stimulate weed growth.
    B. Many types of food can be placed into a compost pile.
    C. Mulch makes plants greener and able to produce more.
    D. Leaves and grass clippings are "cooked" together in a pile.

One Snowy Day

Our boy scout troop was ready to settle in for the night. Most of the tents had been set up, and the sleeping bags were rolled out inside the tents. Instead of setting up, my friends and I started wrestling and playing football. Eventually, we set up our dome tent, but we were too tired to put the stakes into the ground–we just climbed in with our sleeping gear. Ryan, Stuart, and I had placed an electric lantern in our tent. It was very cold outside, and snow had just started falling. We played 20 questions most of the night, using frozen M&Ms as rewards to the winner. Ryan won most of the hands and ate his winnings. Eventually, we got tired of playing 20 questions, so we decided to go to sleep. Somewhere in the middle of the night, all of us woke up with a start. The wind picked up, and the tent we were in started rolling down the hill we had camped on. Hands, feet, and M&Ms came together in a massive tangle. We stopped tumbling when the tent hit a tree. With a loud smack, the lantern broke and we were plunged into darkness. For some reason, all of us were fine and started laughing. We quickly fell back to sleep and woke up to find our tent covered in snow and the rest of the group out looking for us. We hiked the tent back up the hill and told everyone about our roller coaster ride.

11.   What caused the tent to blow down the hill?

    A.   The tent was not tied down correctly.
    B.   The children in the tent did not weigh very much.
    C.   The lantern was left on all night long.
    D.   The other campers decided to roll the tent down the hill.

The Swing

Cindy, Jennifer, Tara, and Amy were all friends and classmates at the local middle school. One day at around 5:00 p.m., they decided they would sit in the playground and tell ghost stories. Cindy told a graveyard ghost story, Jennifer told a haunted house ghost story, and Amy told an abandoned prison ghost story. Now, it was Tara's turn.

All the other girls couldn't wait for Tara to tell her story. She was the best storyteller of all of them. "All right," Tara said, "I'll tell you my story." The girls leaned forward to listen. "Did you know this playground is haunted?"

"Oh, come on," Cindy said. "Who's ever heard of a haunted playground?"

"No, really, it's true," Tara said with a devious grin. The girls waited as Tara began her story. "About twenty years ago, there was a woman who came here every day to let her daughter play on the playground. Her daughter was strong and very healthy, so her mom didn't watch her all that closely. One day, at about this same time, her daughter, Julie, pumped the swings really hard, fell out, and died. The mother, heartbroken by what happened, died about a week later. To this day, it is said that this mother still walks the playground with Julie, watching her play on the swings, and sometimes watches over the other children that play here."

Abruptly, Tara said, "Look, I think there's something in that building over there!" All the girls turned and looked. While they weren't looking in Tara's direction, Tara ran, pushed one swing on the swing set, and ran back to the girls, telling them, "Look at the swing set!" The girls turned around and started screaming. Tara laughed and said, "Tricked you! I pushed the left swing just a few seconds ago."

"Then why are both swings swinging on the swing set?" Amy asked. Tara turned around, saw both swings swinging, and screamed for everyone to run away.

As they ran out, they could hear a woman whispering, "Come on Julie. You can do it. This time I am here to catch you."

12. What is the setting of the story above?

    A. the park
    B. a haunted house
    C. a playground
    D. a graveyard

13. Who is the main character?

    A. Tara
    B. Amy
    C. Jennifer
    D. Julie

When a Friendship is Over

When you are a teenager, if there is one thing that you can count on in life, it is that people change. The person you are today is not the person you will be four years from now. And while you are busy changing, so are your friends. These changes can be painful. Any time you choose to care about another person, you risk a painful, but rarely fatal, broken heart.

Relationships grow and die. Friends grow in different directions. Boy friends and girl friends leave. Children grow up and move away. Parents die. We may even surpass the people we used to look up to. All these events can lead to pain.

Pain comes into everyone's life sooner or later. Painful experiences help us learn. When an important relationship ends, and you feel badly, allow yourself to experience that feeling. It is appropriate to be miserable when you are. It's normal to cry and express your feelings. It's also possible to go to class, study, work, eat, sleep, get your laundry done, and feel miserable at the same time.

If the pain of a broken relationship is getting you down, do something nice for someone who isn't expecting it. When you make someone else smile – well, it can be contagious. If depression is a problem, exercise, study outside in the sunlight, call a friend and talk about it. Whatever you do, don't soak in the pain too long. Get up and do something.

If you feel severely depressed and stay that way, talk to a professional before it starts affecting your health. When friends and family can't help, most schools have counselors available. Take action. There is no need to let the end of a relationship keep you down.

14. According to the passage, how should you react if your relationship ends badly?

    A. Forget about it and go on in life.
    B. Seek professional help.
    C. Express your emotions to others.
    D. Find a way to get revenge.

15. According to the passage, what causes changes in relationships?

    A. People get tired of each other.
    B. natural disasters, wars, and plagues
    C. People move, die, or surpass the people they looked up to.
    D. getting a job

16. According to the passage, what is likely to happen if someone stays depressed?

    A. His or her health will be affected.
    B. Friends will avoid him/her.
    C. He or she will sleep more.
    D. He or she will attempt suicide.

The Hunter

A hunter had been all day looking for deer in the mountains without success until he was completely tired out and sat down on a log to rest and wonder what he should do. A buzzard, a bird which always has magic powers, came flying overhead and spoke to him, asking him what was his trouble. When the hunter had told his story, the buzzard said there were plenty of deer on the ridges beyond if only the hunter were high up in the air where he could see them. The buzzard proposed that they exchange forms for a while. The buzzard would go to the hunter's wife while the hunter would go to look for deer, The hunter agreed, and the buzzard became a man and went home to the hunter's wife, who received him as her husband, while the hunter became a buzzard and flew off over the mountain to locate the deer.

After staying some time with the woman, who thought always it was her real husband, the buzzard excused himself, saying he must go again to look for game, or they would have nothing to eat. He came to the place where he had first met the hunter and found him already there, still in buzzard form, awaiting him. He asked the hunter what success he had had, and the hunter replied that he had found several deer over the ridge, as the buzzard had said. Then the buzzard restored the hunter to human shape and became himself a buzzard again and flew away. The hunter went where he had seen the deer and killed several, and from that time on, he never returned empty-handed from the woods.

– Native American myth

17. In which order did the events in this selection occur?

    A. The hunter flew over the mountains.
       The buzzard became the deer.
       The hunter killed several deer.
    B. The buzzard took on a human shape.
       The hunter killed several deer.
       The buzzard married the hunter's wife.
    C. The buzzard became the hunter.
       The hunter became the buzzard.
       They returned to their original shapes.
    D. The hunter and the buzzard exchanged shapes.
       The hunter saw deer on the ridges.
       The hunter returned empty-handed from the woods.

18. The hunter was tired because he

    A. saw the buzzard in the sky.
    B. could not find any deer.
    C. killed several deer.
    D. flew around the sky as a buzzard.

India

India is the seventh largest country in the world with a population of nearly 1 billion people. Only China contains more people. It is a land of deserts, plains, jungles, and mountains. The people speak about 180 different languages and come from many different races and religious backgrounds.

Many Indian customs have remained the same for hundreds of years, even though many social and scientific advances have also occurred. For example, cows, which are sacred to many Hindus, are allowed to roam freely in modern business districts. Factory workers may wear traditional costumes on the job. In rural areas, girls take care of younger brothers and sisters at home while their brothers go off to school.

For hundreds of years, India was a land of mystery, wealth, and adventure. Columbus thought he was in India when he discovered America. Other European explorers later found India and its famous jewels, rugs, silks, and spices. When the British entered India in the late 1700s, they governed many parts of the country. They built railroads, roads, telephone systems, and established a system of education still in place today. Under Ghandi, India achieved independence from Great Britain in 1947. One year later, he was assassinated. Today India exists as an independent, democratic republic.

19.   Why are cows permitted to live in business areas in India?

   A.   The cows are too old to move.
   B.   Cows provide milk for the people.
   C.   Cows are holy animals.
   D.   Cows can be slaughtered for their meat.

20.   According to the passage, what was one effect of British colonization?

   A.   The British educational system was established.
   B.   All Indians became British citizens.
   C.   Columbus discovered America.
   D.   English became the official language of India.

INFERENCES, GENERALIZATIONS, CONCLUSIONS, PREDICTIONS, AND SUMMARY

An **inference** is information not directly stated in a passage. You have already learned how to locate main ideas and details, but this information is generally stated directly in the passage. However, a skillful reader should be able to combine background knowledge plus facts and details from the passage and make inferences about the information presented.

We make inferences often in our daily lives. For example, if you notice two dogs wagging their tails as you walk toward them, you would infer that they are friendly and eager to meet you. The dogs don't say anything, but their behavior suggests they are friendly. If you observe your football coach jumping for joy after an interception, you might infer that your team gained some yards and a chance to score a touchdown. Even though no words are spoken, the actions speak for themselves.

Types of inference questions you may be asked to answer are listed below:

1. Inferences and Generalizations

2. Conclusions

3. Predictions

4. Summary

INFERENCES AND GENERALIZATIONS

When you draw an **inference**, you are making an educated guess based on facts and details in a passage. By reviewing various ideas and details in a selection, you can infer information that is not directly stated in a passage.

The following is a passage in which the topic must be inferred. Notice how the details in the paragraph contribute to the inference.

These storms occur over land and are the most violent of all atmospheric disturbances. They are highly localized and, therefore, do not affect large areas at one time. The actual path of destruction of these storms is rarely more than 100 yards in width. They take the form of a rotating column of air that extends down to the land from a thundercloud. They happen most frequently in the Great Plains states and in the southeastern part of the United States.

Can you infer the topic of this passage? If you decided that the author was describing **tornadoes**, you were right. The facts and details provided all of the clues. Such information included the following:

- storms occurring over land

- the violence and localized nature of the storms

- a narrow path of destruction

- a rotating column of air

- storms common in Great Plains and the Southeast

You could also draw other inferences about the selection. For example, you could infer that tornadoes cause great damage to people and property. The passage also suggests that since tornadoes emerge from thunderclouds, they occur during unstable weather such as thunderstorms.

Now reread the above selection. Think of two other inferences you could make about the information. Then write your inferences on the spaces provided.

Inference _____

_____

Inference _____

_____

A **generalization** is a type of specific inference in which you apply knowledge in a passage to new situations that are related. You can make generalizations from your reading as well as from your daily life.

Let's read a simple example to see how generalizations work. Then answer the questions that follow.

Many students must deal with stress in their daily living. The sources of this stress may be academic, emotional, or physical. Many students develop positive ways to cope with this stress.

1.   According to the passage, which of the following situations would most likely create stress?

    A.   taking a summer vacation
    B.   studying for a final exam
    C.   eating your favorite breakfast

2. Based on the passage, which of the following would be a positive way of coping with stress?

   A. staying up all night
   B. missing your final exam
   C. talking with friends about a problem

The answer for (1) is B. Studying for a final exam is a specific, academic source of stress. You applied what you learned about stress to a related situation. For question 2, the best answer is C. Talking with your friends about a problem is a specific, positive way of coping with stress. The other choices are negative ways of coping with stress and would be incorrect applications of the information you read. Therefore, both answers are valid generalizations applied to new, related situations.

Now review the previous passage on tornadoes on page 71. Then choose the correct generalizations from the passage.

1. According to the passage, which of the following states would most likely have tornadoes?

   A. New York
   B. Arizona
   C. Mississippi
   D. Connecticut

2. Based on the passage, which of the following generalizations is true?

   A. A funnel-shaped cloud over water would be called a tornado.
   B. A tornado would rarely destroy a big city.
   C. The worst tornadoes have occurred in the Southeast.
   D. Carrying an umbrella will protect you against tornadoes.

Answers: 1 (C), 2 (B). Both answers are valid generalizations based on the information in the passage. Mississippi is the best answer because it is a specific state in the Southeast. Tornadoes are confined to small local areas, so big cities would be less affected.

PRACTICE 1: INFERENCE AND GENERALIZATION

Directions: Read the following passage. Then choose the best inference or generalization for each question.

Turning his head swiftly, the youth saw his friend, Jim, running in a staggering and stumbling way toward a little clump of bushes. His heart seemed to wrench itself almost free from his body at this sight. His friend made a noise of pain. He and the tattered man began a pursuit. There was a singular race.

When he overtook the tall soldier, he began to plead with all the words he could find. "Jim – Jim – what are you doing – what makes you do this way – you'll hurt yerself."

The same purpose was in the tall soldier's face. He protested in a dulled way, keeping his eyes fastened on the mystic place of his intentions.

"No – no – don't touch me – leave me be – leave me be – "

The youth, aghast and filled with wonder at the tall soldier, began quaveringly to question him. "Where yeh goin', Jim? What you thinking about? Where you going? Tell me, won't you, Jim?"

The tall soldier faced about as upon relentless pursuers. In his eyes there was a great appeal. "Leave me be, can't yeh? Leave me be fer a minute."

– Stephen Crane <u>The Red Badge of Courage</u>

1.   Based on the passage, we can infer that

    A.   the tall soldier has been wounded.
    B.   the youth has been injured.
    C.   the youth is trying to arrest the tall soldier.
    D.   the tall soldier wants to walk home.

2.   The passage suggests that

    A.   the youth is angry with the tall soldier.
    B.   the youth is trying to help the tall soldier.
    C.   the youth is indifferent toward the tall soldier.
    D.   the youth is trying to bring the tall soldier back to camp.

3.   Which of the following events is likely to happen?

    A.   The tall soldier will run away from his pursuers.
    B.   The youth will convince the tall soldier to return to camp.
    C.   The tall soldier will tell the youth what he is thinking.
    D.   There is not enough information to make a determination.

4.   Based on the passage, which of the following generalizations is true?

    A.   One soldier out of three will be injured in a war.
    B.   Tall soldiers are more likely to survive a war.
    C.   We must choose whether or not to respond to another person.
    D.   Tall soldiers are more helpful than young soldiers.

PRACTICE 2: INFERENCE AND GENERALIZATION

Directions: Read some passages from newspapers or magazines. What inferences can you make from the information? State any generalizations you can make as well. Cite facts or details to support your inferences and generalizations. Share your passages and inferences and generalizations with other students. Is there agreement about the inferences and generalizations?

CONCLUSIONS

Drawing a conclusion is a common type of inference skill. When you draw a conclusion, you form a judgement or opinion based on the details in a passage. S. I. Hayakawa once said that conclusions are "statements about the unknown made on the basis of the known." To draw conclusions, use all the facts and clues present in the passage.

Look at the picture of a fish with a hook. Check the most logical conclusions that can be drawn from this picture.

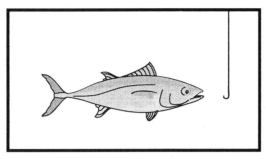

_____ 1. The fish will bite the hook.

_____ 2. The fish will not bite the hook.

_____ 3. The fish is waiting until bait is placed on the hook.

Here is an explanation of the answers:

1. This is not a logical conclusion. Anyone knows that a hook must have bait before a fish will bite.

2. This is a logical conclusion. A fish rarely bites a bare hook even though it may be curious about this strange object in the water.

3. This is a logical conclusion. Fish may wait nearby until bait is placed on the hook. This is particularly true in areas where people fish frequently.

For further practice, read the following paragraph and then answer the question.

At a signal from the captain, the propeller had been disengaged and the fins placed vertically; then the *Nautilus* had shot up at a terrifying speed, like a balloon being carried into the atmosphere. It cut through the water with a loud quivering noise. We could see nothing. In four minutes we had covered the four leagues between us and the surface, and after leaping into the air like a flying fish, we came hurtling back down onto the water, making it splash up to a prodigious height.

– Jules Verne **20,000 Leagues Under the Sea**

Based on this paragraph, we can conclude that

A. the Nautilus was descending into the ocean.
B. the Nautilus was a flying fish named by the captain.
C. the Nautilus rose out of the ocean with great force.
D. the Nautilus raced across the ground at amazing speeds.

To choose the best answer for this question, you should first read the paragraph carefully, paying special attention to the facts and details. Secondly, the question requires you to draw the right conclusion, so you need to narrow your choices to responses that contain stated information from the paragraph. You also should eliminate responses that do not contain facts or details from the passage.

Following this process of logic, you will disregard A. Rather than descending, the author says the Nautilus "shot up" and leapt "into the air like a flying fish." B would be eliminated because the passage does not mention the captain naming the Nautilus after a flying fish. The Nautilus is compared to a flying fish, but this is different from the B response. Choice D is not appropriate because the Nautilus "cut through the water" and made a splash. Therefore, the best answer is C. The facts and details about cutting through water and covering "four leagues between us and the surface," lead us to the conclusion: the Nautilus "shot up" and rose out of the ocean with great force.

PRACTICE 3: CONCLUSIONS

A. **Reading for Conclusions.** Read the following passages. Check only the valid conclusions. Then cite evidence to support your answer.

SLEEPING

Some people think they don't move at all while they sleep. They believe that they go to bed and never change position. Not true. Studies show that everybody makes at least 8 to 12 major posture shifts a night. Insomniacs may double or triple that.

Which is a valid conclusion?

_____ 1. Insomniacs shift positions less often than regular sleepers.

_____ 2. Insomniacs shift positions more often than regular sleepers.

Evidence for your choice_____

_____

HURRICANES

Hurricanes are cyclones caused by very low barometric pressure. Their characteristic center, or eye, is an area of relative calm encircled by powerful winds and storms. Once a tropical cyclone reaches winds of 74 mph, it is technically called a hurricane. The National Hurricane Center in Miami, Florida keeps track of storm formation using all types of monitoring devices to determine location and wind velocity. The center then broadcasts information needed by local weather officials to track the progress of the storm and to take the proper steps to warn citizens and visitors of a hurricane's approach.

Which is a valid conclusion?

_____ 3. A storm with winds of 80 mph is classified as a hurricane.

_____ 4. A storm becomes a hurricane when it reaches winds of 73 mph.

Evidence for your choice_____

_____

FLIGHT

When Orville Wright made the first powered airplane flight in 1903 at speeds of 50 kilometers (31 miles) per hour, the significance of his achievement was barely recognized. Yet in little more than half a century following that historic event at Kitty Hawk, astronauts succeeded in orbiting the Earth at speeds measured in thousands of miles per hour and set foot on the Moon.

Which is a valid conclusion?

_____ 5. Orville Wright was widely praised for the first powered airplane flight in 1903.

_____ 6. Orville Wright was a pioneer of the Space Age.

Evidence for your choice _____

_____

B. **Passage Practice.** Reread several passages from newspapers and magazines. What conclusions can you draw from the information? Cite facts or details to support your conclusions. Share your passages and conclusions with other students. Is there agreement about the conclusions?

C. **Create Riddles.** Cut pictures of people, places, or objects from magazines or newspapers. Each student writes the name of each item in the corner of the picture. Exchange your pictures around the room. Then each person writes a riddle of five clues for each picture. The students in the class number their papers. Then students take turns reading each riddle, and everyone writes the answers on paper. The student solving the most riddles wins a prize.

D. **Riddle Game.** The instructor makes a list of familiar objects for several class teams. Each student must clearly describe one of the objects to his or her team without naming it. If the team guesses the object in 3 minutes, it receives a point. The team with the greatest points wins.

E. **Popular Games.** Practice drawing conclusions by playing **Clue** (board or video version), **Charades, Where in the World is Carmen Sandiego?**, or popular detective games. These games are available at retail stores.

F. **Guilty or Not Guilty?** Attend a real trial or observe one on television or video. Form groups of juries. What are the facts in the case? What conclusions can be drawn from the information? Is the person guilty or not guilty?

G. **Read Riddles.** On your own or with a group, read from **Aesop's Fables** or a book of riddles. Cover the moral or solution to the riddle, and see if you can guess the answer from the information presented.

PREDICTIONS

Another type of inferring is called **making predictions.** **Predictions** involve thoughts or actions than could continue beyond the passage. Sometimes predicting is referred to as **applying ideas.** In other words, you may be asked to relate the information in the passage to a new situation not mentioned in the passage. Once again, clues and facts in the passage will guide your predictions.

To illustrate what predicting is, look at the following signs that are often seen along highways and interstate roads.

You know that the first sign portrays a deer crossing the road. Therefore, you could predict that you should drive with more caution because you could hit a deer up ahead. The second sign is a symbol for two roads intersecting. As a driver, you should apply this knowledge by slowing down since other cars could be crossing the road ahead of you. In both cases, you are making predictions based on information and applying it to new situations.

For further practice, read the following paragraph and then answer the questions.

Many people believe that Africa is full of jungles populated by wild beasts and primitive people with strange customs. From books and movies, others imagine hunters in loincloths throwing spears at elephants and zebras. However, Africa is quite different from what people believe. For example, much of Africa is not jungle but mostly desert or grasslands. You would find less wildlife than expected, and most of these animals live on reserves. Besides small villages, Africa contains large modern cities like Lagos, Nigeria, and Nairobi, Kenya. And instead of hunters in loincloths, many Africans dress just like Americans.

1. According to the passage, if you visited Nairobi, Kenya, how would the men most likely be dressed?

    A. in dashikis   C. in robes
    B. in pants and shirts   D. in loincloths

2. If cities in Africa grow larger, what will probably happen to the wildlife?

    A. Wildlife will be seen only in zoos.
    B. Wildlife will become extinct.
    C. Wildlife will be seen only in its natural habitat.
    D. Most wildlife will be seen only in reserves.

To answer question 1, you would look for any facts in the passage that will support your prediction. Since the last sentence states that "many Africans dress just like Americans," the best answer would be B. Since American men generally wear pants and shirts, many Africans in large cities would probably dress the same way. Men in dashikis (A), robes (C), or loincloths (D) would be less commonly seen, especially in a modern city like Nairobi, Kenya.

The clearest clue for question 2 is sentence 5 in the paragraph. Less African wildlife is now living in jungles and grasslands. Consequently, a logical prediction would be that as cities get bigger, reserves will probably be the only place you will see wildlife like elephants and zebras. Therefore, D is the best answer. The passage never mentions wildlife in zoos (A) or wildlife becoming extinct (B). C would not be a choice because the passage states that fewer animals now live in the wild. Future growth would reduce the wild animal populations even further.

Tips For Answering Questions About Conclusions and Predictions

1. **Read the passage twice.**

2. **Read the question and answer choices.**

3. **Choose your answer based on the stated facts or clues in the passage.**

PRACTICE 4: PREDICTIONS

A.   Reading for Predictions. Read each passage. Then check only the valid predictions. Cite evidence from the passage to support your answer.

Sea Lions Put Fishermen in a Tangle

To sportfishermen of Washington State, a California sea lion feasting on a steelhead salmon is a most unwelcome visitor. Eleven years ago, a small but feisty band of marine mammals began arriving from California waters every fall to gorge on steelhead and other salmon species at Chittenden Locks in Seattle. Repeated efforts to repel or relocate the hungry invaders have met with little success. Now their appetites may cost some sea lions their lives.

"The sea lions could mean the end of this steelhead run," says Joe Scordino of the National Marine Fisheries Service. "Since 1983, the run has fallen from 2,575 steelhead to just 70 last year. In past years, sea lions have taken as much as 65 percent of the returning fish. At this point, every fish they remove is one too many."

Thirty to sixty sea lions cruise the area. About six at a time stake out the locks' fish ladders and waylay steelhead en route to Lake Washington, where they spawn in its tributaries. The run starts in December and peaks in February and March.

Under an amendment to the Marine Mammal Protection Act, Washington State officials are seeking control measures that include killing 10 to 15 sea lions during the next three years. Scordino says no West Coast aquarium will accept the animals; all are males that weigh 600 to 900 pounds.

Which is a valid prediction?

_____ 1. If the number of sea lions is reduced, the steelhead population should increase.

_____ 2. Extra sea lions will be donated to aquariums or zoos.

Evidence for your choice _____

_____

COCAINE

Some 3,000 people a year die in the United States after using cocaine. But the drug has another deadly side. In the rain forests of Bolivia, Columbia, and Peru, hundreds of illegal coca farms are contaminating rivers and streams with millions of gallons of toxic chemicals.

Which is a valid prediction?

_____ 3. Water pollution will increase once cocaine is declared illegal.

_____ 4. Cocaine will destroy more people and the environment as it spreads to other countries.

Evidence for your choice _____

_____

B. **Videos.** On your own or as a class, view a video that you have not seen before. For the first 20 minutes or so, jot down some of the events and traits of the major characters.
Then stop the video periodically, and try to predict what the characters will do next.

C. **Short Stories.** With a partner or in a group, read a high interest short story to the others. Pause at critical points, and see if the others can anticipate the events. Stop just before the climax. Have the other students write an ending. Then read the actual ending and ask which ending was preferred.

D. **Practice Passages.** Review passages from other chapters in this book. Make predictions from the information. Point out facts and details to support your predictions.

MEANING OF A PASSAGE

The **meaning** of a passage is a sentence that contains the message in a passage. It is a concise insight gained from reading a selection.

Read this passage and choose the best meaning.

The youth gave a shriek as he confronted the thing. He was, for moments, turned to stone before it. He remained staring into the liquid-looking eyes. The dead man and the living man exchanged a long look. Then the youth cautiously put one hand behind him and brought it against a tree. Leaning upon this he retreated, step by step, with his face still toward the thing. He feared that if he turned his back the body might spring up and stealthily pursue him.

– Stephen Crane, <u>Red Badge of Courage</u>

Which of the following statements is the best meaning for the passage?

A.   The living and the dead form bonds of love.
B.   Death should not be feared.
C.   Never speak badly about the dead.
D.   Confronting death can be terrifying.

In choosing your answer, you must determine which statement best expresses the message or meaning in the passage. It should be a statement that most appropriately applies to the events described in the selection. Therefore, the correct answer is D.

While the other choices contain general truths, they do not apply specifically to this passage. For example, (A) focuses on love between the living and the dead while the details in the passage convey fear and dread. Likewise, (B) ignores the fear so apparent in the description. Finally, (C) is incorrect because the youth never speaks badly about the dead person. His shock is so great that all he can do is shriek in fear.

```
┌─────────────────────────────────────────────┐
│          Tips for Finding the Meaning        │
│                                               │
│    1.  Read the passage carefully.            │
│                                               │
│    2.  Reread the passage for details.        │
│                                               │
│    3.  Choose the statement that best expresses│
│        the meaning of the passage.            │
└─────────────────────────────────────────────┘
```

PRACTICE 5: MEANING OF A PASSAGE

Directions: Read each passage. Then select the best meaning.

1.   We need to remember as well as to celebrate the end of World War I. We need to remember the dead and the wounded, the widows and orphans, the destroyed and broken homes, farms, and businesses. We need to remember these casualties of war. We must prevent another such war from happening.

– from a newspaper editorial about World War I

A.   Widows and orphans should remember the dead and wounded.
B.   War is part of the human condition.
C.   Remember those who were lost or wounded in the war.
D.   We must prevent war in the future.

2.   An old male elephant was dying in the African wilderness. A group of elephants from his herd gathered around this male, trying to get him to stand up. They tried to stroke him with their trunks, raise him with their tusks, and put food in his mouth. Nothing seemed to work, so the herd left. However, a mother and her calf remained, standing with their backs to the dead elephant. The mother tried to touch the dead elephant with one foot. Then the herd returned and began circling the dead companion. After a time, they gathered tree branches and grass clumps scattering these items on or around the body.

    A.   Elephants often die alone in the wilderness.
    B.   Some animals perform rituals to mourn their dead.
    C.   Death is a fact of life in the African wilderness.
    D.   The elephant population in Africa is declining because they are hunted and killed.

3.   A man was going down from Jerusalem to Jericho, when he fell into the hands of robbers. They stripped him of his clothes, beat him, and went away, leaving him half dead. A priest happened to be going down the same road, and when he saw the man, he passed by on the other side. So too, a Levite, when he came to the place and saw him, passed by on the other side. But a Samaritan, as he traveled, came where the man was; and when he saw him, he took pity on him. He went to him and bandaged his wounds, pouring on oil and wine. Then he put the man on his own donkey, took him to an inn and took care of him. The next day he took out two silver coins and gave them to the innkeeper. "Look after him," he said, "and when I return, I will reimburse you for any extra expense you may have."

                                   – The Bible

    A.   Robbers can be dangerous on the roads.
    B.   Try to avoid areas where there is crime.
    C.   Innkeepers take good care of their customers.
    D.   A good neighbor loves those in need.

4.  It was market-day. The narrow window of the jail looked down directly on the carts and wagons drawn up in a long line, where they had unloaded. He could see, too, and hear distinctly the clink of money as it changed hands, the busy crowd of whites and blacks shoving, pushing one another, and the haggling and swearing at the stalls. Somehow, the sound, more than anything else had done, wakened him up, – made the whole real to him. He was done with the world and the business of it. He let the tin fall, and looked out, pressing his face close to the rusty bars. How they crowded and pushed! And he, – he should never walk that pavement again!

                       – Rebecca Davis <u>Life in the Iron Mills</u>

    A.   We can do little to change past mistakes.
    B.   The world is filled with crowds of friendly people.
    C.   Criticizing the world helps us feel better.
    D.   Jail is a place to relax and enjoy the world.

5.   As the old man walked the beach at dawn, he noticed a young man ahead of him picking up starfish and flinging them into the sea. Finally, catching up with the youth, he asked why he was doing this. The young man explained that the stranded starfish would die if left until the morning sun.

"But the beach goes on for miles, and there are millions of starfish," commented the old man. "How can your effort make any difference?"

The young man looked at the starfish in his hand and then threw it safely in the waves. "It makes a difference to this one," he said.

– Anonymous

A.   The morning sun will kill stranded starfish.
B.   Starfish must be saved from extinction.
C.   Saving even one life can make a difference.
D.   Saving millions of starfish is a waste of time.

6.   Whenever the white man treats the Indian as they treat each other, then we will have no more wars. We shall all be alike–brothers of one father and one mother, with one sky above us and one country around us, and one government for all. Then the Great Spirit Chief who rules above will smile upon this land, and send rain to wash out the bloody spots made by brothers' hands from the face of the earth. For this time the Indian race is waiting and praying. I hope that no more groans of wounded men and women will ever go to the ear of the Great Spirit Chief above, and that all people may be one people.

– The Words of Chief Joseph

A.   Mutual respect and fairness will unite people together.
B.   The Great Spirit Chief rules over heaven and earth.
C.   Unity comes from the Great Spirit.
D.   The White Man's government belongs to the Indian race.

7.   In 1964, Disney Productions bought a chunk of central Florida woodland about the size of San Francisco and began transforming it into a super attraction. Opened in October 1971, Disney World drew 12 million visitors in 1972, more people than live in the state of Florida and twice as many as the number of foreigners who toured the United States that year.

Beneath the Magic Kingdom is an area called Utilidor. Here overhead pipes funnel utilities, including a waste removal system that vacuums trash with a 60 mile per hour "whoosh."

Utilidor houses a huge wardrobe center where seamstresses maintain more than 100,000 costumes. A computer keeps the bears dancing in time, coordinates the groans of the ghouls, and even sniffs the air in the Hall of Presidents to warn against fire.

A.   Disney World has an impressive array of costumes.
B.   An area the size of San Francisco has been transformed into Disney World.
C.   Disney World is a super attraction with state-of-the-art equipment.
D.   Waste tunnels funnel trash at 60 miles per hour.

8.   It was cold and drafty in the second floor apartment. The place was converted from an old farmhouse. It had a kitchenette with a small refrigerator and hot plate just to the right of the entrance. The door had opened to a large room serving as the living room and dining room with a small alcove in the back for a bedroom and a tiny bathroom that used to be a hall closet. It was sparsely furnished in "early attic" furniture. That's all Jake needed right now. He was trying to make it on his own.

     Jake had gotten a job at a gas station doing small repairs and maintenance to cars. The job didn't pay much, but it kept food on the table, put a roof over his head, with a little left over to take in a movie when he had time. Jake had also gotten a little federal grant money and a student loan to pay his books and tuition at the University. He was finally back in school.

     Jake was working toward a degree in sociology. He wanted to help kids like himself, kids who had taken a wrong turn along the way, or were mixed up or in trouble. He wanted to lead them back to a path of success and then give them the push to go forward down the right road. He wanted to be there for at least one kid even though no one was there for him.

A.   Jake faces an easy climb up the ladder of success.
B.   Jake enjoys repairing cars and is trying to open his own garage.
C.   Jake lives in a farmhouse and works at a gas station.
D.   Jake works and goes to school to give others the help he didn't have.

9.   

     Allie was quite bright, and after a few years, her job was just that, a job. Allie wanted a career. So she went back to school at night while she worked. After graduating, she got a position with a company as a computer programmer. It was challenging, and Allie was good at it. Allie was promoted within two years and transferred to the corporate headquarters in South Carolina.

     Moving to another state was difficult. Allie didn't know anyone, and she was young, 28 years old. All the people in her work group were men in their 40s who were already married. Allie decided to pour herself into her work for a while and try to get promoted and transferred again. Allie worked hard, and it paid off. They offered her a promotion and a transfer to Fort Worth, Texas. There was only one problem. She was in love.

A.   Working hard brings happiness.
B.   Education results in better job opportunities.
C.   Choosing between a career and a relationship is a challenge.
D.   In today's society, promotions occur more often than in the past.

100

10.   Dr. Haim Ginott in *Between Parent and Teenager* told this story: Jean walked along the beach with her mother. She asked, "Mom, how do you hold a husband after you've found him?"
       Her mother gave her a silent lesson in love. She scooped up two handfuls of sand. One she squeezed hard. The more she squeezed, the more sand escaped. The other she held lightly, and the sand remained.
       Jean said, "I see."

   A.   Learn the dangers of love.
   B.   Learn the principles of sand science.
   C.   Learn the many meanings of love.
   D.   Learn the difference between love and possessiveness.

PRACTICE 6: MEANING OF A PASSAGE

Directions: Read the following passage. Then write two different statements that would summarize the meaning of this passage. Compare your responses with your group, class, or instructor.

> It rained. The procession of weary soldiers became a bedraggled train, despondent and muttering, marching with churning effort in a trough of liquid brown mud under a low, wretched sky. Yet the youth smiled, for he saw that the world was a world for him, though many discovered it to be made of oaths and walking sticks. He had rid himself of the red sickness of battle. The nightmare was in the past. He had been an animal blistered and sweating in the heat and pain of war. He turned now with a lover's thirst to images of tranquil skies, fresh meadows, cool brooks – an existence of soft and eternal peace.

                              – Stephen Crane <u>Red Badge of Courage</u>

1. _____

    _____

2. _____

    _____

PRACTICE 7: MEANING STATEMENT

Directions: On your own or in a group, review 6 passages found in this book. Write a meaning statement for each one. Then compare your answers with the class or the instructor.

Read the following passages, and answer the questions that follow.

500 Pound Alligator

Pensacola, Fla. - For the past 20 years, hunting dogs have been disappearing in the Blackwater River State Forest. Their owners thought people were stealing their expensive animals.

The thief, it turns out, was a 500-pound alligator that turned a game trail into his private diner, grabbing dogs as they ran across Coldwater Creek in pursuit of foxes or deer.

Their barking apparently was his dinner bell. At least six hunting dogs met their fate in the gator's jaws.

One of the final victims was Flojo, Rufis Godwin's $5,000 Walker fox-hunting hound. The dog disappeared a few weeks ago in the forest about 45 miles northeast of Pensacola. The last Godwin heard of her was her bark as she chased an animal, probably a deer.

Four days later, Godwin was using a tracking device to search for Flojo's electronic collar when he caught a faint signal. The beeps were very weak until he pointed his receiver at a deep swamp hole.

Jamie Sauls, who was with Godwin, also received signals from a collar worn by a dog he had last seen several weeks earlier. They also got a response from a third collar that had been on another friend's dog.

"When we walked up to this hole, all of a sudden the boxes went to beeping wide open," Godwin recalled in a telephone interview from his home in Chumuckla. "So we knew then we were dealing with a gator."

The 10-foot, 11-inch reptile was captured Aug. 15 by state-contracted gator hunters.

1.   Summarize the meaning of above passage._____

    _____

    _____

During the 1880s and 1890s, Andrew Carnegie was a prominent leader in the steel industry and one of the richest men in the world. With his money, he established 1,681 libraries in urban centers across the United States. In 1956, the Library Services Act gave libraries strong federal support.

2.   What would have likely happened if Andrew Carnegie had not promoted libraries in urban areas?

    _____

    _____

Can Snakebites be Healthy?

Bill Haast, an 85 year old Floridian, has developed a reputation as a man with an acquired immunity to snakes. Playing with a cobra is an everyday activity with Mr. Haast, who has been bitten no less than 162 times by venomous snakes.

He began his experimentation with snake venom in 1948 by injecting himself with small amounts of rattlesnake venom. Over the years, he has built up the dosage. He believes the snake venom has kept him healthy. He has not once been sick since he began injecting himself with venom.

He had his near death experiences, though. In 1958, Haast was bitten by a blue krait, an Asian snake which has venom many times more poisonous than a cobra's. It has been known to kill elephants. During his one day ordeal, Haast realized that something as powerful as venom must have something useful for medicine. In the late 1970s, Haast produced a drug called PROven which mirrored the effects produced by his own immunity to snake bites. The drug has been used to treat rheumatoid arthritis and MS (multiple sclerosis). Over 7,000 patients have been treated with this high-demand drug.

He recently purchased a house for snake-keeping in southwestern Florida. Daily he collects venom from over 400 snakes and sells it to laboratories. His own blood is so full of antibodies that it is used as an antidote for victims of snakebites.

3. Summarize the meaning of this passage. _____

_____

_____

4. Based on this passage, what is likely to happen if Bill is bitten again by a poisonous snake?

_____

_____

What I Lived For

An honest man has hardly need to count more than his ten fingers, or in extreme cases he may add his ten toes, and lump the rest. Simplicity, Simplicity, Simplicity! I say, let your affairs be as two or three, and not a hundred or a thousand; instead of a million count half a dozen, and keep your accounts on your thumbnail. In the midst of this chopping sea of civilized life, such are the clouds and storms and quicksands and thousand-and-one items to be allowed for, that a man has to live, if he would not founder and go to the bottom and not make his port at all, by dead reckoning, and he must be a great calculator indeed who succeeds. Simplify, Simplify. Instead of three meals a day, if it be necessary eat but one; instead of a hundred dishes, five; and reduce other things in proportion.

– Thoreau, *Walden*

5. Based on this passage, we can conclude that the writer's philosophy is _____

_____

Explore America's Hands-On Museum of Space Travel

Pilot a spacecraft to the moon's surface. Fire lasers at the speed of light. Feel the force of triple gravity in a spinning moonship. Leap 15 feet high on the zero gravity machine. It's all part of a 21st century adventure of space travel and adventure at The Space and Rocket Center.

Sixty action exhibits involve you in an educational and entertaining experience in which you're an astronaut for the day. You'll see and touch rockets and spacecrafts that have made the fantastic journey into space, watch demonstrations of astronauts' training equipment and meet Baker, the monkeynaut who pioneered space travel.

From the early days of flight to the Space Shuttle and tomorrow's explorations beyond the stars, The Space and Rocket Center offers first-hand experience with the challenges of man in space.

United States Space Camp

Young people from all over the world come to Huntsville for a unique, educational experience. Boys and girls build and launch model rockets, train like astronauts, try on a space suit, and fly a simulated Space Shuttle mission, complete with shuttle cockpit and mission control. From astronaut training with authentic NASA equipment to receiving their wings at week's end, there's no other experience like it on earth! (Open March through November, Huntsville, Alabama)

6.   From the information presented, we can conclude that _____

_____

_____

7.   Based on these articles, who do you think is the intended audience? _____

_____

From an editorial —

In today's Morning News, we heard the Surgeon General's latest report about smoking among young people. Three million teenagers smoke a billion packs of cigarettes every year, and the numbers are growing. The average age to start smoking is now 14! years of age.

What can we do to prevent adolescent smokers from becoming adult smokers? One way is to ban cigarettes from vending machines which are easily accessible to children. Another strategy is to restrict ads featuring glamorous, sexy, and awesome images of smokers portrayed on billboards, appealing to teenagers.

Eliminating the special coupon promotions for tee-shirts and hats on cigarette packs would also reduce smoking. When young people do not hear about or see cigarettes everywhere, they will pay more attention to the health risks associated with cigarette smoking. Smoking-related illnesses kill over 400,000 smokers annually.

Therefore, education and legal action will protect our young people from the smoking habit!

8. What summarizes the writer's viewpoint? _____

_____

9. What does the writer claim is the leading cause of teenage smoking? _____

_____

Harry Houdini

In the summer of 1912, a man was chained and then nailed into a wooden box. Then the box was bound with rope and steel cables and lowered into the East River. Minutes passed as the audience waited to see what would happen. Fearing for the man's life, many gasped for breath themselves. Suddenly, the man emerged from the water, unharmed and freed from his chains. His name was Harry Houdini.

Houdini spent a lifetime performing escapes that left his audiences astonished and clamoring for more. Dangling upside down from a crane, he could wrestle himself out of a straightjacket in minutes. He could be handcuffed and lowered into a steel drum secured with padlocks and filled with water. Three minutes later, he would emerge alive and well.

How did Houdini accomplish his feats? Besides being a master of illusion, he also possessed two unique talents. His body was flexible and muscular which allowed him to untie knots with his fingers and teeth. He also trained himself to hold his breath under water for up to four minutes. Besides that, he could pick apart any lock or chain in the world. In fact, he often showed people from his audience that he could open locks they brought to him. In this way, he proved that the ones he picked were not fake. In 1901, he was handcuffed to a pillar by police who would return in an hour to free him. He escaped before they left the room. In 1903, German police accused him of cheating and encouraging criminals. He escaped in the courtroom and won the case.

10. Which statement above is a conclusion drawn by the author? _____

_____

_____

11. What generalization could accurately describe Houdini's abilities? _____

_____

Moon

Through space exploration, scientists have constructed a history of the moon dating back to its infancy. Rocks collected from the lunar highlands date about 4.0 to 4.3 billion years old. It's believed the solar system formed about 4.6 billion years ago. The first few million years of the moon's existence were so violent that few traces of this period remain. As a molten outer layer gradually cooled and solidified into different kinds of rock, the moon was bombarded by huge asteroids and smaller objects. Some of the asteroids were the size of small states like Rhode Island or Delaware, and their collisions with the moon created huge basins hundreds of kilometers across.

The catastrophic bombardment died away about 4 billion years ago, leaving the lunar highlands covered with huge overlapping craters and a deep layer of shattered and broken rock. Heat produced by the decay of radioactive elements began to melt the inside of the moon at depths of about 200 kilometers (124 miles) below its surface. Then, from about 3.8 to 3.1 billion years ago, great floods of lava rose from inside the moon and poured over its surface, filling in the large impact basins to form the dark parts of the moon called maria or seas. Explorations show that there has been no significant volcanic activity on the moon for more than 3 billion years.

12. From this passage, we can generalize that _____

_____

13. Based on this article, what is likely to happen if an asteroid hits the moon's surface?

_____

_____

The Wild Pitcher

It is the last game of the championship. Tamara, the girl who is always picked last when forming teams, sits on the bench and cheers her team, the Rockets, against the visiting team, the Panthers. Earlier in the game, Louise, the star pitcher of the Rockets, sprained her arm in the opening pitch. Now, in the last inning with a one run Rockets advantage and bases loaded, her replacement, Jenny, also sprained her arm. In a desperate move, Dalia, the coach of the Rockets, told Tamara, "Try your best honey. Just try not to break your hand when you throw the ball." Tamara stumbled clumsily to the mound and readied her first pitch. All she had to do was strike out this one hitter and the game was won. The Rockets fans closed their eyes in fear of what Tamara would do. She threw the ball so strangely it seemed to spin in spirals, yet it passed through the strike zone of the hitter, and she missed it. Tamara continued to throw like this, and by the time the third strike was called, the fans stood up and shouted, "Tamara, Tamara, Tamara!"

14. The lesson to be inferred from this story is _____

_____

15. Based on this story, what is the coach most likely to do with Tamara? _____

_____

CHAPTER 4 TEST

Read the following passages and answer the questions that follow each passage.

The Lost Sea in Sweetwater, Tennessee is the largest underground lake in the world. The temperature inside the cavern remains at 58° F all year long. Many interesting rooms exist inside the cavern. In one room, you can see rare cave flowers called anthodites. Every second of the tour is a fascinating experience you will never forget.

1. Which of the following sentences below is a generalization?

    A. In one room, you can see rare cave flowers called anthodites.
    B. The temperature inside the cavern remains at 58° F all year long.
    C. Every second of the tour is a fascinating experience you will never forget.
    D. The Lost Sea in Sweetwater, Tennessee is the largest underground lake in the world.

Tomorrow's Jobs

In recent years, the level of educational attainment of the labor force has risen dramatically. Between 1975 and 1990, the proportion of the labor force aged 25 to 64 with at least 1 year of college increased from 33 to 47 percent, while the proportion with four years of college or more increased from 18 to 26 percent. Projected rates of employment growth are faster for occupations requiring higher levels of education or training than for those requiring less.

The emphasis on education will continue. Consequently, three out of the four fastest growing occupational groups will be executive, administrative, and managerial; professional specialty; and technicians and related support occupations. These occupations generally require the highest levels of education and skill and will make up an increasing proportion of new jobs. Office and factory automation, changes in consumer demand, and substitution of imports for domestic products are expected to cause employment to stagnate or decline in many occupations that require little formal education – apparel workers and textile machinery operators, for example. Opportunities for high school dropouts will be increasingly limited, and workers who cannot read and follow directions may not even be considered for most jobs.

Employed high school dropouts are more likely to have low paying jobs with little advancement potential, while workers in occupations requiring higher levels of education have higher incomes. In addition, many of the occupations projected to grow most rapidly between 1990 and 2005 are among those with the highest earnings.

2. Based on this passage, we can predict that:

    A. The janitorial profession will increase dramatically in openings.
    B. Textile workers will be in high demand.
    C. Miners will see more demand for their services.
    D. Sales managers will be in high demand.

3. What is the best summary of this passage?

    A. Job openings in many manufacturing fields will increase dramatically in the next century.
    B. Jobs requiring higher levels of education will be in high demand in the next century.
    C. The United States population as a whole has attained a higher level of education.
    D. There will be much fewer jobs available for high school dropouts in the next century.

Blitzkrieg

It was called blitzkrieg – lightning war, and the Germans unveiled it in Poland during September of 1939. It consisted of *stuka* dive bomber attacks, fast tank movements, and mobile infantry deployments, all of which were backed up by heavy bomber attacks. The keys to this whole new tactic were mobility and coordination of a multi-force attack. It was a strategy the Germans developed to avoid the slow, turgid warfare of World War I. It can be reasonably said that this new air-ground, multi-force concept revolutionized modern warfare.

In 1939, the German blitzkrieg overwhelmed Poland. By the end of the first day of the Polish campaign, the Polish airforce had been largely destroyed; most of it was caught on the ground before it could take off, and thus the Germans had almost immediate air supremacy. Also, German high level bombers attacked Warsaw, reducing most of the Polish rear guard to shambles. On the ground, the German military machine streamed across the Polish border - tanks, the armored cars, and the armored infantry and artillery of the mechanized panzer divisions. All of these were supported by waves of Junkers-87 dive bombers, the deadly *stukas*.

4. Which statement from the passage is a conclusion drawn by the author?

   A. It can be reasonably said that this new air-ground, multi-force concept revolutionized modern warfare.
   B. Also, German high-level bombers attacked Warsaw, reducing most of the Polish rear guard to shambles.
   C. It was called blitzkrieg - lightning war, and the Germans unveiled it in Poland that September of 1939.
   D. All of these were supported by waves of Junkers-87 dive bombers, the deadly *stukas*.

Powerboating

For many people, the ideal powerboat would have speeds as high as a jet airplane. For others, fuel efficiency is a primary concern. Whatever features people would enjoy in their powerboat, they will always have to make concessions. Each boat cannot possibly fulfill what everyone desires, regardless of how much money a person has. For example, a boat that is big enough to have a living room and an area for catching and cleaning fish will not be fuel efficient and will be too large to bring close to shore. On the other hand, a smaller boat will have much less space and comfort, but its speed and ability to maneuver will be much greater than a larger boat.

Powerboats also serve various functions. For the risk-taker, power boats built for speed and sharp turns can provide hours of amusement. For the more family-oriented person, larger boats provide enough room for all the family members to sit together comfortably. Some boats built with sturdy hulls can be used on the ocean for deep sea fishing or diving. Regardless of the specialization, powerboats will satisfy whatever desire a person wishes to fulfill on the water.

These boats provide a great deal of excitement and amusement. If used properly, they will continue to provide countless enjoyable outings for the millions who have taken up this sport.

5. After reading this passage, one can conclude that powerboating

   A. will become the most popular sport in America.
   B. is an exciting sport for those who are properly trained.
   C. results in millions of dollars of revenue each year.
   D. is an enjoyable water sport for many people.

Excerpt from the Declaration of Independence

…That whenever any Form of Government becomes destructive of these ends (Life, Liberty, and the pursuit of Happiness), it is the right of the People to alter or abolish it, and to institute new Government, laying its foundation of such principles and organizing its powers in such form, as to them shall seem most likely to effect their Safety and Happiness…

6.   Based on this passage, which of the following conclusions is correct?

    A.   Government, once established, can never be abolished.
    B.   Three branches of government shall rule the nation.
    C.   The government can be abolished or altered if it interferes with rights such as Life or Liberty.
    D.   The rights of Life and Liberty are naturally acknowledged by all governments.

A Life Saved or a Life Lost?

Once in India there was a high priest by the name of Devasha who lived in a certain village. His wife, Yajna, was also of high birth. In time, she became pregnant, and the couple had a son whom they named Kanji. This son was a great gift, a precious diamond to be cherished and treasured.

Shortly after the child's birth, Yajna went to the river to bathe. Devasha stayed with the child and cared for him in his mother's absence. Soon, a messenger notified the high priest that presents for performing sacred ceremonies were arriving. In a hurry, Devasha left a pet mongoose to guard the child.

A few minutes later, a poisonous snake slithered toward the child. At the moment that the serpent was about to strike the child, the mongoose saw the snake and quickly killed it out of love for his master.

When the mongoose saw his master return from his duty, he happily ran toward Devasha with the blood of the snake on his fur. Thinking that the mongoose had killed his son, the high priest strangled the mongoose with his bare hands.

When he arrived home, Devasha discovered his son alive and well. Next to his son, he saw the snake that the mongoose killed. He was stricken with grief and wailed loudly. Returning from the river, his wife, Yajna, learned of the incident and denounced her husband for his foolish action.

7.   Based on this passage, we can infer that

    A.   Yajna was very upset at the mongoose's actions.
    B.   Devasha loved his son very much.
    C.   the mongoose was trying to befriend the snake.
    D.   Devasha does not jump to conclusions.

8.   What is Devasha likely to do in the future?

    A.   Devasha will learn to trust no one.
    B.   Devasha will ask questions before making assumptions.
    C.   Devasha will buy a pet serpent.
    D.   Devasha will always stay near Kanji.

The World of Cyberspace

Is it a person, place, or a thing? Actually, cyberspace is the place where you communicate information using a personal computer and a telephone line. Persons, places, things, and ideas are the information generated in cyberspace. Other names for this world are the information superhighway or the electronic highway.

Why bother with cyberspace? Information 24 hours a day is one reason. Imagine an incredibly rich library of computer software available at any time of the day or night. Add to that newspapers, encyclopedias, magazines, games, discussion groups, and contests with prizes. Most importantly, you can connect with millions of people around the world. You'd never have the chance to meet these people in the real world, but in cyberspace you can. Friendships and businesses can now operate in cyberspace whether you live in the United States or Korea.

What do I need to enter cyberspace? All you need is a personal computer, a modem which connects the computer to the telephone line, and an on-line service provider such as CompuServe, America On-Line or Prodigy. Then you'll be ready to travel, join discussion groups, go shopping around the world, and make new friends too.

9. The best generalization of this passage is that

   A. with a computer and a modem, you can not access the world of cyberspace.
   B. another name for cyberspace is the information superhighway.
   C. encyclopedias and discussion groups are now available on CompuServe, America On-Line, or Prodigy.
   D. cyberspace is the place where you can find people, places, things, and ideas.

Alcohol

Because alcohol is the most widely promoted drug in our society, it is easily abused. Alcohol is the number one problem among youth. By their senior year in high school, almost all students will have tried alcoholic beverages. Four out of ten will consume five or more drinks in a row every two weeks.

Youth who begin drinking alcohol at an early age will most likely experience alcohol related problems later in life.

Alcohol dependence affects relationships with family and friends. Even low doses can impair coordination while driving a car. Higher doses reduce mental abilities and the capacity to remember information. School grades suffer, and students are more likely to skip classes. Other drugs may also be abused and conflicts with the law are more common.

Girls who drink alcohol are more likely to become pregnant. Babies born to such mothers often develop fetal alcohol syndrome. The effects of this condition on these children lead to mental retardation or physical defects. The offspring of alcoholic parents are also at greater risk for alcoholism themselves.

10. Which of the following is a correct generalization found in the passage?

   A. Alcohol dependence affects driving and friendships in school.
   B. Alcohol use by teens in moderation is not a concern.
   C. A nine year old drinking alcohol will experience problems in their mental and physical health..
   D. Some high school students abuse alcohol by their senior year.

The Experiment

"Before you drink, my respectable old friends," said he, "it would be well that, with the experience of a lifetime to direct you, you should draw up a few general rules for your guidance, in passing a second time through the perils of youth. Think what a sin and shame it would be if, with your peculiar advantages, you should not become patterns of virtue and wisdom to all the young people of the age!"

The doctor's four venerable friends made him no answer, except by a feeble and tremulous laugh; so very ridiculous was the idea that, knowing how closely repentance treads behind the steps of error, they should ever go astray again.

"Drink, then," said the doctor, bowing. "I rejoice that I have so well selected the subjects of my experiment."

With shaking hands, they raised the glasses to their lips. The medicine, if it really possessed such virtues as Dr. Heidegger imputed to it, could not have been bestowed on four human beings who needed it more woefully. They looked as if they had never known what youth or pleasure was, but had been the offspring of nature's old age and always the gray decrepit, sapless, miserable creatures, who now sat stooping around the doctor's table, without life enough in their souls or bodies to be excited even by the prospect of growing young again. They drank off the liquid and replaced their glasses on the table.

– Nathaniel Hawthorne, paraphrase from "Dr. Heidegger's Experiment"

11. Based on the passage, we can infer that the drinking of the medicine will probably

   A. make the four persons old and gray.
   B. make the four persons drunk.
   C. restore the youth of the four persons.
   D. make the four persons sick.

The Madman

At last, when his wits were gone beyond repair, he came to conceive the strangest idea that ever occurred to any madman in the world. It now appeared to him fitting and necessary, in order to win a greater amount of honor for himself and serve his country at the same time, to become a knight adventurer and roam the world on horseback, in a suit of armor. He would go in quest of adventures, by way of putting into practice all that he had read in his books; he would right every manner of wrong, placing himself in situations of the greatest peril such as would make him famous to the eternal glory of his name. As a reward for his valor and the might of his arm, the poor fellow could already see himself crowned Emperor...and so, carried away by the strange pleasure that he found in such thoughts as these, he at once set about putting his plan into effect.

– Miguel de Cervantes, adaptation from *Don Quixote*

12. After reading the passage, one could conclude that

   A. someone can be focused on a mission, yet be mentally insane.
   B. the man in this passage will not likely become a great knight and conqueror.
   C. literally putting what you read into practice is always a good idea.
   D. the best way to serve your country is to ride the world on horseback.

13. In this passage, the writer infers that following one's dreams

    A. means reaching for the highest goal.
    B. can also be a great way to escape reality.
    C. is the best way to achieve a healthy, happy life.
    D. requires quick action with little preparation.

Population Density

And what about the assertion that as the world population grows, poverty is the inevitable result?

Actually, the amount of poverty in a country has little to do with its population density or even its supply of resources. It does have a lot to do with each country's economic system and how free it is.

Japan, for instance, is one of the most prosperous countries on earth, but it has many more people per square mile than, say India, one of the world's poorest. Likewise, booming Singapore has a population density of more than 10,000 people per square mile. Yet Singapore's per capita income is over 15 times that of Communist-run Cuba, which has 254 people per square mile.

It is no accident that the world's most prosperous countries are those with the freest and least-regulated, least-taxed economies. Thriving Asian economies like those of Japan, Singapore, Hong Kong, Taiwan, and South Korea are classic examples of these.

14. Based on the information above, one could infer that

    A. Countries with free economies tend to have the lowest population densities.
    B. Communist countries are the most prosperous.
    C. Countries with free economies are the most prosperous.
    D. Communist countries tend to have the highest population densities.

15. Which of the following is an accurate generalization of the passage above?

    A. The world's poorest countries are also the most populous.
    B. Nations with a free economy are the most prosperous.
    C. Communist countries are the most prosperous.
    D. The world's most restricted economies are also the most populous countries.

Tons of Toads

The best laid plans of toads and men. . . . In June 1935, Australia's sugar industry imported 101 cane toads from Hawaii in the hope that they would eat the cane beetles threatening the sugar crop. The toad, described by one person as "ugly even by toad standards" did not have any interest in eating cane beetles. But it made itself at home. It now exists over half of Queensland and is spreading into New South Wales and the Northern Territory. A single female has been known to lay 54,000 eggs in a clutch, and females may lay eggs twice a year. Australia's toad population is now in the millions – and growing.

And the cane toad, which can grow to more than eight inches long, is dangerous. It eats baby snakes and frogs, and when other animals try to eat *it,* it secretes a poison that can kill a dog in 15 minutes. Even humans can die from ingesting the poison. Biologists have suggested introducing a parasite or disease to control the pests.

16. If the cane toad population is not controlled, what is most likely to occur?

    A. The number of cane beetles will increase.
    B. Biologists will find a parasite to kill the toads.
    C. Snakes and dogs will disappear in Australia.
    D. The cane toads will spread to other parts of Australia.

17. What is the best summary of the meaning of this passage?

    A. Australia's cane toad population is very large.
    B. Cane toads can lay 54,000 eggs at a time.
    C. Cane toads are poisonous and can kill humans.
    D. Cane toads were imported to Australia for one purpose, but they have become pests.

Buffalo Soldiers

After the Civil War, many blacks moved to the West to find a better life for themselves. Some became cowhands, ranchers, or shopkeepers. Some farmed the land in a harsh environment with few resources. Several African-American Army regiments served on the frontier and became skilled fighters.

These special soldiers lived among the Indians, but others worked to control and contain the native American population. In their role as soldiers in the military, African-American men were instrumental in patrolling the Great Plains, the Rio Grande, and areas of New Mexico, Arizona, Colorado, and the Dakotas. Under acts of Congress, four segregated regiments were established in 1866 to use the services of African-American soldiers. Two were cavalry regiments and two were infantry units. Black cavalry regiments consisted of the 9th and 10th cavalry, and the infantry units included the 24th and 25th infantry divisions.

The exploits and experiences of the Buffalo Soldiers, a term used by the Indians to describe the black troops, are described in a comprehensive account by William H. Lick, The Buffalo Soldiers: A Narrative of the Negro Cavalry in the West. (Norman: University of Oklahoma Press, 1963)

18. From the passage, one can infer that the writer

    A. admired the African-American soldiers.
    B. thought that African-Americans should not live with Indians.
    C. thought that African-Americans shouldn't move to the West.
    D. was neutral toward the African-American soldiers.

19. What is the best meaning of this passage?

    A. The Buffalo soldiers serve as a great example of Indian valor on the Frontier.
    B. The Buffalo soldiers were not segregated and developed friendships with the Indians.
    C. African Americans became farmers, shopkeepers, and soldiers in the American West.
    D. Segregated regiments of Buffalo Soldiers were established in 1896 to patrol the Western Frontier.

Dr. Dunk

When Dominique Wilkins moved to Washington, North Carolina with his mother and seven brothers and sisters, his favorite game was marbles. "I was the Larry Bird of marbles," he said, but he soon discovered basketball. By the time he was fifteen, he was challenging older players in the schoolyard for a dollar per game.

While he played basketball at Washington High School, sportswriters started calling him "Dr. Dunk," because of his crowd-pleasing dunks on the court. By then, Dominique was six feet seven inches and led his basketball team to two Triple-A state championships. At the University of Georgia, Wilkins continued his astonishing success. The Georgia Bulldogs were able to appear twice in the National Invitation Tournament (NIT). The national Basketball Association's (NBA) coaches selected Wilkins for the All-American squad. After 78 games for Georgia, Wilkins averaged 21.6 points and 7.5 rebounds.

The rest of Wilkins' story is history. He went to play for the Atlanta Hawks for twelve seasons. During this time, he developed into one of the most prolific scorers in NBA history. His flying above the rim style challenged Michael Jordan's status as the NBA's greatest scorer and performer. In fact, in the 1983-84 season, Wilkins won the Gatorade Slam Dunk Contest at the all-star festivities, even beating out rookie Michael Jordan of the Chicago Bulls. Dr. Dunk would continue to be a box-office draw for many years to come.

20. Based on this passage, we can conclude that Wilkins' success in basketball primarily resulted from

    A. luck.
    B. size and height.
    C. crowd-pleasing dunks.
    D. size, hard work, and playing ability.

114

Chapter 5

FACT AND OPINION

Being able to distinguish a fact from an opinion is an important reading skill. A **fact** is a true statement that can be proven by observation, statistics, or research. An **opinion** is a judgment or viewpoint about a person, place, event, or idea. An opinion may not really be true, even though the author may want you to believe it is. Now, let's look at some examples of fact and opinion.

1A. **Fact:**   Many vegetables contain vitamins and minerals that are essential for health.

1B. **Opinion:** Many vegetables are easy to cook and are very delicious.

2A. **Fact:**   Oprah Winfrey was born in Kosciuska, Mississippi on January 29, 1954.

2B. **Opinion:** The Oprah Winfrey Show is my favorite talk show on television.

Statement **1A** about the health benefits of vegetables is a **fact** because researchers have proven that vegetables contain important vitamins and minerals. However, the phrases describing vegetables as "easy to cook and very delicious" in statement **1B** are **opinions.** They express a viewpoint, since not all people think vegetables are delicious or easy to cook.

Statement **2A** about Oprah Winfrey is a **fact** because official birth records indicate the place and date of her birth. On the other hand, statement **2B** is clearly an opinion since the phrase "my favorite" describes one person's belief about the Oprah Winfrey Show.

For practice, read the following paragraph. See if you can distinguish the factual statements from those that are opinions.

1) Viola Clay is 110 years old. **2)** She has a 73 year old grandson on Social Security. **3)** According to her 92 year old daughter, Tillie, Viola is delightful, charming, and civil most of the time. **4)** At precisely 2 p.m. every day, Tillie visits her mother at the Forest Hills Nursing Home. **5)** She brings some cake or cookies to share. **6)** "When she gets cranky, I know its time to leave," her daughter says. **7)** According to birth records, Viola has outlived 22 presidents of the United States. **8)** "It's hard to believe, but my mother's older than the Empire State Building," Tillie whispers to her friends.

On the spaces below, write the sentence numbers for the fact and opinion statements.

Facts: _____

Opinions: _____

PRACTICE 1: FACT OR OPINION

For the following statements, write **F** next to facts and **O** next to opinions. Be able to support your answers.

1. _____ Frog legs are light, tender, and tasty!

2. _____ South Carolina joined the Confederate States of America on December 20, 1860.

3. _____ The United States Department of Agriculture recommends that Americans eat 3 to 5 servings of vegetables each day.

4. _____ Our dog is a comical creature the size of a basketball.

5. _____ Colin Powell would make an outstanding candidate for president.

6. _____ Wayne Beecham was charged yesterday with armed robbery of the Hays Convenience Store on Palm Boulevard.

7. _____ I think that people in small towns are friendly.

8. _____ Highway speed limits vary from state to state.

9. _____ Tom Glavin is one of the hottest pitchers in baseball.

10. _____ A used car often costs less than a new car.

11. _____ The Backstreet Boys will be on channel 32 tonight at 8:00 p.m.

12. _____ The best lunch in the restaurant is spaghetti with meatballs.

13. _____ Atlanta, Georgia was the site chosen for the 1996 summer Olympic games.

14. _____ Everyone attending the Olympic games had a good time.

15. _____ The temperatures at the equator are warmer than those at the North Pole.

PRACTICE 2 - READING FOR FACTS AND OPINIONS

In the following paragraphs, write an **F** in front of statements that are facts and an **O** in front of statements that are opinions. Be able to defend your answers.

Lost Sea

1) The Lost Sea in Sweetwater, Tennessee is the largest underground lake in the world. **2)** The temperature inside the cavern remains at 58 degrees all year long. **3)** Many interesting rooms exist inside the cavern. **4)** In one room, you can see rare cave flowers called anthodites. **5)** Every second of the tour is a fascinating experience you'll never forget.

1._____ 2._____ 3._____ 4._____ 5._____

Wilderness Adventure

1) In the evening, we pitched our tent near Miry Creek. **2)** Our hunters killed a large doe and two bears. **3)** No one loves bear better than men of the woods. **4)** I don't think this is a proper diet for us because we may get sick. **5)** However, we have subsisted plentifully on the bounty of this land. **6)** We arrived at Coggins Point about four in the afternoon and then went on to Westover. **7)** My happiness was complete when I learned my family prospered in my absence.

– adapted from the *Diaries of William Byrd*

1._____ 2._____ 3._____ 4._____ 5._____ 6._____ 7._____

PRACTICE 3: CREATE FACTS AND OPINIONS

On your own or with a partner, think of two persons, places, things, and ideas. Then write a statement of fact and a statement of opinion about each one. Review your statements with a teacher or other students. Revise them based on their feedback.

PRACTICE 4: FIND FACTS AND OPINIONS

Find five facts and five opinions in newspaper or magazine articles, ads, and editorials. Underline them, and then share them with your instructor or classmates for feedback.

PRACTICE 5: LOCATING FACTS AND OPINIONS

Underline all of the **facts** in **Amazing Achievements**. Then underline all of the **opinions** in "Get a Life: Get Unplugged"

Amazing Achievements

Around the world are many amazing achievements. One such structure is the Taj Mahal in India. The Emperor Shah Jahan built this magnificent monument in memory of his wife. Constructed of pure white marble, this building took 20,000 workers 20 years to finish. Sadly, the emperor executed the architect of this structure, so he could never design a more beautiful place.

A similar fate awaited the architect of the impressive St. Basil's Cathedral in Moscow, Russia. Ivan the Terrible ordered this vividly painted church to be built from precious stones. After this structure was completed, he had the architect blinded, so no one could duplicate this masterpiece.

Even more astonishing was the task of building the Great Pyramid Of Egypt over 4,500 years ago. It contains enough stone to construct a 10 foot high wall around Spain. For 30 years, over 4,000 men hauled stones weighing 16.5 tons each. Nearly 2,300,000 of the stone blocks were needed to build the Great Pyramid.

Get a Life: Get Unplugged

It seems to me that there is no sanctuary to turn to, no safe place to go, no place to hide from the scourge of our society–television. Not even our schools are to be held pure from its corroding influence. Despite all the publicity about TV and the national studies that have been done which show a bitter harvest of lower grades, obesity, immaturity, violent role modeling, and a certain level of callousness to the sufferings of others, we are fed a steady diet of television.

Television has often been portrayed as a drug, and I feel rightly so. Remember, the first generation exposed to mind-rotting sitcoms and violent cartoons was the baby boomer generation. After being raised on altered reality, they adopted the anti-social philosophy of "tune in and drop out." Does anyone really think that it is only coincidental that "tune in" refers to both drugs and television? We know each creates an altered state.

In conclusion, as a 17-year-old high school student, I am simply tired of having this despicable stone in my face, 24 hours a day. There is a kid's book my brother got from the library about a group of intelligent, caring, and involved people who found a glowing stone. They sat and watched the thing until they had all lost the will to use their talents and voices, turning into squabbling monkeys. Only when one strong person who had refused to look destroyed the stone and began telling stories from the past, did the people return to their former state.

Please, at least remove the mindless viewing of television from our schools!

CHAPTER 5 REVIEW

For each of the following sentences, write F if it expresses a fact or O if it expresses an opinion.

_____   1.   With outstretched wings, a bald eagle sweeps over a youngster and presents its talons to grasp for the food.

_____   2.   These blue flowers are the most beautiful on the face of the earth.

_____   3.   The new album from this heavy metal band is totally obnoxious.

_____   4.   Andrew Wiles has solved a mathematical equation that has riddled mathematicians for centuries.

_____   5.   George Washington was the first president of the United States.

_____   6.   It takes a brave man to wear a tie that looks like that.

_____   7.   I think that is the best movie that came out last year.

_____   8.   Spending more money on the space program is more important than spending money on cancer research.

_____   9.   Neither New York nor Atlanta has a chance to win the World Series next year.

_____   10.   Beth knew the song because she heard it so many times on the radio.

Read the following passage. For each sentence, write F if the sentence is a fact, and write O if the sentence is an opinion.

King Buck

11) Buck was neither house dog nor kennel dog. 12) The whole world belonged to him. 13) He usually plunged into the swimming tank or went hunting with the judge's sons. 14) He was the king – king over all creeping, crawling, flying things of Judge Miller's place, humans included. 15) During the four years since his puppyhood he had lived the life of a king. 16) He had been fed three times a day and was allowed to roam the countryside. 17) Hunting and other outdoor delights had kept down the fat and hardened his muscles. 18) Buck's love of water had been a help and a health preserver. 19) His massive frame was given a bath two times a week. 20) He seemed to be one of the happiest, most contented dogs alive.

                    – Jack London's *Call of the Wild*

11. _____   16. _____

12. _____   17. _____

13. _____   18. _____

14. _____   19. _____

15. _____   20. _____

CHAPTER 5 TEST

Read the following passages, and answer the questions that follow each passage.

T. J. Sheppard

Suddenly, in the shadow of the Smoky Mountains, as a brilliant light show fills the stage, T.G. Sheppard emerges to the applause of the packed house and smoothly glides into the opening bars of the song. But just as quickly as he appears, he descends from the stage and begins mingling with the hand-clapping audience.

As the melody goes on, he quickly shakes hands and smiles at the ladies in the audience. He pauses for camera shots, hugs young children, breaks the song momentarily to welcome the crowd, and then ascends back to the stage in the closing bars of the song.

Less than five minutes have passed since curtain time, but in these brief moments T.G. Sheppard has won the heart of his audience, and it's a bond that is drawn tighter over the next two hours. He weaves his own hit songs, popular melodies and big-band sounds, personal glimpses into his life, and comedy routines into a theatrical presentation that ends in somewhat of an emotional parting that seems to end all too soon.

1. Which of the following statements is a **fact**?

    A. T. G. Sheppard glides smoothly into the opening bars of the song.
    B. T. G. Sheppard pauses for camera shots and hugs young children.
    C. T. G. Sheppard has won the heart of his audience.
    D. T. G. Sheppard's show ends in an emotional parting that seems to end all too soon.

After the Blast

At first glance, the beach at Bikini Atoll, a small island in the Pacific Ocean, looks like a tropical paradise. But in truth, the land and water share a poisoned past, from the era when 23 atomic tests were conducted at Bikini Atoll.

In 1946, all 167 Bikini residents were relocated. Then 42,000 people and 90 vessels used the island for target practice. This was to be the first peace time testing of nuclear weapons.

Testing continued until November 1958. The most damaging explosion came on March 1, 1954, when a 15 megaton hydrogen bomb, code-named Bravo, was exploded on the island. This bomb was the most powerful ever exploded by the United States. It was a thousand times more powerful than the bomb dropped on Hiroshima. Not only did it open a mile-wide crater on Bikini Atoll, but it also vaporized one small island and part of another.

To this day, the soil on Bikini contains too much radioactive cesium to permit the Bikinians, now numbering 2,025, to return from their exile.

2. Which of the following statements is an **opinion**?

    A. In 1946, all 167 Bikini residents were relocated.
    B. This bomb was the most powerful ever exploded by the United States.
    C. Bikini Atoll should not be used for nuclear testing.
    D. 42,000 people and 90 vessels used the island for target practice.

Movie Review

A 1991 release, <u>Terminator 2: Judgement Day</u> stars Arnold Schwarzenegger as the hero. This sequel to the 1984 <u>Terminator</u> is far less satisfying than the original. The movie contains many spectacular special effects and some exciting action sequences. However, the story line is weak, and the movie's obvious message is "Don't use nuclear bombs."

The new advanced terminator is given the name T-1000, the Ultimate Destructive Machine. In the movie, Schwarzenegger plays the underdog which doesn't make much sense considering his size and strength. The movie also stars Linda Hamilton, Edward Furlong, and Joe Morton. Special effects are by Sean Winston and Dirk Reeves. At the King Mall Cinema through May 10.

3. Which of the following statements expresses an **opinion?**

   A. The movie contains many spectacular special effects and some exciting action sequences.
   B. Special effects are by Sean Winston and Dirk Reeves.
   C. The new advanced terminator is given the name T-1000, the Ultimate Destructive Machine.
   D. A 1991 release, <u>Terminator 2: Judgment Day</u> stars Arnold Schwarzenegger as the hero.

Let the Good Times Roll

The new development and growth in this area are incredible! We are so happy that we now have many modern conveniences at our doorstep. The new mall has made shopping so much easier. The architecture of the mall is beautiful, and all of the shops have been carefully arranged. In addition, the new office parks have brought over 500 jobs to this area. Furthermore, the tax dollars from the new residents and businesses are paying for much needed repairs at the local schools. We understand that environmentalists are upset with the destruction of natural resources, but the economic improvement to this area is more than worth this loss.

−The Residents of Green Park Subdivision

4. Which of the following statements is a **fact?**

   A. The new mall has made shopping so much easier.
   B. The new development and growth in this area are incredible!
   C. The architecture of the mall is beautiful, and all of the shops have been carefully arranged.
   D. In addition, the new office parks have brought over 500 jobs to this area.

The Beginning of Hollywood

From as early as the 1920s, millions of Americans have been regular moviegoers. In the beginning, movies had simple plots and were quickly over. Often, they lasted only fifteen minutes. The first western, <u>The Great Train Robbery</u>, had three small scenes – a train robbery, a pursuit on horseback, and a surprise ending where the crook pointed his gun at the movie audience and fired.

During the early 1900s, Hollywood and New Jersey were competitors for the movie industry. New Jersey was desirable because so many actors and actresses worked on Broadway, which is near New Jersey. However, all filming had to take place outside where the light was strong enough. As a result, Hollywood, nestled in the hills of sunny southern California, became the better choice for year-round filming. By 1911, fifteen film companies had made their home there.

By the 1920s, Hollywood became a booming industry. Actors such as Charlie Chaplin were making $10,000.00 per week instead of a few dollars per day on Broadway. Directors began producing longer movies with more complicated plots. In time, Hollywood stood for films and the rich, sophisticated people who starred in them.

5. Which of the following statements states a **fact**?

   A. The people were more polite in Hollywood than in New Jersey.
   B. New Jersey was attractive because the best actors and actresses worked on Broadway.
   C. Because of its sunny weather, Hollywood became the capital of film making.
   D. Unlike New Jersey, Hollywood people enjoy being in front of a camera.

State Playoffs Start Today

Five months ago, 220 high school football teams started their journey to the state championship. As of Friday, only three of the teams remain in the playoffs, and only one will become the state champion.

North Metro (15-1) plays Long Hill (13-1) for the class AAA title at 7 PM in Dodge Memorial Stadium. North Metro's star quarterback, Rob Sanders, leads the league in pass completions. He will be a challenge for the Long Hill Raiders, but Long Hill's offense will keep Sanders on his toes while he looks for openings in the line.

The winner of tonight's playoff will meet the undefeated Washington Warriors (14-0). Stunning victories in their last two games of the season make them the team to beat in the state. The final playoff will be next Saturday at Roger's Stadium in Jones County. A crowd of 8,000 spectators is expected, and WHIA will televise the game from the stadium.

6. Which of the following statements is an **opinion?**

   A. The final playoff will be next Saturday at Roger's Stadium in Jones County.
   B. Stunning victories in their last two games of the season make them the team to beat in the state.
   C. Rob Saunders leads the league in pass completions.
   D. As of Friday, only three of the teams remain in the playoffs, and only one will become the state champion.

Mark Twain

Mark Twain was the pen name of Samuel Clemens. Clemens was born in 1835 in Florida, Missouri. When he was four, his parents moved to the town of Hannibal, Missouri, where he experienced some of the adventures he wrote about in his novels *Tom Sawyer* (1876) and the *Adventures Of Huckleberry Finn* (1884). These two novels are some of his best known works and are still enjoyed over 100 years later by children and adults around the world.

In his 20s, Clemens was an apprentice pilot on a Mississippi River steamer. Life didn't just stop there. With the West opening up, he followed and went to California. This is where he won literary success with his reading and journalism. In San Francisco, he began his career as a lecturer, delighting audiences with his manner and wit. By the late 1860s, he traveled Europe and the Middle East and wrote about these trips in *Innocents Abroad.*

After some financial ups and downs, Clemens built a mansion in the 1890s, now a museum at Redding Connecticut, where he passed away in 1910, at the height of his fame. Clemens' legacy to the world is his literary style which produced several wonderful books, many more than are mentioned here. Readers of all ages should choose books by Mark Twain. They are some of the best stories written.

7.   Which of the following statements expresses a **fact?**

   A.   Readers of all ages should choose books by Mark Twain.
   B.   Clemens was born in 1835 in Florida, Missouri.
   C.   These two novels are still enjoyed by children and adults around the world.
   D.   They are some of the best stories written.

Glacier Meltdown

Glaciers are huge ice masses which slowly flow over land. They tend to form in high mountains and in the polar regions. Low temperatures year round allow snow to build up and become compacted into very dense ice. The thickness of the ice varies between 300 and 10,000 feet.

Throughout many parts of the world, glaciers are shrinking in size. Researchers suspect this shrinkage is related to global warming. This glacial shrinkage should be the top priority in future global warming research.

Since the late nineteenth century, researchers from the United States and Russia have recorded an eleven percent reduction in the total volume of ice in the world's smaller glaciers. In Central Europe, the mountain glaciers have been reduced to half their original size.

All is not lost, however. Greenland and Antarctica, which contain ninety percent of the world's ice, have not shown this shrinkage in glacier size. Nevertheless, the retreat occurring among the 500,000 smaller glaciers in the world does provide another convincing fact that the earth's climate is getting warmer.

8.   Which of the following statements expresses an **opinion?**

   A.   Glaciers are shrinking in size.
   B.   The shrinking of glaciers is worldwide.
   C.   The retreat of smaller glaciers indicates the earth is getting warmer.
   D.   Glacial shrinkage should be the top priority in future research.

Brighten Up Your SAD Days

Have you wondered why you might have less energy, feel like sleeping longer, feel blue, or experience varying degrees of depression? Have you observed these feelings more in winter than in spring or summer? Well, you are not alone. It is estimated that about 35 million Americans may be affected by Seasonal Affective Disorder (SAD) – also referred to as Light Deprivation Syndrome. It is a form of wintertime depression that can become so severe that some people are incapable of working or maintaining relationships.

Studies by Dr. Daniel Kripke of University of California, San Diego, and others have shown that low levels of exposure to daylight or its indoor equivalent may be a risk factor for seasonal as well as major depression.

SAD is characterized by a tendency to sleep too much, tire easily, crave carbohydrates or sweets, and increased irritability. An encouraging treatment is now being used with special light boxes which supply the extra light SAD sufferers seem to be lacking. Dr. Karl Doghramji, director of a sleep disorder center in Pennsylvania, found that an effective treatment is sitting in front of the light box for an hour or more each day–in the morning or at noon.

Just how the light helps is not quite known, but there are many theories. It is known, however, that the nerve impulses created by light waves reach the hypothalamus–the brain center that controls sleeping, eating, and mood. It is thought that SAD sufferers have some biochemical abnormality in the hypothalamus that becomes aggravated by lower levels of light.

9. Which of the following statements is an **opinion**?

    A. An interesting and encouraging treatment is now being used with special light boxes.
    B. It is estimated that about 35 million Americans may be affected by SAD.
    C. SAD is characterized by sleeping too much, tiring too easily, craving carbohydrates or sweets, and increased irritability.
    D. Dr. Karl Doghramji found an effective treatment is sitting in front of a light box for an hour or more each day.

Wilma Rudolph

Nothing has been easy for Wilma Rudolph. Born in Clarksville, Tennessee, she was the twentieth of 22 children. Her mother worked as a domestic, and her father was a railroad handyman. As a child she suffered pneumonia, scarlet fever, and polio and wore a brace on her leg when she was six years old. It was not an auspicious beginning for an Olympic medal winner, but her mother's determined effort to take her to Meharry Medical College in Nashville for weekly treatment continued until she would walk.

Encouragement of track coach Ed Temple inspired her to run. Wilma ran in America, in Australia, and in the 1960 Rome Olympic games where she won three gold medals, broke two world records, and brought the crowd to its feet in waves of applause. When she joined the Women's Sports Hall of Fame in 1980, she became the first black woman to receive that honor and the first to so honor the Hall of Fame.

10. Which of the following statements is an **opinion**?

    A. Wilma Rudolph won three gold medals in the Rome Olympics.
    B. Nothing has been easy for Wilma Rudolph.
    C. Wilma brought the crowd to its feet in waves of applause.
    D. Wilma wore a brace on her leg when she was six years old.

Injuries to Teenagers

Motor vehicle-related deaths are responsible for nearly 80% of all injury deaths in teenagers. One out of every fifty teens requires hospitalization for motor vehicle (occupant) related injuries each year. Auto safety classes and use of seat belts are very important as protective measures for the safety of our teens.

The second leading injury threat to the lives of teenagers is drowning, while burns are third and poisoning fourth. The most common poison ingestions in teens involve alcohol and drugs.

The most common type of nonfatal injury in teenagers is sports injuries. Approximately one out of fourteen teenagers has required hospitalization for a sports injury. Football caused nearly 20% of these injuries, with basketball, roller-skating, and baseball causing most of the other injuries.

11. Which of the following statements from the passage is an **opinion?**

    A. Motor vehicle-related deaths are responsible for nearly 80% of all injury deaths in teenagers.
    B. One out of every fifty teens requires hospitalization for motor vehicle (occupant-related) injuries each year.
    C. The second leading injury threat to the lives of teenagers is drowning, while burns are third and poisoning fourth.
    D. Auto safety classes and use of seat belts are very important as protective measures for the safety of our teens.

Road Reflections

Everyone who knows me understands that I would gladly trade in my husband's thirty year old foreign car for a newer vehicle if I had the money. I have often forewarned my husband that if I, perchance, would die in his vehicle, I would haunt him unceasingly. Well, last Tuesday I thought the moment had finally come. Normally, I would dare not speed in his trusted rickshaw, as I like to arrive breathing and in one piece. Unfortunately, this morning my watch told me that top velocity was needed to get to school on time, so I depressed the accelerator recklessly. Everything was going well until **the noise**. It started down at my feet – a strange whirling, metal screech and traveled rapidly up the steering column to my anxious ear. My brain immediately identified this dire noise as death's horn sounding for me. Then, I carefully assessed the traffic flow, changed lanes, and calmly parked on the shoulder of the highway. After I had time to sit quietly and absorb the fact that I had not been forced to meet God through a windshield and twisted metal, I spontaneously poured out tears and laughter of gratitude, relief, and happiness. Death by a Volkswagen was not to be that day; it had only been the speedometer cable whining about the cold weather and its old age.

– Mary Hawkins

12. Which of the following statements is a **fact?**

    A. I have often forewarned my husband that if I, per chance, would die in his vehicle, I would haunt him unceasingly.
    B. I do not like speeding in his old car, as I like to arrive breathing and in one piece.
    C. My brain immediately identified this dire noise as death's horn sounding for me.
    D. Death by a Volkswagen was not to be had that day; it had only been the speedometer cable whining about the cold weather and its old age.

Recycling Efforts Increasing

The Cobb Solid Waste Department is moving forward aggressively with its efforts to divert recyclable materials from the county landfill and increase community awareness regarding recycling opportunities.

According to Jocelyn Moore, recycling education manager for the Solid Waste Department, increasing recycling efforts by residents and department staff resulted in more that 5.7 million pounds of recyclable material being diverted from the landfill during a recent 12-month period.

"These efforts not only benefited Cobb by reducing landfill demands, but by selling the recyclable materials we realized more than $150,000 in revenue for county government," she said.

One of the most successful recent programs involves recycling mattresses and bedding materials. The program began last May and took in more than 32,000 pounds during its first two months. By mid-October, the total had risen to 75,000 pounds.

Other recycling programs recently started include the collection of mixed-color glass and plate glass such as automobile windows. Recycling bins for each of these materials are located at the Solid Waste Transfer Station on County Farm Road. No ceramic pieces can be accepted.

Still another program gets under way this month as the department adds textiles to its impressive lists of recycled materials.

Residents are encouraged to drop off clothing, blankets, towels, sheets, shoes, and purses at a collection site at the Transfer Station.

13. Which of the following statements from the passage is a **fact**?

    A. Other recycling programs recently started include the collection of mixed-color glass and plate glass such as automobile windows.

    B. The Cobb Solid Waste Department is moving forward aggressively with its efforts to divert recyclable materials...

    C. One of the most successful recent programs involves recycling mattresses and bedding materials.

    D. The department added textiles to its impressive list of recycled materials.

Starting an Ant Colony

Her greatest labor ahead, the mated harvester queen lands and breaks off her now useless wings. Working alone, she is vulnerable to predatory birds, lizards, and other ants; only one in 100 to 1,000 queens survives these first days.

Quickly, the queen digs her nest with mandibles and forelegs, making balls of the moist soil to lift around the entrance. Once enchambered below the surface, she lays eggs. When they hatch into larvae, she feeds her brood on secretions from metabolized fat reserves and wing muscles. After a few weeks, the first generation of 10 to 20 daughter-workers takes over nest digging and foraging. Harvesters gather and store seeds, often affecting the spacing and number of desert plants. When the colony's population reaches several thousand, the queen produces winged males and females. Truly, she is queen of all she surveys.

14. Which of the following statements form the passage is an **opinion**?

   A.   Working alone, she is vulnerable to predatory birds, lizards, and other ants.
   B.   Once enchambered below the surface, she lays eggs.
   C.   After a few weeks, the first generation of 10 to 20 daughter-workers takes over nest digging and foraging.
   D.   Truly, she is queen of all she surveys.

From an editorial -
Forget the Speed Limits

The federal government now lets the states decide on a speed limit or no speed limit at all. I think this is great news for drivers in our state since many of us think the speed limits should be raised.

In my opinion, our legislators should vote to remove the speed limit on Interstate Highways like 1-95,1-20, I-26 and I-85. This change would reduce the driving time between Spartanburg and Charleston, for example, without fear of getting a speeding ticket. Of course, motorists would still have to be careful and prudent about their speed at night. They would also have to use proper judgment in heavy traffic or if there is an accident.

Speed limits could also be raised to 75 mph on the loops around Columbia and Greenville. Drivers would use the fast lanes to maintain this speed. On county roads, I believe the speed limit should be no more than 65 mph because driving conditions change quickly as you enter or leave small towns and intersections.

If everyone uses common sense and good judgment, we could safely raise the speed limits in our state and get where we're going a lot faster.

LeRoy Byrd, Florence

15. Which of the following statements from the passage is a **fact**?

   A.   I think this is great news for drivers in our state since many of us think the speed limits should be raised.
   B.   The federal government now lets the states decide on a speed limit or no speed limit at all.
   C.   In my opinion, our legislators should vote to remove the speed limit on Interstate Highways like 1-95,1-20, I-26 and I-85.
   D.   If everyone uses common sense and good judgment, we could safely raise the speed limits in our state and get where we're going a lot faster.

READING GRAPHIC AIDS

Graphic aids present complex information in a simplified, visual format. In this chapter, you will read and answer questions about graphic aids.

SCHEDULES

Schedule - information arranged in a timetable with dates and times. Schedules may contain departure and arrival times, such as a bus or plane schedule. They may also include programs or meeting times, like a television schedule or a class schedule.

OAKDALE BUS SCHEDULE									
Weekdays gray and white — Saturday and Sundays gray only OUTBOUND from downtown (Bus sign reads Oakdale)					INBOUND from Oakdale Mall (Bus sign reads Downtown)				
1st & Hyatt	10th & Lake	18th & Miami	25th & Water	Oakdale Mall	Oakdale Mall	25th & Water	18th & Miami	10th & Lake	1st & Hyatt
6:10	6:18	6:22	6:28	6:35	6:40	6:47	6:53	6:57	7:05
7:10	7:18	7:22	7:28	7:35	7:40	7:47	7:53	7:57	8:05
8:10	8:18	8:22	8:28	8:35	8:40	8:47	8:53	8:57	9:05
9:10	9:18	9:22	9:28	9:35	9:40	9:47	9:53	9:57	10:05
10:10	10:18	10:22	10:28	10:35	10:40	10:47	10:53	10:57	11:05
11:10	11:18	11:22	11:28	11:35	11:40	11:47	11:53	11:57	12:05
12:10	12:18	12:22	12:28	12:35	12:40	12:47	12:53	12:57	1:05
1:10	1:18	1:22	1:28	1:35	1:40	1:47	1:53	1:57	2:05
2:10	2:18	2:22	2:28	2:35	2:40	2:47	2:53	2:57	3:05
3:10	3:18	3:22	3:28	3:35	3:40	3:47	3:53	3:57	4:05
4:10	4:18	4:22	4:28	4:35	4:40	4:47	4:53	4:57	5:05

1. T or F   The gray areas are for weekends only.

2. When does the 9:18 bus from 10th & Lake arrive at the Oakdale Mall? _____

3. Where does the 12:53 bus pick up passengers? _____

4. How many minutes does it take to travel from 1st and Hyatt to 25th and Water? _____

5. Where would you be if you left the Oakdale Mall at 8:40 and noticed the time was 9:05?

_____

6. T or F   The Oakdale Mall is closer to 10th and Lake than it is to 18th and Miami.

7. When is the earliest you can catch an inbound bus at 18th and Miami on Sunday? _____

TABLES

Table - a way to present data and statistics. It is a concise way to present a large quantity of information using rows and columns to organize the information.

Directions: Carefully read the table below. Then answer the questions that follow.

LIFE INSURANCE RATES

	MONTHLY RATES SMOKERS					MONTHLY RATES NON-SMOKERS			
Issue Age	$100,000 Male	Female	$250,000 Male	Female	Issue Age	$100,000 Male	Female	$250,000 Male	Female
40	22.56	17.58	50.22	37.58	40	12.98	12.62	26.08	25.25
41	23.38	18.79	52.12	40.68	41	13.04	12.71	26.31	25.46
42	24.21	20.06	54.22	43.79	42	13.15	12.81	26.50	25.72
43	25.07	21.31	56.29	46.93	43	13.21	12.89	26.72	25.92
44	25.89	22.48	58.38	50.06	44	13.31	12.99	26.91	26.10
45	27.15	23.42	61.52	52.16	45	13.39	13.05	27.15	26.31
46	28.79	24.21	65.70	54.26	46	13.81	13.16	28.20	26.51
47	30.12	25.13	68.84	56.32	47	14.62	13.22	30.26	26.75
48	32.18	25.91	74.05	58.47	48	15.54	13.31	32.36	26.95
49	34.25	27.18	79.28	61.62	49	16.32	13.42	34.42	27.16
50	37.18	28.82	86.53	65.71	50	17.16	13.82	36.52	28.20

1. What is the monthly rate for a $250,000 policy for non-smoking males who are 44 years of age?

   _____

2. If a 47 year old female smoker wanted a $100,000 policy, what would be her monthly payment?

   _____

3. What is the monthly rate for a $250,000 policy for a 46 year old, male, non-smoker?

   _____

4. If a smoker is paying $68.84 for a $250,000 policy, what age and sex is the person?

   _____

5. What is the monthly rate for a $100,000 policy for non-smoking females who are 47 years of age?

   _____

6. Looking at the insurance rates for men and women of the same age, which group has higher rates, smokers or non-smokers?

   _____

7. Looking at the insurance rates of men and women of the same age, which rates are lower, men's rates or women's rates?

   _____

8. If a smoker is paying $22.48 for a $100,000 policy, what age and sex is the person?

   _____

9. If a 48 year old non-smoking male wanted a $250,000 policy, what would be his monthly payment?

   _____

10. What is the monthly rate of a $100,000 policy for a 42 year old male smoker?

   _____

LINE GRAPHS

Line graphs can present a large quantity of data in a small space. Be sure to read the title of the graph and the horizontal and vertical headings as well as the key.

Study the line graph below, and answer the questions that follow.

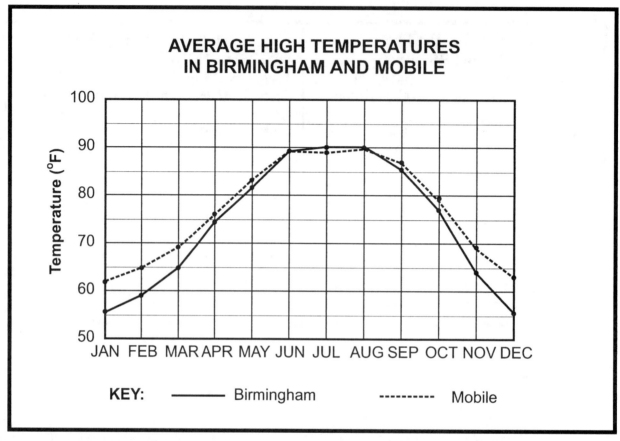

1. What is the average high temperature in Birmingham for the month of July? _____

2. How many months is the average temperature the same in both cities? _____

3. What are the 2 coldest months in Mobile? _____ , _____

4. What are the three coldest months in Birmingham? _____ , _____ , _____

5. In which month is the average high temperature 65° in Birmingham? _____

6. What is the average high temperature in Mobile for the month of April? _____

7. In which two months is the average high temperature 69° in Mobile? _____ , _____

8. Are the degrees in the above graph in Celsius, Fahrenheit, or Kelvin degrees? _____

9. If you disliked cold weather, would it be better to live in Birmingham or Mobile? _____

10. What is the average high temperature in May for the city of Mobile? _____

BAR GRAPHS

Bar graphs are another way of presenting data. **Study the bar graph below, and then answer the questions that follow.**

The President's Proposed 2002 Discretionary Spending

Billions of dollars

Energy	$3
Agriculture	$5
Social security & medicine	$8
Economic development	$15
Other income security	$16
General government	$16
Employment, social services	$20
Transportation	$22
Science & space	$23
International affairs	$25
Veterans benefits	$27
Natural resources	$28
Housing assistance	$29
Justice	$33
Health	$49
Education	$52
Military	$396

Source: Center for Defense Information

1. How much money did the president propose be spent on the military? _____
2. How much more does the president propose Congress spend on Agriculture than on Commerce? _____
3. Which two departments does the president propose funding at the sum of $16,000,000,000? _____ , _____
4. How much does the president propose spending on transportation? _____
5. How much does the president propose that the Department of Justice receive? _____
6. What is the source of information for the graph above?_____
7. What conclusions can you draw from this bar graph? _____
_____

SYMBOL GRAPHS

Sometimes, graphs use symbols or pictures to represent data.

Study the graph below, and answer the questions that follow.

WORLD PRODUCTION AND CONSUMPTION OF PETROLEUM

● Production   ○ Consumption

Each symbol signifies one million barrels per day

Middle East
● ● ● ● ● ● ● ● ● ● ● ● ● ● ● ● ● ● ●
○ ○ ○ ○ ○

Europe
● ● ● ● ● ● ● ● ● ● ● ● ●
○ ○ ○ ○ ○ ○ ○ ○ ○ ○ ○ ○ ○ ○ ○ ○ ○ ○ ○

United States and Canada
● ● ● ● ● ● ● ● ● ●
○ ○ ○ ○ ○ ○ ○ ○ ○ ○ ○ ○ ○ ○ ○ ○ ○ ○

Latin America
● ● ● ● ● ● ● ● ●
○ ○ ○ ○ ○ ○

Asia
● ● ● ● ● ● ●
○ ○ ○ ○ ○ ○ ○ ○ ○ ○ ○ ○ ○

Africa
● ● ● ● ● ● ●
○ ○

Australia & Pacific islands
●
○

---

1. What part of the world consumes the most oil?   _____

2. How many parts of the world produce more oil than they consume?   _____

3. How many parts of the world consume more oil than they produce?   _____

4. How many more barrels of oil does Europe produce daily than Africa?   _____

5. How many barrels does the Middle East produce every day?   _____

6. Which three areas of the world consume more than twice as much oil as they produce?   _____

_____

_____

MAPS

A **map** is a flat drawing of all or part of the earth. A **globe** is a model of the earth shaped like a ball or sphere. North, south, east, and west are called **cardinal directions**. North is usually at the top of a map or globe, south is at the bottom, east is to your right, and west is to your left.

Maps and globes also contain a symbol to help you find directions. This symbol is called a **compass rose** like the one shown on the world map below. A compass rose shows the four cardinal directions. It may also show the **intermediate directions** (in-between directions). These intermediate directions are **northeast (NE), northwest (NW), southeast (SE), and southwest (SW)**.

Now practice finding directions on the world map shown below.

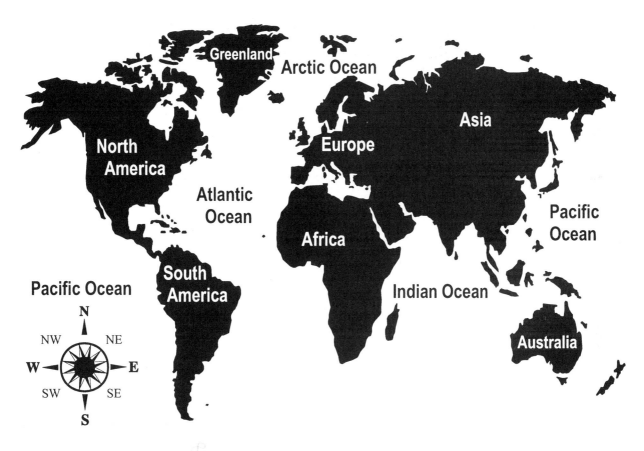

1. Which continent is south of Europe? _____
2. Which ocean is north of Europe? _____
3. Which continent is east of Europe? _____
4. Which continent is west of Europe? _____
5. What ocean is northwest of Australia? _____
6. What continent is southeast of Asia? _____
7. What direction is Africa from South America? _____
8. What direction is South America from Europe? _____
9. What island is northeast of North America? _____
10. Which ocean lies east of Asia? _____

READING A HISTORICAL MAP

A **historical map** shows places and events from the past. The purpose of this kind of map is to help us understand and interpret historical events.

Study the historical map below. It shows how the German submarine U 20 sank American and British ships during World War I. **Then answer the questions that follow.**

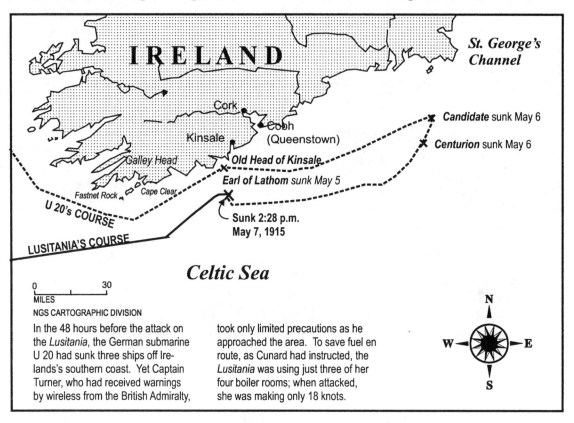

In the 48 hours before the attack on the *Lusitania*, the German submarine U 20 had sunk three ships off Ireland's southern coast. Yet Captain Turner, who had received warnings by wireless from the British Admiralty, took only limited precautions as he approached the area. To save fuel en route, as Cunard had instructed, the *Lusitania* was using just three of her four boiler rooms; when attacked, she was making only 18 knots.

1. Which line shows the U 20's course? _____

2. In which direction was the U 20 moving right before it sank the *Candidate*? _____

3. Name the ships that the U 20 sank. _____

   _____

4. When was the *Lusitania* sunk? _____

5. In which body of water was the *Lusitania* sunk? _____

6. Why was the *Lusitania* traveling so slowly? _____

7. Which ship sank the closest to land? _____

8. In which direction was the *Lusitania* moving when it was sunk? _____

9. In which direction was the U 20 moving when it sank the *Lusitania*? _____

READING A GRID MAP

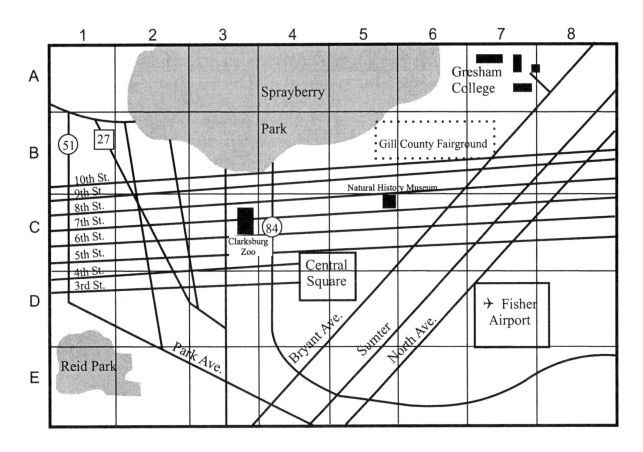

A **grid** is a pattern of lines drawn to make rows and columns on a map. These lines divide the map into squares. Each square can be identified by numbers and letters. The numbers appear on the top of the map, and the letters are located on the left side of the map.

Look at the letters on the side of the map above. The letters identify the rows of squares. The numbers label the columns of squares. If you were asked to locate Reid Park on the map, you would look to see which row and column it is in. Most of Reid Park is at the intersection of row E and column 1. Therefore, the answer is E-1.

Identify the row and column for each of the following places.

1. Gresham College _____

2. Fisher Airport _____

3. Natural History Museum _____

4. The center of Gill County Fairground _____

5. The intersection of Bryant Avenue and 6th Street _____

6. What is the location of 10th Street and Highway 27? _____

7. Where is Clarksburg Zoo? _____

DEGREES OF LATITUDE AND LONGITUDE

World maps and globes contain two sets of lines that form a grid around the earth. This grid helps us locate places. Horizontal lines that run parallel around the earth are called **lines of latitude**. The 0^0 line of latitude is the **equator.** It divides the earth into the **Northern Hemisphere** and the **Southern Hemisphere.** Lines of latitude are numbered 0^0 to 90^0 north and 0^0 to 90^0 south. The United States is in the Northern Hemisphere because we are north of the equator.

The second set of lines on the global grid is **lines of longitude**. The 0^0 line of longitude is the **prime meridian** which goes through Greenwich, England. It divides the earth into the **Eastern Hemisphere** and the **Western Hemisphere.** Lines of longitude are numbered from 0^0 to 180^0 east and 0^0 to 180^0 west. The United States is in the Western Hemisphere because we are west of England. The latitude measurement for a location is always listed first, followed by longitude.

Now look at Mexico's lines of latitude and longitude. Then answer the questions about this part of the globe. Example: Monterrey is located at 27^0 N 102^0 W.

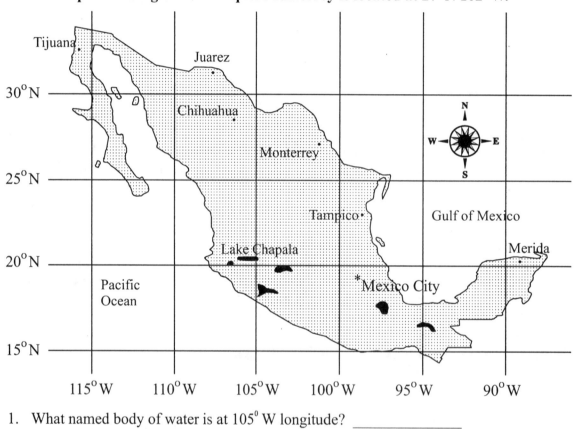

1. What named body of water is at 105^0 W longitude? _____
2. Is Mexico north or south of the equator? _____
3. Is Mexico east or west of the Prime Meridian? _____
4. Estimate the longitude of these cities: Monterrey _____, Chihuahua _____, Mexico City _____.
5. Estimate the latitude of these same cities: Monterrey _____, Chihuahua _____, Mexico City _____.
6. Estimate the latitude and longitude of Juarez _____, Tampico _____, and Merida _____.
7. What city lies at latitude 34^0 N and longitude 116^0 W ? _____

136   Copyright © American Book Company

READING A WORLD MAP

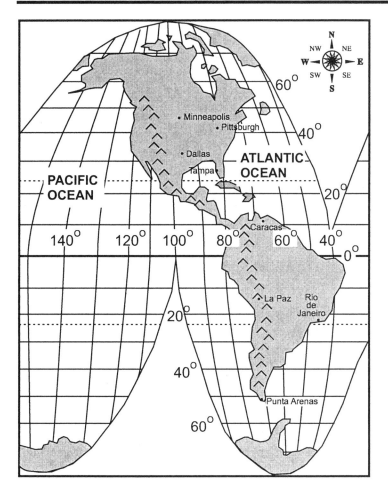

When reading a world map, it is important to remember that the warmest part of the earth is near the **equator** at 0° latitude. The coldest part of the earth is at the north and south poles. Also, the higher the altitude, like the top of a mountain, the cooler the temperature. Seasons in the Northern and Southern Hemispheres are opposite. For example, when it is summer in the United States, it is winter in Chile.

The latitude line at $23\frac{1}{2}^{\circ}N$ is called the **Tropic of Cancer**. The latitude line at $23\frac{1}{2}^{\circ}S$ is called the **Tropic of Capricorn**. These lines are denoted by dashes on the world map. Between these two lines of latitude is the area of the world that is called the **tropics**. The tropics grow fruits such as pineapples, coconuts, bananas, and mangos that do not grow well anywhere else. In addition, there is no noticeable change of seasons at these latitudes.

Use the world map above to answer the following questions.

1. Which city labeled in the southern hemisphere would tourist most likely find sunny, warm beaches? _____

2. Which city labeled in the southern hemisphere would likely have the coldest winter temperature? _____

3. If you flew from Dallas to Minneapolis, which direction would you be going? _____

4. Which city labeled in the northern hemisphere would have the coldest average temperature in the winter? _____

5. Which city is located $40^{\circ}N$ $80^{\circ}W$? _____

6. If you flew from Dallas to Rio de Janeiro, in which direction would you travel? _____

7. If you flew from Pittsburgh to Punta Arenas in July, would you need to pack warm clothing? _____

8. Which city would likely have a cooler climate, La Paz or Rio de Janeiro? _____

ROAD MAPS

Reading a **road map** requires paying close attention to the key. The **key** gives information about what all the symbols mean. Reading the key will help you find the location of airports, railroads, camp sites, and more. In addition most state maps will have little numbers on the roads showing you how many miles it is between towns. By adding the numbers together, you can determine the distance between two towns.

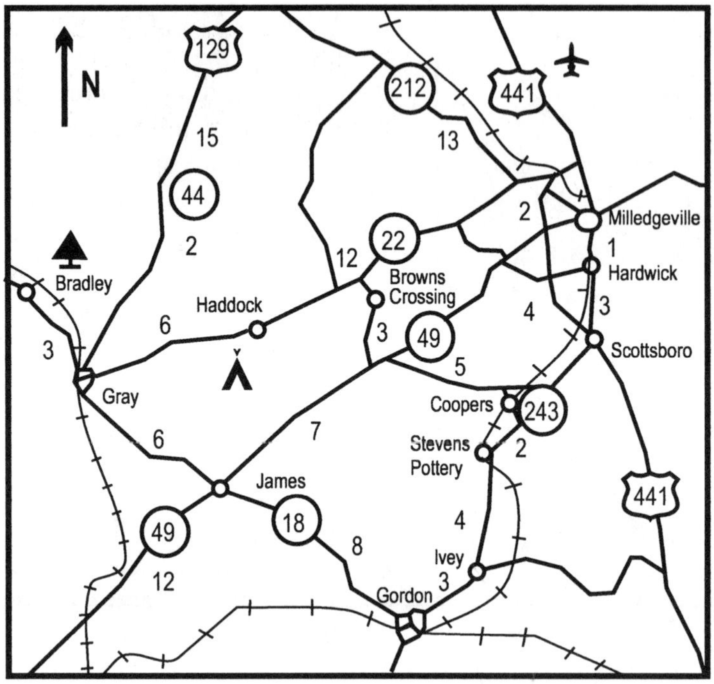

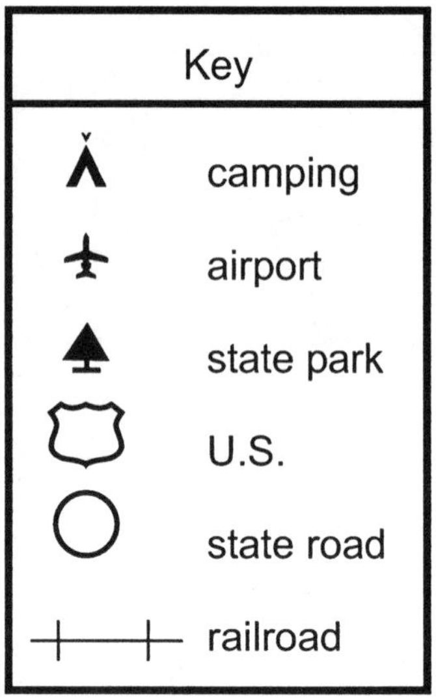

Carefully read the map and key above to answer the following questions.

1. How far is it from Milledgeville to Scottsboro traveling US 441? ________________

2. How far is it from Coopers to Stephens Pottery ? ________________

3. Is it shorter to go from Gordon to Brown's Crossing through James or Coopers? ________________

4. Which highway is closest to the airport? ________________

5. Where would this sign be found? | Haddock ⟶ 6 |

   A. at the intersection of State Roads (18) and (49)

   B. at the intersection of State Roads (212) and (49)

   C. at the intersection of State Roads (18) and (243)

   D. at the intersection of State Roads (18) and (22)

6. In which town can a train switch from a north-south track to an east-west track? ________________

7. How many miles apart are Gray and Gordon on state route (18)? _____

8. Which town is closest to a camping area? _____

9. Which town is closest to a state park? _____

10. What is the shortest route to take from Scottsboro to Gordon? _____

ECONOMIC MAPS

An **economic map** shows resources and products of a country. These resources and products provide an income and standard of living for the people. **Study the following map of Australia, and then answer the questions.**

MAJOR MINERAL DEPOSITS AND AGRICULTURAL PRODUCTS IN AUSTRALIA

B	Bauxite	L	Lead
	Coal	N	Nickel
C	Copper		Silver
	Gold	U	Uranium
I	Iron Ore	Z	Zinc
	Wheat		Cotton
	Rice		Sugar Cane

1. Based on this map, which agricultural crop is most prolific in New South Wales? _____

2. Based on this map, which mining industry is the largest in Western Australia? _____

3. Which region of Australia contains the most minerals? _____

4. Which three provinces in Australia show no agricultural development? _____

   _____

5. Which provinces have mines for precious metals (gold or silver)? _____

   _____

DIAGRAMS

Sometimes a **diagram** can be used to explain a concept more clearly than an explanation written in paragraph form. The diagram below shows the earth's water cycle.

EARTH'S WATER CYCLE

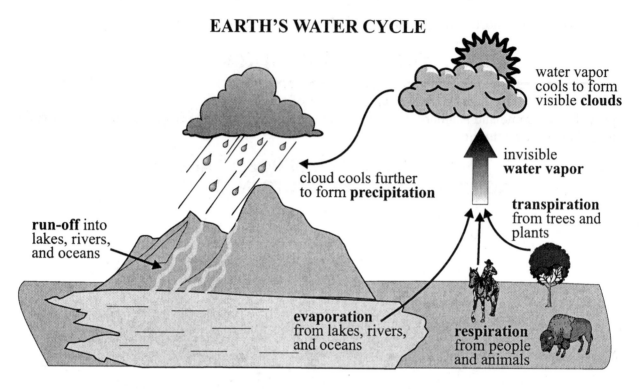

water vapor
cools to form
visible **clouds**

invisible
water vapor

cloud cools further
to form **precipitation**

transpiration
from trees and
plants

run-off into
lakes, rivers,
and oceans

evaporation
from lakes, rivers,
and oceans

respiration
from people
and animals

Study the diagram, and answer the questions below.

1. In what 3 ways does water get from the ground to the sky? _____

    _____

    _____

2. How are clouds formed? _____

    _____

3. What must happen to water vapor before it is visible? _____

    _____

4. Define precipitation. _____

    _____

5. What must happen to clouds before precipitation can occur? _____

    _____

6. Describe how the respiration of people and animals becomes rain. _____

    _____

7. When you blow on a cool glass or mirror, what do you see? _____

Use the schedules, tables, maps, graphs, and diagrams presented to answer the questions that follow.

LIFE SPAN OF DOMESTIC ANIMALS

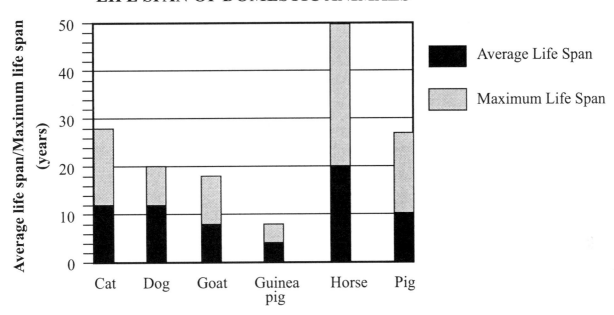

1. Which animal has the longest maximum life span?   _____

2. What is the average life span of a Guinea pig?   _____

3. Which animal lives longer on average, a dog or a pig?   _____

4. What is the maximum life span of a cat?   _____

5. How many more years does the average horse live than the average goat?   _____

6. Which animal has a maximum life span of 8 years?   _____

7. Which two animals are closest in maximum life span?   _____

8. Which two animals are closest in average life span?   _____

9. Which animal has an average life span of 20 years?   _____

TEAM STATISTICS
1995-96 CHICAGO BULLS

Player	Minutes Played	Field Goal %	Free Throw %	Rebounds	Assists	Total Points	Avg. Pts./ Game
Jordan	3,090	49.5	83.4	543	352	2.491	30.4
Pippen	2,825	46.3	67.9	496	452	1,496	19.4
Kukoc	2,103	49.0	77.2	323	287	1,065	13.1
Longely	1,641	48.2	77.7	318	119	564	9.1
Kerr	1,919	50.6	92.9	110	192	688	8.4
Harper	1,886	46.7	70.5	213	208	594	7.4
Rodman	2,088	48.0	52.8	952	160	351	5.5
Wennington	1,065	49.3	86.0	174	46	376	5.3
Salley	673	45.0	69.4	140	54	185	4.4
Buechler	740	46.3	63.6	111	56	278	3.8
Simpkins	685	48.1	62.9	156	38	216	3.6
Brown	671	40.6	60.9	66	73	185	2.7

10. When Rodman attempted a free throw, what percent of the time did he score? _____

11. Who had the most assists? _____

12. Which two players scored the lowest number of points? _____

    _____

13. Who made the highest percentage of field goals? _____

Top U.S. Commercial Advertising Spending by Category

$ represents 1 billion dollars

Automotive $$$$$$$$$$

Retail $$$$$$$$

Consumer Services $$$$$$$

Entertainment $$$$$

Food $$$$

Toiletries & Cosmetics $$$

14. How much money was spent on food advertising?

    _____

15. How much money was spent on automotive advertising?

    _____

16. Was more money spent on entertainment or for retail stores?

    _____

17. What category spent the most on advertising?

    _____

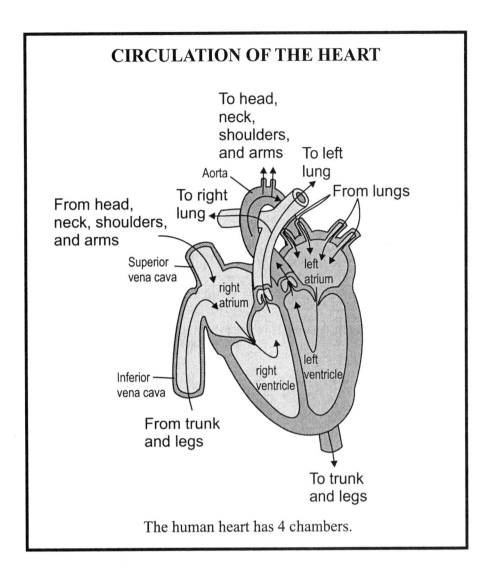

CIRCULATION OF THE HEART

To head, neck, shoulders, and arms

To left lung

Aorta

To right lung

From lungs

From head, neck, shoulders, and arms

Superior vena cava

right atrium

left atrium

Inferior vena cava

right ventricle

left ventricle

From trunk and legs

To trunk and legs

The human heart has 4 chambers.

18. Where does the blood go when it leaves the right atrium? _____

19. Which chamber does blood coming from the lungs enter? _____

20. Through which vessel does blood travel to get from the trunk and legs to the right atrium? _____

21. Which vessel carries blood from the left ventricle to the neck and head? _____

22. Where does blood go that leaves the left atrium? _____

23. Which vessel carries blood from your head and neck to your right atrium? _____

24. Where does blood go next when it leaves the right ventricle? _____

AVERAGE TEMPERATURES FOR TAMPA AND MIAMI

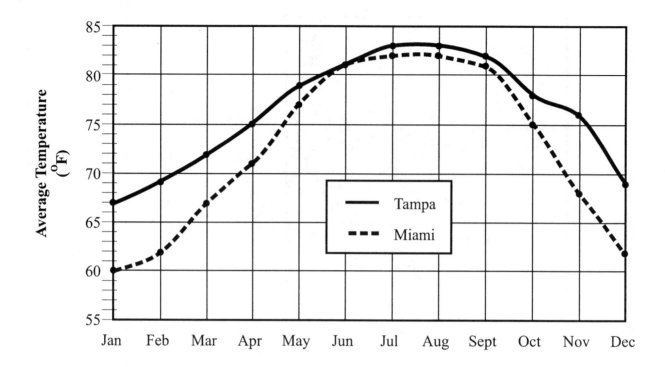

25. In which month is the average temperature in Miami and Tampa the same? _____

26. What is the average temperature of Tampa in August? _____

27. Between which two months does the average temperature fall the fastest in Miami? _____

    and _____

28. What is the lowest average temperature for Miami during the coldest month of the year? _____

29. For how many months of the year is the average temperature above 80°F in Tampa? _____

30. During how many months of the year does the average temperature fall below 70°F in Miami? _____

31. What is the average temperature in Miami in the month of March? _____

ROAD MAP

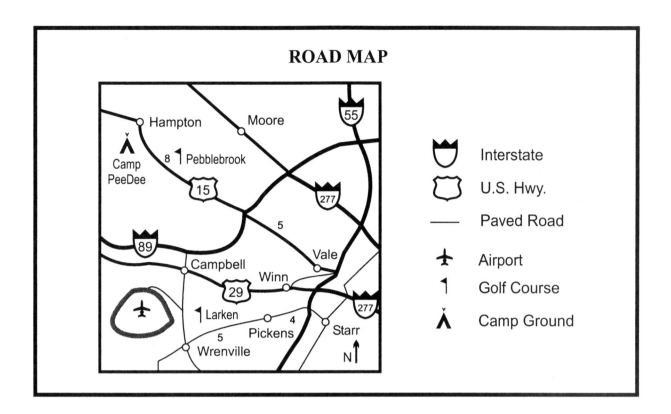

32. How many miles is it from Vale to Hampton?   _____

33. If you are in Pickens, which direction is the Larken golf course?   _____

34. What kind of road is closest to the campground?   _____

35. Which interstate highway is closest to Vale?   _____

36. How many miles will you drive to go from Pickens to Wrenville?   _____

37. Which highway do you use to drive from Interstate 89 to Pebblebrook?   _____

38. If you are in Campbell, which direction is Vale?   _____

39. If you are in Wrenville, which direction is Campbell?   _____

40. How many golf courses are on the map?   _____

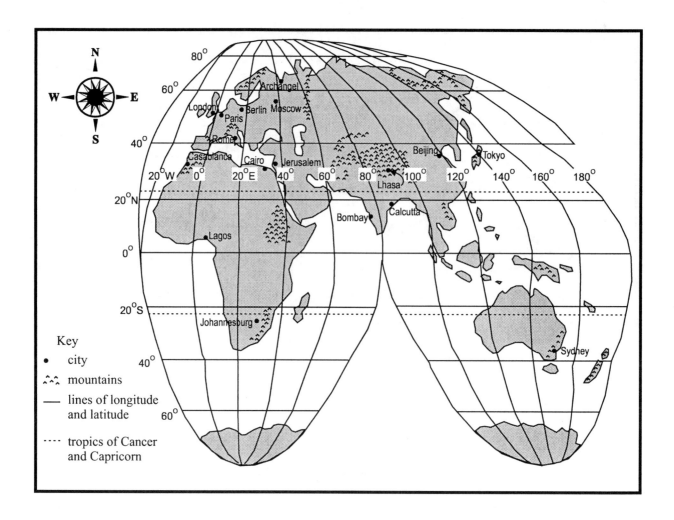

41. Which city would have cooler temperatures, Cairo or Lhasa?   _____

42. Which city would have a warmer average temperature, Bombay or Beijing?   _____

43. What is the latitude of the city of Lagos?   _____

44. What is the longitude of the city of Johannesburg?   _____

45. If you were in Rome, which direction would Beijing be?   _____

46. If you were in Moscow, which direction would Jerusalem be?   _____

47. Which city is located at 19°N, 87°E?   _____

48. Which city is located at 34°S, 151°E?   _____

49. Which city is located at 52°N, 1°W   _____

50. If you were on an airplane traveling from Sydney to Johannesburg, what direction would you be going?   _____

CHAPTER 6 TEST

Use each schedule, table, map, graph, or diagram to answer the questions that follow.

MARTA RAIL WEEKDAY TIMETABLE
NORTHBOUND

Airport	East Point	Lakewood	Oakland	West End	Five Points
4:08a	--	--	--	--	--
4:31a	4:35a	4:39a	4:41a	4:43a	4:47a
4:47a	4:51a	4:55a	4:57a	4:59a	5:03a
5:01a	5:05a	5:09a	5:11a	5:13a	5:17a
5:11a	5:15a	5:19a	5:21a	5:23a	5:27a
5:19a	5:23a	5:27a	5:29a	5:31a	5:35a
5:27a	5:31a	5:35a	5:37a	5:39a	5:43a
5:35a	5:39a	5:43a	5:45a	5:47a	5:51a
5:43a	5:47a	5:51a	5:53a	5:55a	5:59a
5:51a	5:55a	5:59a	6:01a	6:03a	6:07a
5:59a	6:03a	6:07a	6:09a	6:11a	6:15a
6:07a	6:11a	6:15a	6:17a	6:19a	6:23a
6:15a	6:19a	6:23a	6:25a	6:27a	6:31a
6:23a	6:27a	6:31a	6:33a	6:35a	6:39a
6:31a	6:35a	6:39a	6:41a	6:43a	6:47a
6:39a	6:43a	6:47a	6:49a	6:51a	6:55a

1. When the train leaves the Airport station at 6:07 a.m., when is it scheduled to arrive at Five Points station?

   A.   6:23 a.m   C.   Monday
   B.   6:23 p.m.   D.   5:51 a.m.

2. What is the next stop after Oakland?

   A.   Lakewood   C.   East Point
   B.   West End   D.   Five Points

3. If you needed to get to Five Points by 6:00 a.m., what time would you need to leave from the Lakewood station?

   A.   5:47 a.m.   C.   5:43 a.m.
   B.   5:59 a.m.   D.   5:51 a.m.

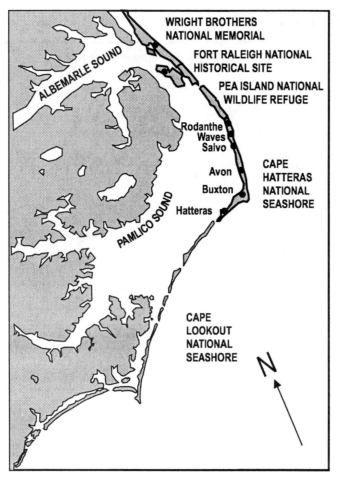

4. Based on this map, if tourists traveled from Buxton to the Fort Raleigh National Historical Site, what direction would they be traveling?

   A. Northwest
   B. North
   C. East
   D. Southeast

5. Traveling east of the city of Hatteras, which of the following places will someone discover?

   A. Pamlico Sound
   B. Albemarle Sound
   C. Cape Lookout National Seashore
   D. Buxton

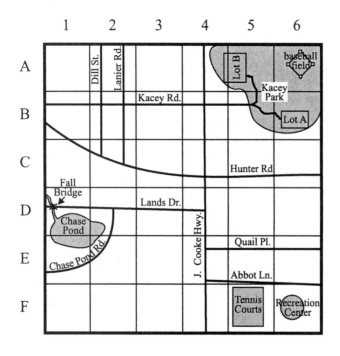

6. In which row and column do you find the recreation center?

   A. E5   C. E6
   B. F5   D. F6

7. Which of the following landmarks would be found in A6?

   A. Chase Pond
   B. baseball field
   C. tennis courts
   D. recreation center

8. In which row and column do you find the intersection of Chase Pond Road and Lands Drive?

   A. D2   C. D4
   B. E1   D. E2

148

COLUMBUS' SECOND VOYAGE
November 3, 1493 to March 10, 1496

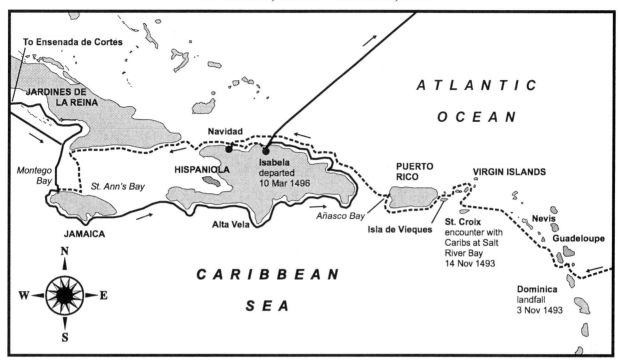

9. Based on this map of Columbus' second voyage, how many months was Columbus in the Caribbean?

    A. 34
    B. 28
    C. 24
    D. 16

10. When Columbus departed from Isabela, which direction did he sail?

    A. North
    B. West
    C. Northwest
    D. Northeast

11. Of the four islands listed below, which island did Columbus see first?

    A. St. Croix
    B. Jamaica
    C. Virgin Islands
    D. Puerto Rico

TOP 10 FASTEST ANIMALS

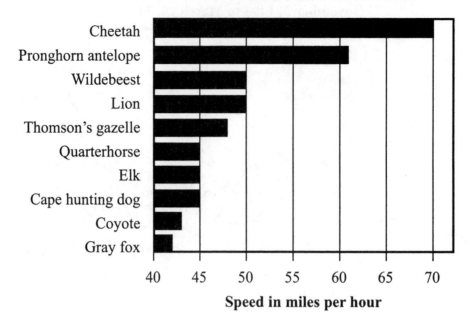

12.   How fast can a gray fox run?

   A.   41 mph   C.   43 mph
   B.   42 mph   D.   44 mph

13.   How much faster is a cheetah than a lion?

   A.   10 mph   C.   50 mph
   B.   20 mph   D.   70 mph

14.   Which two animals can go the same speed?

   A.   quarterhorse and coyote   C.   lion and gazelle
   B.   gray fox and coyote   D.   elk and cape hunting dog

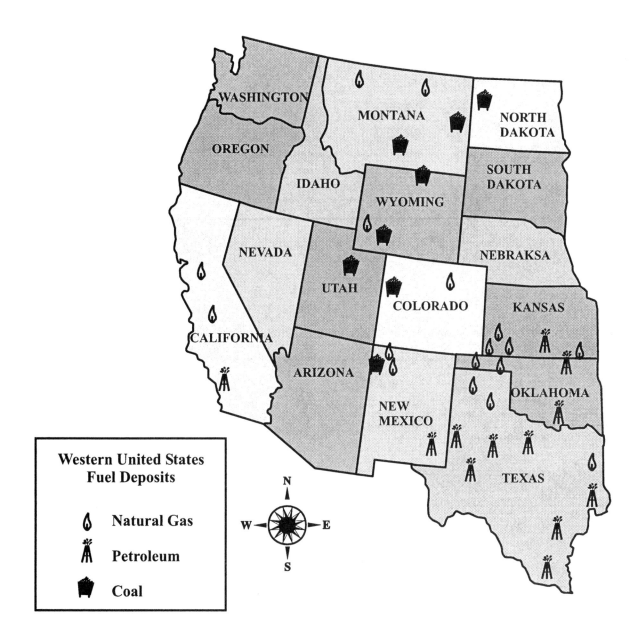

Western United States Fuel Deposits

💧 Natural Gas

🛢 Petroleum

⬟ Coal

15. According to the map, which state has the most petroleum reserves?

    A.   Texas   C.   Nevada
    B.   California   D.   Oklahoma

16. Which kind(s) of fuel deposits does New Mexico have?

    A.   natural gas, coal, and petroleum   C.   natural gas and coal
    B.   only natural gas   D.   only petroleum

17. Which state has the most natural gas fuel deposits?

    A.   North Dakota   C.   Oklahoma
    B.   Wyoming   D.   Kansas

In May of 1961, two Navy men went so high up in a hot air balloon, 113,740 feet, that they were at the edge of space. The following chart shows the time, height, and temperature as they ascended to the edge of space.

Read the chart below, and answer the questions that follow.

time	altitude (ft)	temperature ($^{\circ}$F)
7:08 am	0	74
7:34 am	26,000	-27
7:50 am	43,000	-73
8:10 am	53,000	-94
8:25 am	65,000	-80
9:05 am	95,000	-41
9:47 am	113,740	-29

18. What was the altitude when the temperature was the lowest?

    A. 43,000 feet   C. 65,000 feet
    B. 53,000 feet   D. 95,000 feet

19. What was the temperature when they were on the ground?

    A. 74°F   C. −73°F
    B. −27°F   D. −29°F

20. Which of the following statements is true?

    A. The higher they went, the colder it was.
    B. It was warmer at the edge of space than at 26,000 feet.
    C. It was warmer at the edge of space than at 43,000 feet.
    D. The coldest altitude was the edge of space.

CABLE TV SUBSCRIBERS
(1983-2005)

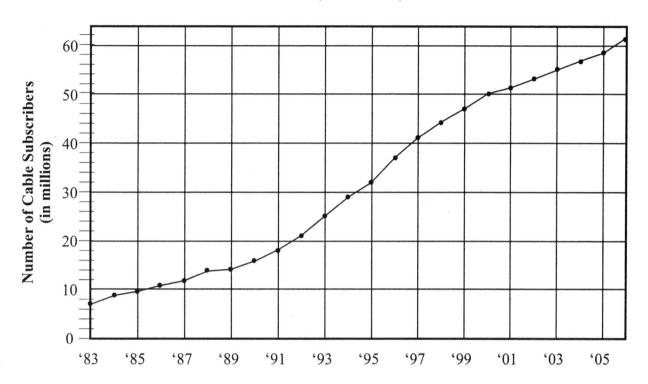

21. How many subscribers were there in 2000?

    A. 50,000   C. 5,200,000
    B. 50,000,000   D. 54,000,000

22. What was the first year that there were more than 20 million subscribers?

    A. 1991   C. 1993
    B. 1992   D. 1994

23. Which of the following statements is false?

    A. There were over 10 million more subscribers in 1991 than in 1983.
    B. There were over 30 million subscribers in 1995.
    C. There were less than 45 million subscribers in 1997.
    D. There were more than 59 million subscribers in 2001.

Average Television Viewing Time, 2005

📺 represents 2 hours of viewing time per week

Category	Age	Hours of Viewing Time
Women	18-24	📺📺📺📺📺📺📺
	25-54	📺📺📺📺📺📺📺📺📺📺📺⌐
	55+	📺📺📺📺📺📺📺📺📺📺📺📺📺⌐
Men	18-24	📺📺📺📺📺📺
	25-54	📺📺📺📺📺📺📺⌐
	55+	📺📺📺📺📺📺📺📺📺⌐
Teens	12-17	📺📺📺📺📺⌐
Children	2-5	📺📺📺📺📺📺⌐
	6-11	📺📺📺📺📺⌐

24. Which group spends the most time watching TV?

    A. Men 25-54
    B. Women 25-54
    C. Men 55+
    D. Women 55+

25. How many hours do children age 2-5 spend watching TV per week?

    A. $6\frac{1}{2}$ hours
    B. $5\frac{1}{2}$ hours
    C. 13 hours
    D. $8\frac{3}{4}$ hours

DICTIONARY SKILLS

Dictionary - a reference book listing words in alphabetical order. For each word, a dictionary generally includes spelling, pronunciation, definitions, parts of speech, usage, etymology or word origin, and sometimes synonyms and antonyms. The kinds of information given in a dictionary are described in detail below.

Word Division - Each word is divided into a syllable or syllables. Each syllable is pronounced with a single sounding of the voice. For example, the word **swallow** is divided into two syllables, **swal** and **low**. In a dictionary, this is written as **swal·low**.

Principal parts - Each verb in a dictionary entry is immediately followed by the principal parts of that verb. For instance, the verb **see** is found in the different verb tenses as **saw, seen,** and **see′ ing**.

Pronunciation - Each entry in a dictionary is followed by its pronunciation. For example, the word **radius** is pronounced **ray-dee-uhss (rā′ dē us)**. Consult a pronunciation guide in the in the front of the dictionary if you are unsure of how to pronounce a symbol. **(Example: ē is ee)**.

Plural form - Some words in a dictionary entry are also shown in their plural form. For example, the word **child** in the dictionary is immediately followed by the plural form, **children**.

Part of speech - Each dictionary entry also notes which part of speech the entry word is. Before the first definition or entry, the part of speech will appear in italics as an abbreviation. Here is a list of each part of speech and its abbreviation:

transitive verb = *vt.*	adjective = *adj.*
intransitive verb =*vi.*	preposition = *prep.*
noun = *n.*	conjunction = *conj.*
adverb = *adv.*	interjection = *interj.*
pronoun = *pron.*	article = *article*

Example: the word **holiness** is a noun, so the abbreviation *n.* appears after the word.

Definition - Each dictionary entry also contains a definition. A definition is the meaning of the entry word. **(Example: mascot - any person, animal, or thing supposed to bring good luck)** Sometimes there are several definitions listed for each entry word.

Etymology — The etymology (word origin) of each word is also part of each dictionary entry. Consult the etymology guide in the front of the dictionary to discover the meanings of the abbreviations. **(Example: OE means Old English, Fr means French, L means Latin, GR means Greek)**

Synonyms — Synonyms (words having similar meaning to the entry word) and antonyms (words having the opposite meaning to the entry word) are also commonly placed at the end of a dictionary entry. **(Example: raise - *v.* to cause to rise. SYN. See LIFT)**

The following is an example of a dictionary entry:

> **gris·ly** (griz′ lē) ***adj.*** [ME *grislich*] terrifying; horrible - SYN. See GHASTLY

From this definition, we know that the word **grisly** is divided into two syllables as gris·ly. We also know that **grisly** is an adjective. This word came from Middle English and has **ghastly** as a synonym.

Here is another dictionary entry:

> **cher·ry** (cher′ ē) ***n., pl.* -ries.** [OFr. *cerise*] 1. a small fleshy fruit containing a smooth, hard pit and ranging from yellow to very dark red 2. any of various trees (genus *Prunus*) of the rose family which bear this fruit.

From this entry, we know that the word **cherry** is correctly divided as cher·ry. We also know that **cherry** is a noun and that the plural form is spelled **cherries**. The word is derived from Old French and does not have any synonyms or antonyms.

PRACTICE 1

Read the following dictionary entries. Fill in the appropriate blanks with the correct answer.

1.
> **know** (nō) ***vt.* knew, known, know′ing** [ME *knowen*] 1. to have a clear perception or understanding of; to be sure or well-informed about (to *know* the truth) to be aware or cognizant of; have perceived or learned (to *know* that one is in control). SYN. See UNDERSTAND

A. Word Division _____   D. Pronunciation _____

B. Part of Speech _____   E. Verb Parts _____

C. Etymology _____   F. Synonym _____

2.

> **flur·ry** (flur′ i) **n., pl, -ries** [unk] 1. a sudden, brief rush of wind; gust 2. a gust of rain or snow   3. a sudden confusion or commotion.

A. Word Division   _____   D.   Plural Forms   _____

B. Part of Speech   _____   E.   Pronunciation   _____

C. Etymology   _____   F.   Synonym   _____

PRACTICE 2

Use the sample dictionary page below to answer the questions that follow.

> ## Sample Dictionary Page
>
> **366 dashboard - dastardly**
>
> **dash•board** *n.* a panel under the windshield of the vehicle, containing indicator dials, compartments, and sometimes control instruments. [Scand. origin]
>
> **da•sheen** *n.* the taro (sense 2). [Orig. unknown]
>
> **dash•er** *n.* **1.** One that dashes. **2.** The plunger of a churn or ice cream freezer. **3.** a spirited person.
>
> **da•shi•ki** *n.* A loose, brightly colored African tunic, usually worn by men. [Yoruba origin]
>
> **dash•ing** *adj.* **1.** Audacious and gallant; spirited. **2.** Marked by showy elegance; splendid. **-da•shing•ly** *adv.*
>
> **dash•pot** *n.* A piston-and-cylinder device used to damp motion.
>
> **das•sie** *n.* The hyrax. [Afr. origin] dim. of das, badger [MDV]
>
> **das•tard** *n.* A base, sneaking coward. [Middle English origin]
>
> **das•tard•ly** *adj.* Cowardly and mean-spirited; base. **-da•stard•li•ness** *n.*
>   **Usage:** *Dastardly* is employed most precisely when it combines the meaning of "vicious" and "cowardly." It is loosely used to mean simply "base" or "reprehensible." Thus, a gunman who shoots his victim in the back is committing a *dastardly* act.

1. What is the name for a brightly colored African tunic?   _____

2. What is the adverb form of dashing?   _____

3. What word would best describe a person who shoots someone in the back?   _____

4. **Das** is a shorter form of which word?   _____

5. What is the second definition for **dasher**?   _____

PRACTICE 3: DICTIONARY SKILLS

A. **Look Alikes - Sound Alikes.** Look up each of the following words in a dictionary. Identify the part(s) of speech, the various meanings, and then use each word in a sentence:

affect	allusion	capital	cite
effect	illusion	capitol	sight
			site

conscious	desert	device	elicit
conscience	dessert	devise	illicit

heard	loose	passed	personal
herd	lose	past	personnel

principal	stationary	than	threw
principle	stationery	then	thorough
			through

B. **Words to Know.** How many of these words do you know? Find out their meanings and parts of speech. See if you can use them in a sentence:

antidote	gratify	narrate	urban
bilingual	hybrid	ordeal	visualize
concoct	induce	prism	wean
divert	jovial	replica	zest
essence	khaki	spontaneous	flagrant

C. **Personal Word List.** To improve your knowledge of words, create a personal word list. Divide pages in your notebook into four columns. For each word entry, list the word (1) followed by the pronunciation and part of speech (2), the use of the word in a sentence (3), and finally the dictionary definition (4). As you find new words, add them to your personal word list, and review them periodically. Use the chart below as a model. Review your words periodically.

Word	Pronunciation Part of Speech	Word in Sentence	Dictionary Definition
surname	sur′ nām v. n.	Her <u>surname</u> is Garcia.	family name, last name
annual	an′ yoo wəl adj.	New Year's Eve is an <u>annual</u> celebration in the United States.	once a year; yearly

CHAPTER 7 REVIEW

Read each dictionary entry below. Then fill in the blanks appropriately.

1. | **jerk** (jûrk) *n.* [unk] a very quick pull or twist; (*slang*) a person thought of as rude or foolish

A. Part of speech _____   C. Plural form _____
B. Pronunciation _____   D. Etymology _____

2. | **ox·y·mo·ron** (äk′ si mō′ rän) *n.* [LGr. *oxymōron*] a figure of speech in which opposite or contradictory words are combined

A. Part of speech _____   C. Word division _____
B. Pronunciation _____   D. Etymology _____

3. | **ex·plor·a·tor·y** (ik splô′r′ a tôr′ ē) *n., pl* [L. *exploratorius*] **-ries** a class period in which the student has the option to choose between several different classes

A. Part of speech _____   C. Plural Form _____
B. Pronunciation _____   D. Etymology _____

4. | **se·cede** (si sēd′) *vi.* [L. *secedere*] to withdraw formally from a society, federation, or organization

A. Part of speech _____   C. Word division _____
B. Pronunciation _____   D. Etymology _____

5. | **cool** (kōōl) *adj.* [OE. *Col*] barely cold; free from excitement

A. Part of speech _____   C. Word division _____
B. Pronunciation _____   D. Etymology _____

CHAPTER 7 TEST

Use the sample dictionary entry below to answer each question.

> **in·vent** (in vent′) *vt.* 1. to think up, devise, or fabricate in the mind 2. to think out or produce; originate, as an experiment; devise for the first time 3. to find; discover

1. What part of speech is the entry word?

   A. interjection C. preposition
   B. verb D. noun

2. What is the correct division of the dictionary entry?

   A. inv·ent C. in·vent
   B. inven·t D. i·nvent

> **des·tine** (des′ tin) *vt.* -tined, -tining. 1. To predetermine, as by fate: usually in the passive 2. to set apart for a certain purpose; intend

3. What is the correct spelling of the past tense of the dictionary entry?

   A. destind C. destiny
   B. destining D. destined

4. What is the correct division of the dictionary entry?

   A. destin·e C. de·stine
   B. des·tine D. dest·ine

> **stud·y** (stud′ ē) *n., pl.,* **stud′ ies**. 1. the act or process of applying the mind so as to acquire knowledge or understanding, as by reading, investigating, etc. 2. Careful attention to, and critical examination and investigation of any subject, event, etc.

5. What is the correct spelling of the plural form of the dictionary entry?

   A. studys C. studyes
   B. studiys D. studies

6. What part of speech is the entry word?

   A. noun C. verb
   B. adjective D. preposition

> **speak** (spēk) *vi.* **spoke, spo′ ken, speak′ ing.** 1. to utter words with the ordinary voice; talk 2. to express or communicate opinions, feelings, ideas, etc. by or as by talking to make a request or reservation (for): usually in the passive voice.

7. What are the principal parts of the entry word?

   A. speak, speaked, spoken, speaking
   B. speak, speek, spoke, speaking
   C. speak, spoke, spoken, speaking
   D. speak, spoked, speaked, speaking

8. What part of speech is the entry word?

   A. noun
   B. verb
   C. adjective
   D. preposition

> **i·tal·ic** (i tal′ ik) *adj.* Designating or of a type in which the characters slant upward and to the right, used in different ways, as to emphasize words, indicate foreign words, set off book titles, etc.

9. What part of speech is the entry word?

   A. adjective
   B. conjunction
   C. adverb
   D. noun

10. What is the correct division of the dictionary entry?

    A. i·ta·lic
    B. it·al·ic
    C. i·tal·ic
    D. ita·lic

Chapter 8

USING AND CHOOSING REFERENCE SOURCES

If you were thinking about getting running shoes, where would you buy them and how much would you pay? If you're a smart shopper, you would browse through the newspaper ads for a shoe sale. Or you might scan the phone directory. Then you might call some stores near you to check prices and shoe sizes available. If you decided to shop at a mall or shopping center, you'd probably look over the mall directory, so you could find the shoe stores that carry the brand you want.

The ability to choose and use reference sources is an essential life skill in today's society. Whether you are buying shoes, doing research in the library, or reading a schedule or diagram, you will face situations where you will need the right resources. Obtaining and using the information from these sources can help you answer questions or complete a task in school, at home, or on the job.

LEARNING AND USING REFERENCE SOURCES

In this part of the chapter, you'll learn about important reference sources. You'll also practice answering questions about these sources. Here are the main ones:

Alphabetizing	**Glossary**
Thesaurus	**Encyclopedia**
Telephone Directory	**Internet and Databases**
Sections of a Book	**Dewey Decimal System**
Table of Contents	**Electronic Library Catalog**
Index	**Newspaper Index**
Bibliography	**Newspaper Ad**

Review the **Tips for Reference Sources** at the end of this section. Study the definition and example for each reference source. Then answer the questions about each one.

ALPHABETIZING

When lists of words are organized in some manner, the most common method of organization is **alphabetical order**. When words are alphabetized, they are arranged from the letters A - Z in the alphabet.

Many times, words in alphabetical order will begin with the same letter. In these cases, use the second letter of the word to decide which will go first. If the second letter is also the same letter, use the third letter, etc.

Example: raw - first letter   lemon - second letter   Harding - third letter
           sail   loan   Hascal

All reference sources list their topics by alphabetical order. Telephone books and dictionaries post two guide words at the top of each page. Any entry can be found by simply looking for the entry between the guide words.

Example: Realtors - Temporary are guide words. Telephone is a word you could find on that page.

Other reference sources alphabetize by putting the first letter of the volume or drawer in which you will find all words starting with that letter or letters. Encyclopedias and card catalogs use this system.

Example: The letters N - O are listed on the front of a card catalog drawer. The subject oriental can be found in this drawer.

One reference source, the directory, alphabetizes by putting the last names of persons or the names of companies on a large sign. The names are placed in alphabetical order from top to bottom.

		Room Number
Example:	Atley & Company	106
	Durham Foundation	210
	Hands On Office Products	113
	Lip Saver Technologies	302
	Narcotics Recovery Counseling Service	111
	Penn & Schuman Message Center	205
	Vibrant Voices, Inc.	303

    ** If you wanted to add Car Care, Inc. to the directory, it would have to be placed between Atley & Co, and Durham Foundation.

PRACTICE 1: ALPHABETIZING

Directions: Select the correct answer.

1. If you are looking for the entry aggravation in the dictionary, which words could you find at the top of the page?

    A.   afraid - against   C.   aflame - agrarian

    B.   agriculture - ajar   D.   agree - amount

2.

**ARTS & SCIENCES
BUILDING**

	Office Number
Dr. Greg Ainsley	105
Dr. Vicky Greene	206
Dr. Steve Loxley	203
Dr. Richard Planter	312
Dr. Laura Shannon	113
Dr. George Tinley	109
Dr. Sarah Vanderbilt	308

Dr. Zell Manford, a new faculty member in the Arts & Sciences Building, will have his name added to the above alphabetized building directory between

A.   Dr. Steve Loxley and Dr. Richard Planter.
B.   Dr. Richard Planter and Dr. Laura Shannon.
C.   Dr. Vicky Greene and Dr. Steve Loxley.
D.   Dr. Greg Ainsley and Dr. Vicky Greene.

3.   If you are looking through the card catalog for the word <u>zoology</u>, which drawer would you look in to find the card?

A.   A   C.   N - O
B.   W - Z   D.   Q - R

4.   If the guide words <u>Furniture</u> - <u>Garage</u> were at the top of a page in the yellow pages, which listing could be included on that page?

A.   Flooring   C.   Garbage Collection
B.   Fender Repair   D.   Futons

5.   If you were looking for the word <u>roundhouse</u> in the dictionary, which words would you find at the top of the page?

A.   roar - runt   C.   rat - roadhouse
B.   ranch - rill   D.   rouse - rust

6.   If you are looking in the <u>J-K</u> encyclopedia, which of the following articles will you find?

A.   Catholicism   C.   Lithuania
B.   Indiana   D.   Jakarta

7.   If you are looking for the name <u>Gulianni</u> in the white pages of the telephone book, which guide words could be listed at the top of the page?

A.   Guthrie - Gylord   C.   Goodrum - Guff
B.   Goethe - Gusman   D.   Gunther - Guy

164

Atwater National Bank	
	Suite No.
Ms. Nancy Birch	524
Mr. Phillip Dorman	213
Mrs. Gail Keckley	406
Ms. Monique Givens	106
Mr. Randall Landover	301
Mr. Jay Pickard	227
Mrs. Terri Tyler	408
Mr. Dan Williams	505

8. Mr. Al Sharpe, a newly hired CPA (certified public accountant), will have his name added to the above alphabetized building directory between

    A. Mr. Randall Landover and Mr. Jay Pickard.
    B. Mr. Jay Pickard and Mrs. Terri Tyler.
    C. Mrs. Terri Tyler and Mr. Dan Williams.
    D. Mrs. Gail Keckley and Ms. Monique Givens.

Fairview Health Clinic	
	Suite No.
Mrs. Amanda Chadwick, LPN	105
Dr. Ray Fiorio	213
Mr. Trent Hesnor, RN	113
Dr. Colleen Lebont	201
Ms. Patricia Mason, RN	302
Dr. Enrique Petrarch	109
Mrs. Joan Quincy, LPN	212
Dr. Evelyn Spinnaker	307
Mr. Bill Thornton, LPN	311

9. Dr. Tad Ross, a new general practitioner in the Fairview Health Clinic, will have his name added to the above alphabetized directory between

    A. Dr. Colleen Lebont and Ms. Patricia Mason, LPN.
    B. Dr. Enrique Petrarch and Mrs. Joan Quincy, LPN.
    C. Dr. Evelyn Spinnaker and Mr. Bill Thornton, LPN.
    D. Mrs. Joan Quincy, LPN and Dr. Evelyn Spinnaker.

10. If the guide words graft - grubby were at the top of a page in the dictionary, which entry could be included on that page?

    A. gross
    B. graduation
    C. grudge
    D. graceful

THESAURUS

THESAURUS - a book containing lists of synonyms and antonyms in alphabetical order. A thesaurus improves writing and one's knowledge of words.

Thesaurus Entry

88. HEIGHT

NOUNS:

1. height, tip, stature, elevation
2. top, highest point, ceiling, zenith
3. hill, knoll, volcano, mountain

VERBS:

4. heighten, elevate, raise, rear, erect
5. intensify, strengthen, increase, advance
6. command, rise above, crown, surmount

ADJECTIVES:

7. high, towering, exalted, supreme

Antonyms: depth, descent

For Questions 1-3, circle the word that would best provide a synonym for the italicized word in each sentence below. Then answer questions 4-8.

1. With a *height* of 20,320 feet, Mt. McKinley is an impressive sight.
    stature   **top**   **elevation**

2. The *high* skyscraper stood in the center of the city.
    exalted   **supreme**   **towering**

3. The frequent thunder *heightened* our fears for Latasha's safety.
    intensified   **erected**   **crowned**

4. T or F   **Increase** is the same part of speech as heighten.

5. T or F   A mountain is lower than a hill.

6. What part of speech is **height**? _____

7. What are the antonyms for **height**? _____

8. List the synonyms for **high**. _____

TELEPHONE DIRECTORY

Telephone Directory - a book listing names, addresses, and phone numbers of persons, businesses, or organizations in alphabetical order. The phone directories provide a network for locating information. The white pages contain home phone numbers and sometimes business numbers. The yellow pages contain listings for businesses and organizations. In some cities, there are now blue pages for government listings.

STEPHEN'S SEAFOOD RESTAURANT

Family owned and operated
Open Daily for Lunch and Dinner
Major Credit Cards Accepted

Stephen's Seafood Restaurant
    3822 Vista Drive Surf City............ 684-3210
Stone's Oyster Grill
    112 Breeze Road North Beach...... 823-9434

Strike's Burgers
    3340 Shore Blvd. Surf City 684-3288
Sub Stop
    725 Ocean Road Coraltown 459-4666
Sunshine Diner
    Rib and Shrimp Specials
    2941 Vista Drive Surf City 683-7443
Supper Club
    Fine Cuisine
    603 Breeze Road North Beach 824-6000
Tastee Yogurt
    810 Ocean Highway Linnville 572-8420

1.   What is the phone number for the Sunshine Diner? _____

2.   Where is Stephen's Seafood Restaurant located? _____

3.   T or F   The phone number for Strike's Burgers is 684-3288.

4.   T or F   Stephen's Seafood Restaurant is open on Mondays.

5.   What is the main attraction at the Supper Club? _____

6.   T or F   Only two restaurants serve seafood.

7.   How many restaurants are there in Surf City? _____

8.   Where could you go to eat in Coraltown? _____

9.   T or F   The address of Stone's Oyster Grill is 1112 Breeze Road North Beach.

10.   What is served at the Sunshine Diner? _____

PRACTICE 2: TELEPHONE DIRECTORY

On your own or in a group, review telephone directories. List the various kinds of information you find. In groups, see how many of the following you can find.

an attorney's phone number
emergency numbers
the name of a hospital, church, and park
state government offices
the phone number for your nearest post office

long distance dialing directions
the address of a steak restaurant
a local radio and television station
the address of the closest movie theater
area code for New York City and Dallas

SECTIONS OF A BOOK

Each textbook will include each of several sections to help the reader acquire knowledge. Listed below is each of the sections of a book found when reading from front to back.

Title Page - This page displays the title of the book, the name(s) of the author(s), edition (if the book has been published before), copyright (date the book was published), publishing company, and place of publication.

Preface - This section provides an explanatory statement about the book, telling the book's history, purpose, or plan.

Table of Contents - This section lists all the parts of the book including the introduction, the chapter titles, chapter subheadings, and page numbers indicating where each chapter begins, as well as the additional material pages.

Appendix - This part of the book contains additional material that is not essential to the text itself. This material includes charts, documents, tables, illustrations, and/or photographs. The appendix is located at the end of the text.

Glossary - This section is a dictionary of the specialized terms at the end of a book. Definitions are written in a clear and brief manner; they are also arranged in alphabetical order. The glossary contains all the terms and words that were boldfaced or italicized in the text of each chapter.

Index - This part appears at the end of the book and contains the most important topics, headings, and subheadings discussed in the textbook. The index items are arranged alphabetically with their page number reference and include important people, places, events, locations, equations, and/or books.

Bibliography - This section contains the references or citations the author(s) used while writing their book. Each reference includes the title of the work, the name(s) of the author(s), the date of publishing, publishing company, location of the publisher, and page numbers.

PRACTICE 3: SECTIONS OF A BOOK

Directions: Read the following questions and select the best answer based on the information above.

1. Which part of the book would you use to locate a table referred to in the book?

   A. bibliography
   B. appendix
   C. title page
   D. glossary

2. The preface is the part of the book that gives

   A. the explanatory statement of the book.
   B. the citations of authors who wrote the textbook.
   C. the publisher's name and address.
   D. the chapter subheadings.

3. Which part of the book is used to find the sources used in writing this book?

A.   table of contents
B.   appendix
C.   bibliography
D.   title page

4. Which part of the book would you use to locate the definition of "paleontology"?

A.   index
B.   glossary
C.   bibliography
D.   preface

5. The table of contents is the part of the book that gives a list of

A.   the author's name and publisher.
B.   the title of the book.
C.   the key words and definitions.
D.   the section and chapter names with their starting page numbers.

6. Which part of the book is used to find the name of the publishing company for the book?

A.   title page
B.   index
C.   appendix
D.   bibliography

7. Which part of the book would you use to locate the page number for a reference on the word "self-actualization"?

A.   index
B.   table of contents
C.   glossary
D.   bibliography

8. The appendix is the part of a book that gives information about

A.   chapters and page numbers.
B.   contributing author's names.
C.   tables, charts, and graphs referenced in the book.
D.   the definition of a particular word found in the book.

9. Which part of the book is used to find the introduction to the book?

A.   preface
B.   glossary
C.   table of contents
D.   bibliography

10. Which part of the book is used to find the page number for the beginning of chapter 5?

A.   appendix
B.   glossary
C.   preface
D.   table of contents

TABLE OF CONTENTS

Table of Contents - a listing of chapters and topics. A table of contents appears in the front of a book and provides an overview of the content and organization of a book.

1. In which chapter would you find information on Life expectancy? _____

2. On which page does the section on Religion start? _____

3. If you wanted to find statistics about marriage and divorce, on which page of the book would you look? _____

4. Which chapter would you read if you wanted to find out how much money is spent on health? _____

5. In which chapter would you find facts about immigration? _____

6. What is the last page dealing with Insurance coverage? _____

INDEX

Book Index - an alphabetical list of topics in a book with page numbers. The index generally contains every topic mentioned in a book and tells you which pages discuss the topic. An index appears at the end of a book.

SAMPLE INDEX

Namibia, diamonds 22
Naples 13
neap tide 21
nectar 32, 34
Neptune 4
New Guinea, area 42

New Zealand, geysers 12
             waterfalls 44
nickel 11
Nile River 18-19, 43
noise, loudest 42
nomad 37
North Africa, deserts 37, 44

---

1. On which pages are deserts discussed?_____

2. Where would you read about the loudest noise? _____

3. On which page is a major city in Italy mentioned? _____

4. What are New Zealand's two famous attractions? _____

5. Where would you find out more about the Nile River? _____

6. On which pages is nectar discussed? _____

7. In what country can you find diamonds? _____

8. On what page would you find information about nickel? _____

9. Look up six topics in another book index. List each topic and the page numbers about the topic here.

    _____   _____

    _____   _____

    _____   _____

BIBLIOGRAPHY

Bibliography - a list of writings about a particular author or topic. The writings consist of books or periodicals in alphabetical order by author's last name. A periodical is a magazine such as **National Geographic** or **Reader's Digest.** If the source is a magazine, the title of the article is in quotation marks. The name of the magazine is underlined. Titles of books are also underlined.

Read the sample bibliography below, and answer the questions that follow.

SAMPLE BIBLIOGRAPHY

Burnett, Frances Hodgson. The Secret Garden. New York: TDA, 1988.

Byars, Betsy. The Summer of the Swans. New York: Scholastic, 1970.

Keller, Helen. The Story of My Life. New York: Dell, 1965.

Reagan, C. & Stoner, G. "Great Stories For Children." Children Today 23 (1998): 76-77.

Sterling, Dorothy. Freedom Train. New York: Scholastic, 1954.

Verne, Jules. 20,000 Leagues Under The Sea. New York: Bantam, 1962.

Zeller, Hellen. "Games Children Play." Social Issues 11: (1997): 331-334.

1. Which listing in the bibliography is listed first? _____

2. Who is the author of *Story Of My Life*? _____

3. Which publishing company published the book by Jules Verne? _____

4. Which magazine has an article about children playing games? _____

5. Which book was published in 1962? _____

6. Where was *The Secret Garden* published? _____

7. How many sources listed are magazine articles? _____

8. Which book is the story of Helen Keller? _____

9. Which article has two authors? _____

10. Who is the author of The Summer of the Swans? _____

GLOSSARY

Glossary - an alphabetical list of specialized words with their definitions. The glossary is placed at the end of a book. Glossaries are found in science, social studies, literature, math books, and many others as well.

Sample Glossary Page

monogamy - marriage to one person at a time.

monopoly - one company dominating a particular market such as cars or telephones.

monotheism - belief in one God.

mores - standards of conduct that are held by a particular culture.

multiculturalism - respecting and accepting many cultures.

national health service - health care for all citizens regardless of income.

nationalism - one nation having more rights than another nation.

net financial assets - what we own minus what we owe.

nuclear family - a group consisting of two parents and their children.

occupation - a job for pay.

---

1. What is belief in one god called? _____

2. True or False. Volunteering to care for pre-school age children is an occupation.

3. True or False. Arriving at school on time is an example of a more.

4. True or False. A savings account is part of net financial assets.

5. Affordable medical care is called _____

6. True or False. Racism is part of muticulturalism.

7. What is being married to one person called? _____

8. True or False. Nationalism occurs when everyone in the world is treated equally.

9. True or False. A single father with two children is a nuclear family.

10. When does a company become a monopoly? _____

_____

ENCYCLOPEDIA

Encyclopedia - a reference work, found in libraries or on the Internet, containing articles on a variety of subjects such as people, places, historical events, science, and technology. The articles are arranged alphabetically in volumes. Specialized encyclopedias on art, music, law, technology, and literature are also available in libraries and on the Internet.

Sample Encyclopedia Page

CAVY, *KAYvee,* is the common name for several related South American *rodents* (gnawing animals). Common cavies are called *guinea pigs*. Other cavies include *maras (Patagonian hares) and mocos*. Most cavies have fat bodies, short legs, and stiff, bristly hair. Maras have long, thin legs. A few kinds of *domesticated* (tamed) guinea pigs have long hair. All cavies eat plants or seeds.

CAYENNE PEPPER, a hot spice made from a plant called capiscum frutescens.

CAYMAN ISLANDS, A British dependency, located about 200 miles (320 kilometers) northwest of Jamaica in the Caribbean Sea. The three islands that make up the Cayman Islands are named Grand Cayman, Little Cayman, and Cayman Brac. They range over 100 square miles (259 square kilometers), and have 14,000 persons. The capital and largest city, Georgetown, is on Grand Cayman, the largest island.

CAYUGA INDIANS. See Iroquois Indians.

CAYUGA LAKE. See Finger Lakes.

CBR WARFARE. See Chemical-Biological-Radiological Warfare.

---

1. In what volume would you find more information on Cayuga Lake? _____

2. What is the common name for guinea pig? _____

3. What is another name for the Iroquois Indians? _____

4. Where are the Cayman Islands? _____

5. How many islands make up the Cayman Islands? _____

6. What kind of food do maras eat? _____

7. What does CBR stand for? _____

8. What is capiscum frutescens? _____

INTERNET AND DATABASES

Computer Research: The process of using computers for research is both similar and yet different from other means of research. There are two forms of research that can be accessed on a computer. The first form is **computer software** and the second is the **Internet**. Both can be reliable and complete in the information they contain; however, there are steps students need to take to ensure the quality of research when using these two sources.

Computer Software: Some computer software programs are arranged or formatted like encyclopedias while some are formatted like their predecessors, arcade games. For most any type of educational software, there will be instructional text written into the program. Usually this text can be accessed through clicking on a "HELP" tab or button found on the screen.

When choosing software for research, you will need to ask yourself some questions about the program(s) before using them.

1) Is the program written by a well-respected company?
2) Has the program been updated recently?
3) Is the material in the program appropriate for your grade level?
4) Can the information found on the software program be verified in other sources?

The Internet: The Internet has become one of the most common research tools today. If you are finishing up a research paper and you have not yet gone "on-line," should you consider your research completed? Most likely the answer is no. The way we gather and publish information has changed drastically since the development of the Internet. Even popular culture and the media have been affected by the wide reach and use of the Internet.

The ability to best choose and use Web sites is a vital skill in this rapidly growing world of Internet access. Whether you are looking for the best price for your spring break travel, finding out the details of a job you are applying for, or writing a paper for class, the Internet is a valuable resource if used wisely and efficiently.

Using the Internet can challenge your research skills. First, you must decide which **key words** to use and how to frame them in the search mode to find the material you want, instead of a lot of marketing sites or opinion based information. In addition, you must access various **search engines** such as Google, Yahoo, or MSN to find the best Web sites about your topic. Then, you must **validate** the material, checking the site for its credibility or the material for accuracy. Next, you must decide how best to use the material and if it is the **appropriate** source for your particular topic. Read at least the first two paragraphs of a passage before printing. This should give you an idea of its tone, its supporting research, and often an overview of its contents. Last, but perhaps most important, is the skill of **safe research** on the information highway. These topics will be discussed in more detail in Appendix D, "Using Electronic Resources."

PRACTICE 4: ENCYCLOPEDIA, INTERNET AND DATABASES

A. Encyclopedia. Write the key word or heading you would use to find the following information. It would be helpful to look in the index of your encyclopedia set to start. Then mention the page where you found the information, and answer the question.

1. Where and in what year did Columbus make his second voyage to the New World?

2. Describe the Zulu culture.

3. How do you care for a baby?

4. How large do leatherback sea turtles get?

5. What were the teachings of Mahatma Gandhi?

6. Which vitamins are found in beef?

7. Teaching Chimpanzees American sign language.

8. How did jazz music start?

9. Name the seven wonders of the world.

10. Where did Joseph Stalin die?

11. What are the cures for sea sickness?

12. List four famous American humorists.

13. Explain how a telescope works.

14. How do microwave ovens work?

15. What products come from pine trees?

B. Internet and Databases. Read over the following topics. Choose three to research, using at least one software program and the Internet, or develop your own with teacher approval. Write about your findings on 3 × 5 note cards, one for each topic. Share your findings with others in your class. Discuss your preferred search engines and sites for research.

Mad Cow Disease	Earthquakes	Bird songs	Holidays
History of Chocolate	Lunar Eclipses	Calendars	Teddy Roosevelt
Pastas	Teeth	Mahatma Gandhi	History of Writing
Herbs for healing in South Carolina	Maple Syrup in Vermont	Washington Apples	Zimmermann Telegram

DEWEY DECIMAL SYSTEM

Many libraries use the **Dewey Decimal System** to organize their books and make them easy to find. The numbering system is divided into the 10 categories listed below.

Section Numbers	Category	Examples
000 - 099	General Works	Encyclopedias
100 - 199	Philosophy	psychology, ethics
200 - 299	Religion	mythology, world religions
300 - 399	Social Sciences	law, government, economics, education
400 - 499	Languages	dictionaries, grammars
500 - 599	Science	astronomy, biology, chemistry, physics, math
600 - 699	Technology	medicine, business, engineering, farming, homemaking
700 - 799	Arts & Recreation	dance, painting, music, hobbies
800 - 899	Literature	poetry, plays, short stories, novels
900 - 999	History	biography, geography, travel

Use the chart above to determine what section or category you would use to find the following books.

1. Which section would have a book about a United States president? _____

2. Which category would have a book about Buddhism? _____

3. Which category would have a book about shooting stars? _____

4. Between what numbers would you find a book about painting with acrylics? _____

5. Which category would have a book about what to see in India? _____

6. In which section would you find a book about the causes of storms? _____

7. In which section would you find the book The Mystery of the Missing Necklace? _____

8. In which category would you find a Spanish-English/English-Spanish dictionary? _____

9. Which section would have a book about starting your own business? _____

10. In which category would you find a book on Freud's contributions to modern psychology? _____

ELECTRONIC LIBRARY CATALOG

A library catalog is an alphabetical listing of books in a library. These used to be on 3″× 5″ cards filling lots of drawers in a large cabinet! Now they are found on a computer system or on microfilm. A computerized catalog can search for books and other library items by **author, title,** or **subject**. A book or item will be listed at least three times in the catalog--once by author, once by title, and once by subject. Each entry for an item or book will contain the following information: the author's full name, the title of the book, place of publication, name of publisher, date of publication, number of pages, and brief facts about the book. The **call number** is listed. Below is a sample entry that you might find on the electronic catalog.

Subject Card

Famous Americans - Biographies

Palacios, Argentina, 1953- comp.
    Standing Tall: The Stories of Ten
    Hispanic Americans.
    New York: Scholastic, Inc, 1994.
    234 pp.

Includes Selected Bibliography and Sources
1. Famous Americans - Biographies   I. Title
HA 922.43TS4
ISBN 0-590-47140-6

Answer the following questions based on the sample catalog entry above.

1.   How many pages does the book contain?

    _____

2.   Under what subject is the book classified?

    _____

3.   What is the book's call number?

    _____

4.   Where and when was the book published?

    _____

5.   What is the book's title?

    _____

NEWSPAPER INDEX AND NEWSPAPER AD

Newspaper Index - an alphabetical list of sections in a newspaper. This index helps you locate articles on a particular topic.

Sample Newspaper Index

Sections	
Main News/Front Page	A
Editorials	B
Travel	C
Sports	D
Entertainment	E
Obituaries	F
Advertisements	G
Classified Ads	H

Main News/Front Page - the page and section where the most important news items are printed.

Editorial Section - the section where the editors' or publisher's opinions on some subjects are printed.

Travel Section - the section where information about different areas of the world and prices of travel are printed.

Sports Section - the section where the latest sports events and famous sports players are discussed.

Entertainment Section - the section where the latest movies, theater performances, and musical concerts are posted and discussed.

Obituaries - the section where funeral notices and brief biographies of the deceased are posted.

Advertisements - public notices or announcements recommending certain products or services.

Classified Section - the section where notices of employment opportunities, homes for sale, apartments for rent, lost and found, etc. are posted.

Tell which section you would look for the following articles.

1. Where would you find an article about a major earthquake in China? _____

2. Where would you find news about the state basketball playoffs? _____

3. What would you find in the obituaries? _____

4. Where would the movie listings appear? _____

5. Where would you find the time and place of a movie you want to see? _____

6. Where would you look for the cheapest plane fare to New York? _____

7. Where would you look to find the details on the time for a funeral? _____

8. Where would you find the editors' opinions on the latest government crisis? _____

9. Where would you find the department store sales this week? _____

10. What would you find in the classified section? _____

11. What would you expect to find on the front page? _____

NEWSPAPER AD

Newspaper (Classified) Ad - a notice designed to promote a product, service, or business. Newspaper ads vary in size, shape, and color and are often created to increase sales or to offer employment.

> Fine dining restaurant in Liberty now hiring hostess, cooks, servers, and bussers. Will work around your school schedule. Jobs pay between $5 - $8 per hour. Ask for Sandra or Keva. Apply at 461 Whistle St. or phone 889-4200.

12. What is the address of the restaurant? _____

13. When are the workers needed? _____

14. Whom should you speak with about the positions? _____

15. Since the employer works around a school schedule, who is the main audience for the ad?

_____

PRACTICE 5: NEWSPAPER AD

A **magazine** is a publication issued weekly, semimonthly, monthly, or quarterly which contains nonfiction articles or fictional stories from different contributors. Magazines also publish current information on the latest events and trends around the world.

For homework, each student finds an ad in a newspaper or magazine and then develops four questions about it. Students bring their ads and questions to class, and exchange them with other students. Answers are given after students reply to the questions.

QUESTIONS ABOUT REFERENCE SOURCES

TIPS FOR QUESTIONS ABOUT REFERENCE SOURCES

1. **Skim through the reference source.**

2. **Read the reference source two or three times.** Become familiar with the format and organization of the reference.

3. **Read the question carefully.**

4. **Scan the reference source to find your answer.**

5. **Confirm your answer by reviewing the evidence in the source.**

CHOOSING THE RIGHT REFERENCE SOURCES

In the first part of this chapter, you learned about important **resource materials**. Then, you practiced answering questions about them. Now is a good time to learn to choose the best resource material for your needs.

Let's say that you are doing a report on cowhands. Several sources may give some information about cowhands, but only a few sources will give you enough material for a report. For example, a **dictionary** will give you a definition of cowhand. A **bibliography** might list some books about cowhands. The **electronic card catalog** can help you locate the books about cowhands if you have any in your library. You might even locate a **map** of states where cowhands live. However, only one or two reference sources will provide enough information for a report. Most likely this information will come from longer articles in an **encyclopedia** (in book form or in **computer software**), or from educational sites on the **Internet**.

Based on the above example, you can see that choosing the right reference source means:
1) Clearly defining your own research needs,
2) Being familiar with different resources and their strengths, and
3) Being able to use each form of resource material easily.

In the chapter review, you'll be identifying the best resource for obtaining information on a particular topic or problem. Before you start answering the questions, review the main resource materials from this chapter.

CHAPTER 8 REVIEW

Directions: Read each question. Then choose the appropriate source for finding the information.

1. Which source will help Tyrone fix his computer?

   A. encyclopedia   C. electronic library catalog

   B. dictionary   D. telephone directory

2. Sonya wants to write to Danny Haren of the St. Louis Cardinals. Where would she look?

   A. dictionary   C. Internet

   B. thesaurus   D. index

3. Josh found a gold watch in the woods with no identification. Where would he find the owner?

   A. newspaper ad   C. telephone directory

   B. encyclopedia   D. thesaurus

4. Diane is writing a paper and needs another word to use for the word "trip." Which reference should she use?

   A. appendix   C. thesaurus

   B. bibliography   D. encyclopedia

5. Shawn is buying his first car. Where would he look for the best price?

   A. computer software   C. table of contents

   B. newspaper ads   D. bibliography

6. Where would Maria look to find books of African-American folktales?

   A. encyclopedia   C. ad

   B. computer software   D. electronic library catalog

7. Aaron wants to find out which page in his history book tells about the causes of World War I. What part of the book should he look in?

   A. bibliography   C. index

   B. appendix   D. title page

8. Zack needs to know the page number for the beginning of Chapter 6. Where should he look?

   A. index   C. bibliography

   B. table of contents   D. appendix

9. Brittany needs to know the definition of the word "lugubrious." Where should she look?

   A. dictionary
   B. thesaurus
   C. electronic library catalogue
   D. encyclopedia

10. Charles needs to do a report on sea creatures that dwell on the bottom of the ocean. Which of the following resources would he most likely **not** turn to?

    A. encyclopedia
    B. Internet
    C. newspaper index
    D. electronic library catalog

11.

Marketing and Sales Division Building	Office No.
Mr. Arnold Bass	218
Ms. Susan Chapel	128
Mr. Dale Fletcher	222
Mr. Ken Greene	207
Mrs. Cheryl Love	105
Ms. Gail Spears	109
Mr. Ben Tinley	215
Mrs. Jessie Ulrich	112
Mr. Sam Walton	111

Ms. Stone, a new accounts manager in the Marketing and Sales Division Building, will have her name added to the above alphabetized building directory between

A. Mrs. Cheryl Love and Ms. Gail Spears.
B. Mr. Ben Tinley and Mrs. Jessie Ulrich.
C. Ms. Gail Spears and Mr. Ben Tinley.
D. Ms. Susan Chapel and Mr. Dale Fletcher.

12. If the guide words <u>lance - late</u> were at the top of a page in the dictionary, which word could be included on that page?

    A. laundry
    B. laser
    C. lamp
    D. lake

13. Where would you find alphabetized definitions of terms describing the body in a biology book?

    A. table of contents
    B. index
    C. bibliography
    D. glossary

14. Where would you look for a book on speed reading?

    A. electronic library catalog
    B. telephone directory
    C. an index
    D. a table of contents

```
┌─────────────────────────────────────────┐
│              Statistical Index            │
│                                           │
│  Space Research and Technology,           │
│       Federal Outlays......................509, 983│
│  Spain. See Foreign Countries             │
│       Spanish-American War, cost.............548│
│  Spices, imports......................1105,1107,1109│
│  Sporting and athletic goods              │
│       Sports.............................407,408,1130│
│  Consumer Price Indexes.....................748│
│  Sporting goods and bicycle shops,        │
│       retail.................................1278│
│  Sports........................309,404,412│
│  Expenditures...........................393,407│
│  Sports Associations..........................92│
│  Sports Industry Receipts..................395│
│  Spot Market Price Index.....................760│
│  Squid......................................1152,1158│
└─────────────────────────────────────────┘
```

15. On what page(s) would you find information about pepper and cloves?

A. 1109		C. 983	
B. 760		D. 393	

Use the following information on the Dewey Decimal System to answer questions 16-20.

Section Numbers	Category	Examples
000 - 099	General Works	Encyclopedias
100 - 199	Philosophy	psychology, ethics
200 - 299	Religion	mythology, world religions
300 - 399	Social Sciences	law, government, economics, education
400 - 499	Languages	dictionaries, grammars
500 - 599	Science	astronomy, biology, chemistry, physics, math
600 - 699	Technology	medicine, business, engineering, farming, homemaking
700 - 799	Arts & Recreation	dance, painting, music, hobbies
800 - 899	Literature	poetry, plays, short stories, novels
900 - 999	History	biography, geography, travel

16. What section would have a book entitled <u>The Cry in the Night</u>? _____

17. In which category would you find a book on the catfish farming? _____

18. Which category would have a book on battles during the Civil War? _____

19. In which section would you find a book of poems by Emily Dickenson? _____

20. In which section would you find a book titled
     <u>Plants that Eat Insects</u>? _____

184

CHAPTER 8 TEST

Use the following chart of the Dewey Decimal System to answer questions 1-5.

Section Numbers	Category	Examples
000 - 099	General Works	Encyclopedias
100 - 199	Philosophy	psychology, ethics
200 - 299	Religion	mythology, world religions
300 - 399	Social Sciences	law, government, economics, education
400 - 499	Languages	dictionaries, grammars
500 - 599	Science	astronomy, biology, chemistry, physics, math
600 - 699	Technology	medicine, business, engineering, farming, homemaking
700 - 799	Arts & Recreation	dance, painting, music, hobbies
800 - 899	Literature	poetry, plays, short stories, novels
900 - 999	History	biography, geography, travel

1. Where would you find a book entitled *Dairy Farming in the Year 2000*?

   A. 900-999   C. 300-399
   B. 600-699   D. 000-099

2. Where would you look for a book on decorating your living room?

   A. 900-999   C. 300-399
   B. 600-699   D. 000-099

3. In which category would you find a book about how to get a bill through Congress?

   A. General Works   C. Social Sciences
   B. Religion   D. History

4. In which category would you find a book about how cells in your body multiply?

   A. Philosophy   C. Technology
   B. Science   D. Literature

5. Where would you go to look for a book on the life of President Truman?

   A. 100-199   C. 800-899
   B. 300-399   D. 900-999

Directions: Read each question, and then choose the appropriate source for finding the information.

6. Which source would you use for buying a portable compact disc player?

   A. newspaper   C. glossary
   B. encyclopedia   D. book index

7. If Kelsey were lost in the mall, where would she look for help?

   A. index   C. map
   B. dictionary   D. Internet

8. Saturday is prom night, and Luis decides to go. What source might help him find a tuxedo?

   A. electronic library catalogue
   B. telephone directory
   C. bibliography
   D. atlas

9. Where would you search to find the origin of the word **numeral?**

   A. diagram   C. dictionary
   B. sign   D. table of contents

10. Orlando wants to watch the Super Bowl on television tomorrow, but he can't remember when it starts. Where should he look?

   A. encyclopedia   C. newspaper
   B. index   D. Internet

11. Teresa is doing research on the Ebola virus for a class project. Which is the best source for her to use to get started?

   A. thesaurus   C. dictionary
   B. Internet   D. glossary

12. The senior class trip will be a long bus drive from Miami to New York. What is the best source for travel plans?

   A. atlas   C. directory
   B. encyclopedia   D. bibliography

13. Don wants to find out what the weather will be like at the beach this weekend. What source would be the most helpful?

   A. glossary   C. thesaurus
   B. newspaper   D. encyclopedia

14. The International Food Festival is next week, and everyone must bring food from another country. Where will Fatima find a dish to make?

   A. schedule   C. index
   B. directory   D. recipe book

15. Where would you look for a list of the players on this year's All-American high school basketball team?

   A. table of contents   C. ad
   B. Internet   D. glossary

16. Where would you look for a picture of the current Miss America?

   A. encyclopedia   C. atlas
   B. Internet   D. glossary

17. Sondra wants to write to the publishing company of a book that she has. Where should she look for the address?

   A. index
   B. glossary
   C. table of contents
   D. title page

18. If the guide words <u>Bland - Blevins</u> were at the top of a page in the telephone book, which listing could be included on that page?

   A. Blair   C. Blanton
   B. Blalock   D. Bligen

19. If you were looking for the name Terrell in the telephone book, which words could you find at the top of the page?

   A. Tennison - Tharp
   B. Terryberry - Thisse
   C. Terza - Thackston
   D. Tener - Terranova

20. **Participating Dentists**

   Lisa Andu, DDS
   Stephen Campbell, DDS
   John Glasser, DDS
   Peggy King, DDS
   Paul McLendon, DDS
   D. Janet Taylor, DDS
   Gary Terkiewicz, DDS
   Leigh Thomaston, DDS
   Marysia Triggs, DDS
   Brenda Warner, DDS

   Harry K. Telzig will be added to the alphabetized list of participating dentists in the dental plan. His name will be added between

   A. Leigh Thomaston, DDS and Marysia Triggs, DDS.
   B. D. Janet Taylor, DDS and Gary Terkiewicz, DDS.
   C. Gary Terkiewicz and Leigh Thomaston, DDS.
   D. Marysia Triggs, DDS and Brenda Warner, DDS.

21. In the entertainment section of the newspaper, you would find information about

   A. where to purchase concert tickets.
   B. a missing dog.
   C. plane crashes.
   D. the editors' opinions.

22. In what section of the newspaper would you find opposing views on a current event?

   A. Front page
   B. Classified section
   C. Advertisements
   D. Editorial section

23. In the obituaries of a newspaper, you would find

   A. restaurant reviews.
   B. biographies on the recently deceased.
   C. news on medical advancements.
   D. information about basketball championships.

24. In what section of the newspaper would you find the latest department store sale?

   A. Classified section
   B. Advertisements
   C. Obituaries
   D. Front page

25. Which part of a book would you use to locate additional charts and graphs not found in the book's chapters?

   A. Appendix
   B. Glossary
   C. Table of contents
   D. Bibliography

26. The <u>title page</u> is the part of the book that gives information on

   A. page references for the names, places, and subjects in a book.
   B. the author, title, and publication of the book.
   C. books, articles, etc., used or referred to by an author.
   D. supplementary material not essential to the text itself.

27. Which part of a book would you use to locate the page numbers that discuss the Cuban Missile Crisis?

   A. Title page   C. Glossary
   B. Index   D. Appendix

28. Which part of a book would you use to find other writings on a specific subject referred to by the author?

   A. Preface   C. Glossary
   B. Appendix   D. Bibliography

29. If the guide words <u>Towing - Trailer</u> were at the top of a page in the yellow pages, which listing could be included on that page?

   A. Travel Agencies
   B. Tire Dealers
   C. Transmissions
   D. Toys

30. If you have the encyclopedia volume labeled <u>So-Sz</u>, which subject could you find in that volume?

   A. Race Relations
   B. Temperature
   C. Snow
   D. Spelling

Chapter 9

ANALYSIS OF LITERATURE

Analyzing literature improves your understanding of what you are reading. Then you can learn to think critically about reading selections taken from speeches, short stories, poems, plays, articles, essays, ads, and editorials. You will be taught how to analyze the following elements of literature:

1) **Argument and Fallacy**
2) **Propaganda**
3) **Author's Purpose**
4) **Structural Devices**
5) **Rhetorical Devices**
6) **Types of Literature**

In this chapter, you will be learning about these elements. You will also complete practice exercises about analyzing literature.

ARGUMENT AND FALLACY

An **argument** often presents opinions that have a positive or negative slant. A writer will use reasons to support a claim or assertion about a topic or issue. You may be asked to analyze an ad, article, or editorial taken from a newspaper or magazine. An **advertisement** tries to persuade you to purchase a product such as a car or a service such as trash collection. An **editorial** presents a viewpoint on a controversial issue, such as violence on television or raising the speed limits.

When you read a selection from a book, magazine, or newspaper, you will usually need to identify the statement that best describes the argument. Follow these tips for analyzing an argument:

Tips for Analyzing an Argument
1. **Identify the opinion or viewpoint on the issue.** It will generally appear near the beginning of the selection, but it may also appear at the end as a conclusion.
2. **Read the supporting reasons for the opinion.**
3. **Decide whether the reasons or examples support the argument.**

Hint 1: A **valid argument** contains good logic, solid evidence, or clear reasons and examples from the reading selection.

Hint 2: A **fallacy** or **false argument** contains poor logic, weak evidence, or faulty reasons and examples from the reading selection.

To identify the statement that best describes the argument, you should also learn the main kinds of fallacies used in arguments. **Fallacies** are information that try to falsely persuade you to accept an opinion or viewpoint about an issue.

Main Types of Fallacies

Name	Example
1. **Jumping to Conclusions -** a claim with little proof to support it.	Vote for the people's choice! Sun Soap is the best!
2. **Ad Hominem -** attacking the person rather than his or her ideas.	Tom dresses like a nerd! How could he run for president of the Student Council!
3. **Circular Argument -** part of an argument is used as evidence to support it.	Looks are more important than talent because looks mean everything.
4. **Testimonial -** famous persons endorse a product, even though they aren't experts.	Bill Cosby loves Jell-O. Robin Williams drives a Lexus.
5. **Either-Or Fallacy -** there are only two sides to an issue.	Either we eliminate all weapons from this earth, or we'll blow each other up!
6. **Glittering Generalizations -** unprovable praises	Our candidate is a "true American"

Now let's read some selections and answer questions about the arguments.

Metabolism refers to how the body burns energy. People with high metabolisms burn more calories than people with low metabolisms. Consequently, they have an easier time losing weight. One-half of the women and one-fourth of the men in the United States are trying to lose weight and become fit. The sad truth is that most of us will regain our weight in a year or less.

What's the real secret for losing weight and keeping it off? The answer is developing and maintaining a healthy metabolism. Here are some tips for improving your metabolism and melting away that extra fat:

1) **Drink plenty of cold water.** Filling up on water decreases the appetite. Three quarts of water each day are ideal.
2) **Don't skip meals, especially breakfast.** Eat small meals every two to three hours. In this way, carbohydrates and protein will not be converted into fat.
3) **Eat fat-burning foods.** Raw vegetables, whole grains, fruits, and legumes are your best choices. Consume fruits between meals for extra energy, so they won't be converted to fat.
4) **Exercise regularly.** Aerobic exercises like running and walking are best. Also try lifting weights - a good muscle builder and fat burner. Exercise before you eat. It will decrease your appetite and increase your metabolism.

1.   Which one of the following statements best describes the writer's argument?

   A.   The writer states that people with high metabolisms lose weight easier, which is an invalid argument.
   B.   The writer develops a valid argument.
   C.   The writer jumps to conclusions based on limited information.
   D.   The writer does not support the argument with valid reasons.

Rapidly Burn Off Pounds And Inches

   This is it! The diet pill researchers around the world have hailed for its powerful, quick-working ingredients that help people shed stubborn fat – fast! People can lose up to 5 pounds the first 48 hours without complicated calorie counting or suffering from biting hunger pains.

People Can Lose 10, 20, 50, Even 100 pounds!

Super Diet Pill Satisfies Need For Fast Action Without Strenuous Dieting

   So fast-working, people can see a dramatic difference in just two days. Users, even those with long-time weight problems, find they can burn off up to a pound of fat and fluid every five hours over a weekend alone.

50% Fat Loss In 14 To 21 days

   Incredibly, testing showed people lost 15, 20, 30, or more pounds without making major sacrifices or drastic changes! What's more, it works so fast that people shed as much as 50% of their fat in just two to three weeks.

---

2.   Which one of the following statements best describes the argument of the writer in the above selection?

   A.   The writer constructs a valid argument.
   B.   The writer explores only two sides of an issue.
   C.   The writer uses the personal testimony of famous people.
   D.   The writer jumps to a conclusion.

Responding to the Metabolism Passage

   To find the right answer for question 1, you must locate the statement that best describes the argument of the writer in the above selection. As you read the passage, you must decide whether the argument is valid, which is always one of your choices, or whether there are fallacies in the argument. **The best way to select your answer is to read each answer choice and see which one accurately describes the argument in this passage.**

The best answer for question 1 is B. The writer constructs a valid argument by presenting substantial evidence about the proven methods of increasing metabolism. Choice A is wrong because it is a known fact that individuals with higher metabolisms by definition burn their body's energy supply faster. Choice C is wrong because the passage provides a great deal of information to support the argument. Choice D is incorrect because the writer does offer valid reasons for the argument. These reasons are based on the widely accepted evidence about how the body metabolizes food.

Responding to the Diet Pill Passage

Choosing an answer for the second passage requires you to read the ad carefully.

First, you must identify the writer's opinion or viewpoint about losing weight.

Basically, the ad promotes a powerful diet pill that helps you shed pounds fast.

Secondly, you must review the supporting reasons to see whether the argument is valid or whether it is a fallacy.

Thirdly, you must find the statement that best describes the argument.

When you analyze the supporting reasons for this fast-working diet pill, you realize that the writer offers very limited information about the diet pill. Little proof is presented to support the claims. The writer never mentions the names of the diet pill researchers, the people who lost weight, or where or when the testing was done. Therefore, D is the best answer because the ad jumps to conclusions.

Choice A would be wrong because the supporting evidence about the diet pill is not well documented. Choice B is incorrect because the ad focuses on only the favorable aspects of the product. Choice C is wrong because no famous celebrities are quoted for anything in the passage.

PRACTICE 1: ARGUMENTS AND FALLACIES

Read each of the following selections. Check "Valid" if the all the sentences in the argument are valid and explain why the arguments are valid. Check "Fallacies" if one or more of the sentences in the argument are fallacies. Then list any fallacies and explain why they are fallacies.

1. When you bite into a Dreambar, you'll sail into a galaxy of gooey goodness. Chewing that rich chocolate center sends waves of delight zooming through you. And who can resist that peanuts and oatmeal wrapped around the outside. "That's why kids like Dreambars for snacks," says football linebacker Denzel Conner. "They provide that extra energy kids need to do their homework." Make your dreams come true. Have a Dreambar today!

    Valid _____

    Fallacies _____

    Explanation _____

    _____

    _____

2. There can be no question that Congress is more efficient than it was in its early days. Legislative business in both houses can now be conducted effectively; many weapons of obstruction that the rules once permitted have been eliminated. It is in the nature of a partisan body that some members will object to the manner in which the rules and procedures are applied. Congress would not be Congress – indeed, democracy would be in danger – if there were not complaints about how the institution was being run. But the long view yields the conclusion that, although Congress might conduct its business better in the future, it is operating more effectively now than it did in the past.

–from *To Make Laws* by James H. Hutson

Valid _____

Fallacies _____

Explanation _____

_____

_____

3. We either follow Trey Weiner, or we support Curtis Dornsky for district representative. Trey is a true leader who walks his talk. It doesn't matter that he wears old clothes and drives around in a beat-up pickup truck. He speaks for the people of this city. On the other hand, Curtis Dornsky wants the voters to focus on his good looks and his flashy Fifth Avenue suits. He talks about reducing taxes, but look how he dresses. He also drives a shiny new Lexus and a fancy Cadillac. Either you vote for the defender of the common people or the champion of the rich and famous. The other candidates just don't have a chance against these two competitors. When I vote next Tuesday, there's only one candidate I'll choose. His name is Trey Weiner.

– editorial in *The Wilson Gazette*

Valid _____

Fallacies _____

Explanation _____

_____

_____

4.   In the Catskills I found something I'd missed after four decades of living in cities: simple courtesy. Like a friendly wave, for example. It is unthinkable not to return one…Walt Meade, a naturalist who lives in Roxbury, on the Catskill's northern slope, says, "I was going to Grand Gorge when Jane Hubble drove by and waved. But I didn't see her till it was too late. The next time I saw her, she berated me, "I wasted a perfectly good wave on you, Walt Meade. And I don't know if I'm going to wave at you again." Time after time, stories of compassion come out of the Catskills. "When my dad's barn burned down, the neighbors put a new one up in three days." "When our daughter was killed, the neighbors just came in and took over." The genuineness of the Catskills calls out like a distant memory…

– Paraphrase from *National Geographic*

Valid _____

Fallacies _____

Explanation _____

_____

_____

5.   Doctors are a regular set of humbugs, and most of them are quacks. They go off to school and learn some recipes for curing diseases. Then they manage in one way or another to get the teachers in their school to give them a certificate, and then they'll go out into some town or village or city and rent some space over a drugstore and get some bones and an old skull and a lot of books and spread them around the room and call it an office. They put up a sign and call themselves doctors. Then they guess what your illness is and collect their money.

–from *Shams* by John S. Draper

Valid _____

Fallacies _____

Explanation _____

_____

_____

PRACTICE 2: ARGUMENT AND FALLACY

A.   Other Fallacies. Two other fallacies that are important are **False Cause** and **Ignoring the Question.** Find definitions and examples of these fallacies in an English or Language Arts book.

B. Reasons for Arguments. Mark either **Agree** or **Disagree** next to each statement. Then write reasons for your opinion. Exchange your opinion and the reasons for it with a partner or in a group. Then determine whether the argument is valid or whether it contains fallacies.

		Agree	Disagree
1.	A black cat crossing your path brings bad luck.	_____	_____
2.	Looks are more important than intelligence.	_____	_____
3.	Jeans and pants must be worn with belts.	_____	_____
4.	Students who cheat in school should be expelled.	_____	_____
5.	The speed limit should be increased.	_____	_____
6.	A school dress code is necessary.	_____	_____
7.	Money solves your problems.	_____	_____
8.	A high school diploma is important.	_____	_____
9.	Children are just like their parents.	_____	_____
10.	Television has too much violence.	_____	_____

C. Fallacies in Ads. Find examples of valid arguments and fallacies from this chapter in newspaper and magazine ads, articles, editorials, or television commercials. Then share your examples with the class and your teacher. See if they agree with your findings.

D. Perform Skits. In a small group, create a television advertisement for a product or service. Use scenes, props, posterboard, etc. to create a realistic presentation. Perform two versions of the advertisement, one with a valid argument and one with fallacies. The class then analyzes each version to determine which is a valid argument and which has fallacies. Discuss your findings.

PROPAGANDA

A writing that purposely tries to influence others is called **propaganda**. It is found in editorials, magazines, television commercials, political statements, and everyday conversation.

TYPES OF PROPAGANDA

Testimonials – a frequently used technique in which famous persons endorse a product even though they are <u>not</u> qualified as experts.

Example: Chuck Norris endorses anti-perspirant. Michael Jordan endorses cereal.

Transfer — a technique in which the public's feelings on one thing are somehow connected to another unrelated thing.

> **Example:** "If federal employees are hired based on their political membership, then this nation is not truly a democracy." Democracy, rule by popular consent of the governed, is not related to one employer's hiring policy.

In-Crowd Appeal — a kind of flattery which encourages viewers to identify with an admired, envied group.

> **Example:** A super model stands in front of a new sports car. The viewers are supposed to connect the desirability of the woman to the desirability of the new car.

Bandwagon — a technique in which the reader is made to feel that a great movement is beginning. The reader would be an idiot or an enemy if he/she does not join the movement.

> **Example:** "Millions of people sign on to the Internet everyday and receive the latest information. If you don't get on-line, you will be left behind." Do you have to jump on this bandwagon? No qualifications are required to put information on the Internet.

PRACTICE 3: RECOGNIZING PROPAGANDA

Read the following passages. Write "balanced" if the statement seems to be truthful or fair. Write "propaganda" if the statement seems to distort or slant information. Then explain your choices.

1. Buy Youth-filled Vitamin E supplements today. They're going to make you look younger and feel happier! Over one hundred thousand people are already taking advantage of this supplement to look years younger. Why shouldn't you?

    _____

    _____

2. Do you want the state government to tax even more of your income? Don't let greedy Uncle Sam pocket more of your money. Write to your congressman today, and send a "no more taxes" message to the leaders of our state.

    _____

    _____

3. Bring your friends to see the latest Laser Light Show at the Gigantic Gold Dome. Penny Starway, the best new voice in country music, was thrilled: "This show has the prettiest lights and images I have ever seen! If you want to see the best in laser technology, come on down to the dome."

    _____

    _____

4. There is still a great deal of controversy about the future of the space program. While some people believe it is a waste of much needed funds, others point to the great scientific and technological advances that have resulted from the exploration of space. Supporters of the program most frequently cite the wide uses of microprocessors as one of the major contributions to space-related research.

   _____

   _____

5. The County Government meeting broke up after a long debate. The man's supporters claim he is the duly elected representative of the people and should be allowed to take his seat on the council. His opponents disputed this, saying that his previous protests of council activities disqualified him from holding public office.

   _____

   _____

6. When looking for the best travel agency, try Globe World Travel. Thousands of satisfied customers have been on the tours we offer. Imagine a moonlight walk in Paris, a lion safari in East Africa, or a shopping spree in Singapore! Many of the nation's top business leaders choose Globe World Travel for their vacations. Why don't you?

   _____

   _____

7. Grace Chisolm, the well-known newscaster, has this to say about the Cheetah XR71A: "It drives like a sea breeze. I can definitely tell this car is going to redefine the future of the automotive industry." Like Ms. Chisolm, we at Sunrise Motors believe this sports car looks better, rides better, and feels better than anything else in its class.

   _____

   _____

8. I stand as firm as the rock of Gibraltar on the right that women have to shape the thoughts, socially and politically, of the world. They can make our country better and purer, just as they appreciate their own rights. I am in favor of women's rights—in their rights to rise up in the majesty of the nature their Creator gave them and emancipate themselves from the foolish fashions and sentiments of the age. When they do rise, they will be more respected by all mankind than all the rulers of the earth from Adam down to the present day.

                                            – Clarissa's speech in *Shams* by John S. Draper

   _____

   _____

AUTHOR'S PURPOSE

Author's purpose refers to the reason why an author writes a selection. Knowing the author's purpose helps us to better understand a reading passage. For example, if the author is telling a story with characters, plot, and setting, then the author's purpose is **to relate an adventure**. Technically, this purpose is **to narrate**. A **narrative** means to tell a story through a series of related events.

You should become familiar with the various reasons an author communicates information in a reading selection. These purposes are listed below with definitions and examples.

Purpose	Definition	Reading Selection
To inform	To present facts and details	"Ocean Fishes"
To entertain	To amuse or offer enjoyment	"Time I Slipped in the Mud"
To persuade	To urge action on an issue	"Raise Penalties for Polluters"
To instruct	To teach concepts and facts	"Tips For Healthy Living"
To describe feelings	To communicate emotions through words	"When My Dog Died"
To create suspense	To convey uncertainty	"Will Tom Win the Race?"
To motivate	To incite	"You Can Lose Weight!"
To cause doubt	To be skeptical	"Are Adults Responsible?"
To describe an event	To narrate	"My Trip to Mobile"
To teach a lesson	To furnish knowledge	"Mastering Exponents"
To introduce a character	To describe a person's traits	"First Look at Captain Nemo"
To create a mood	To establish atmosphere	"Gloom in the House of Usher"
To relate an adventure	To tell an exciting story	"Lost in a Cave"
To share a personal experience	To tell about an event in your life	"The Time I Learned to Share"

PRACTICE 4: AUTHOR'S PURPOSE

Directions: Based on the previous list of author's purposes, identify the author's purpose for the following reading passages. Then discuss your choices with your class or the instructor.

1.   The fire crackled musically. From it swelled light smoke. Overhead the foliage moved softly. The leaves, with their faces turned toward the blaze, were colored shifting hues of silver, often edged with red. Far off to the right, through a window in the forest, could be seen a handful of stars lying, like glittering pebbles, on the black level of the night.

                                                      – Stephen Crane <u>Red Badge of Courage</u>

   A.   To describe an event   C.   To persuade
   B.   To create a mood   D.   To teach a lesson

2.   The blood carries oxygen from the lungs to each cell in the body. In addition, the blood carries carbon dioxide from the cells to the lungs where it is expelled as a waste product. Nutrients like protein and glucose depend on the blood for their dispersal throughout the body.

   A.   To motivate   C.   To relate an adventure
   B.   To entertain   D.   To inform

3.   **Letter to His Son**

      The South, in my opinion, has been aggrieved by the acts of the North, as you say. I feel the aggression and am willing to take every proper step for redress. It is the principle I fight for, not individual or private benefit. As an American citizen, I take great pride in my country, her prosperity and institutions, and would defend any state if her rights were invaded. But I can anticipate no greater calamity for the country than a dissolution of the Union. It would be an accumulation of all the evils we complain of, and I am willing to sacrifice everything but honor for its preservation. I hope, therefore, that all constitutional means will be exhausted before there is a resort to force.

                                                      – Gen. Robert E. Lee, Jan. 23, 1861

   A.   To introduce a character   C.   To persuade
   B.   To cause doubt   D.   To entertain

4.      Columbus' own successful voyage in 1492 prompted a papal bull dividing the globe between rivals Spain and Portugal. But the Portuguese protested that the pope's line left them too little Atlantic sea room for their voyages to India. The line was shifted 270 leagues westward in 1494 by the Treaty of Tordesillas. Thus, wittingly or not, the Portuguese gained Brazil and gave their language to more than half the people of South America.

   A.   To motivate   C.   To relate an adventure
   B.   To describe feelings   D.   To inform

5.   At the start of every school year, each student is given a handbook that lists all the school rules. The conduct code in our high school requires that students be respectful and responsible toward each other and their teachers. When disruptive behavior threatens the safety of the students or teachers, the school administrator will determine a penalty which will be communicated to the parents.

     Yesterday, between classes at our high school, David spray painted the back of Sam's new leather jacket. Ignoring the pleas of students and teachers, Sam chased David down the hall, wrestled him to the floor, and punched him in the stomach twice. Students nearby quickly grabbed Sam and David and pulled them apart just as Mr. Freel, the principal, arrived on the scene. Based on what students and teachers observed, Mr. Freel suspended Sam and David for ten days.

A.   To persuade
B.   To create a mood
C.   To teach a lesson
D.   To describe feelings

6.   Twelve-year-old Nadia told us a story that seemed unbelievable but true about her family's journey to the United States. In Romania, her father was involved in the politics of Romania, opposing the communist regime of Ceausescu. Because of death threats made against her family, Nadia and her family had to leave the country in the middle of the night. They had arranged for a boat to meet them so they could sail the Black Sea to freedom in Bulgaria. Because they left in a hurry, they took nothing with them except their clothes. The boat never came, so they swam into the sea until a boat from Bulgaria discovered her family swimming. All of them survived the swim except for Nadia's little brother, Dimitry. From that country, they obtained refugee status and traveled to the United States. This experience made Nadia and ourselves very thankful for the lives we have here.

A.   To instruct
B.   To describe an event
C. To cause doubt
D. To persuade

7.   During Napoleon's war with England, both England and France seized neutral ships and goods. In addition, they were conscripting United States merchant sailors into their navies, enraging the people of the United States. In August 1810, Napoleon publicly repealed his previous decrees and declared that neutral ships could freely trade in France without risk of confiscation or conscription. President Madison believed Napoleon's words. When Britain refused to promise the same thing, Congress declared war on England and began invading Canada, starting the War of 1812.

A.   To inform
B.   To describe an event
C.   To relate an adventure
D.   To persuade

8.   Hand grippers can help give your arms those bulging biceps you're after, but only if they offer enough resistance. If you can squeeze them repeatedly for one to two minutes, and your hands don't get tired, they're too weak for you. You can keep buying stronger ones or make something at home that can do the same job.

A.   To instruct
B.   To persuade
C.   To describe an event
D.   To entertain

9.   There was no escape from the severe regimen Ida was compelled to follow. The work she had to do, the rules she had to observe. Breakfast at seven-thirty sharp because the store had to be opened by her father at eight, which meant rising at seven; luncheon at twelve-thirty, so as to satisfy her father and her own noon recess hour which was completely filled in by this; dinner invariably at six-thirty because there were many things, commercial and social, which fell upon the shoulders of William Zobel at night. And between whiles, from four to six on weekdays and later from seven to eight at night, as well as all day Saturdays, store duty in her father's store.

– Theodore Dreiser

  A.   To relate an adventure   C.   To persuade
  B.   To introduce a character   D.   To teach a lesson

10.   My family came to America in 1985. No one spoke a word of English. In school, I was in an English as a Second language class with other foreign-born children. My class was so overcrowded that it was impossible for the teacher to teach English properly. I dreaded going to school each morning because of the fear of not understanding what people were saying and the fear of being laughed at.

– Yu-Lan (Mary) Ying, an eyewitness account about learning English

  A.   To cause doubt   C.   To share a personal experience
  B.   To entertain   D.   To create suspense

PRACTICE 5: AUTHOR'S PURPOSE

Directions: In a group or on your own, review 6 passages from a newspaper or magazine. Using the list of purposes from this section, identify the author's purpose in each selection. Exchange your passages with a classmate to see if he/she identifies the same purpose. Then discuss your findings with the class or with your teacher.

STRUCTURAL DEVICES

     Structural Devices refer to elements that help you understand a story, poem, or play. In this part of the chapter, you will be learning about these structural devices. These devices are **plot, character, setting, point of view, mood,** and **theme** or **interpretation.**

     Now let's review these structural devices and some of their features. Study them and then apply what you learn to some sample passages of literature.

Setting and Its Features

setting	- includes the <u>place</u> and <u>time</u> in a story. The setting of Poe's *Cask of Amontillado* is a murky wine cellar.
place	- location where a story takes place. The Uncle Remus tales of Joel Chandler Harris take place in rural Georgia.
time	- when the story occurs. Crane's *Red Badge of Courage* takes place during the Civil War.

Plot and Its Features

plot - pattern of events in a story leading to a conclusion. The plot of *Moby-Dick* centers around Captain Ahab's pursuit of a great white whale.

climax - the turning point in a story. In Poe's "Fall of the House of Usher," the climax occurs when the reader discovers that his dead sister is alive.

conflict - the struggle between different forces in a story. These struggles can be with nature, with one's self, with others, or with society. In Jack London's *Call of the Wild*, the dog Buck struggles with nature and society until he joins a wolf pack.

foreshadowing - clues or hints of events to come. In *The Wizard of Oz*, a harsh wind blows through the trees before the wicked witch appears.

suspense - anticipation about what will happen in a story. In "Little Red Riding Hood," we worry about what the wolf will do to the little girl.

Character and Its Features

character - an imaginary person that appears in a literary work. Celie and Nettie are the main characters in Alice Walker's *The Color Purple*.

antagonist - an opponent or rival of the hero. The antagonists in Hemingway's *Old Man and the Sea* are the sharks.

dialogue - conversation between two people in a story. Huck and Jim engage in many dialogues as they travel along the Mississippi River in Mark Twain's *Huckleberry Finn*.

narrator - the person telling a story. In Angelou's *I Know Why the Caged Bird Sings*, the narrator is a young girl who is also the main character.

protagonist - the hero or main character. The protagonists are Romeo and Juliet in Shakespeare's famous play of the same name.

Point of View and Its Features

point of view - the perspective from which a writer tells a story. Harper Lee writes *To Kill A Mockingbird* from the point of view of Scout, a young girl living in a small town in Alabama.

first person point of view - narrator tells the story from the "I" point of view. In *House On Mango Street*, Esperanza tells her story as the main character.

third person point of view - writer tells story describing characters as "he," "she," or "they." Irving's *Rip Van Winkle* is an example of this point of view.

Mood and Its Features

mood - the atmosphere of a literary work. The writer often creates a mood through details in the setting and plot. The mood is also a feeling or impression conveyed to the reader in the work of literature. In "The Cask of Amontillado," Poe creates a mood of mystery and gloom. A mood of humor and mischief pervades *Tom Sawyer* by Mark Twain.

Types of Moods (Learn what these words mean.)

angry	dramatic	mocking	sad
anxious	fearful	optimistic	satirical
boring	happy	pessimistic	suspenseful
calm	humorous	poetic	sympathetic
cynical	lighthearted	relaxed	tragic
depressed	lofty	threatening	remorseful
lackadaisical	gloomy	tense	nervous
hysterical	lethargic	pensive	tearful
expectant	disgusting	macabre	beguiling

Theme or Interpretation

theme or interpretation - the message or meaning in a story, poem, or play. The reader is then able to gain insights into literature and life. The theme of Paul Laurence Dunbar's "We Wear the Mask" is that we all must wear masks that hide our true selves. One interpretation of Kate Chopin's "Story of an Hour" is that life is full of surprises that can kill you.

Tips for Understanding Structural Devices

1. Study the definitions and examples of plot, character, setting, point of view, mood, and theme from this section.

2. Complete the following practice passages.

3. Apply them to the exercises at the end of this chapter.

PRACTICE 6: STRUCTURAL DEVICES

Directions: Read each of the following passages. Then answer the questions about structural devices.

20,000 Leagues Under The Sea

When I got up, I saw that Captain Nemo and his first mate were on the platform. They were examining the ship's position, exchanging several words in their incomprehensible language.

Here was our situation. Two miles to starboard rose Gueboroar Island, whose coast extended from north to west like an immense arm. Toward the south and east, we could already make out the tops of several coral formations which the ebb tide was beginning to uncover. We had gone aground at high tide, which would make it difficult to refloat the *Nautilus*. Nevertheless the ship had suffered no damage, for her hull was solidly joined. But even though it could never sink or spring a leak, there was a serious danger of its remaining grounded forever on these reefs, and that would be the end of Captain Nemo's submarine.

I was thinking of all this when the captain came over looking as cool and calm as ever. He seemed neither disturbed or unhappy.

"An accident?" I asked.

"No, an incident," he replied.

"But an incident," I retorted, "that will force you once again to live on that land you have been fleeing!"

– Jules Verne

1. The story is told from the point of view of

    A. the first mate.   C. first person narrator.
    B. Captain Nemo.   D. the third person.

2. At the end of the selection, the mood is

    A. tense.   C. relaxed.
    B. happy.   D. boring.

3. The main conflict in this passage is a struggle with

    A. society.   C. Captain Nemo.
    B. one's self.   D. nature.

4. The setting of this passage is

    A. near the sea.   C. under the sea.
    B. on a reef.   D. on an island.

5. The best statement of the plot in this passage is that

    A. the Nautilus ran aground near shore, so Captain Nemo and the narrator argue.
    B. Captain Nemo and the narrator disagree about where the Nautilus will land.
    C. Captain Nemo found a submarine near Gueboroar Island and wants to own it.
    D. the Nautilus will be sailing out to sea after a few days of rest.

The Hermit's Hut

Thomas, bearing the unconscious monk in his arms, and somewhat faint from his own wounds, staggered in the direction of the chiming bell. He had but a short distance to go from the scene of combat to the tiny chapel, where a hermit was saying his prayers.

At the sound of Thomas' clattering footsteps, the hermit turned with a start and hastened toward him disclosing a kindly face lit by large brown eyes.

"Brother," said Thomas, "here is a holy man badly wounded for my sake. I beg you to use your skill with herbs to heal him."

The hermit responded quickly and led them into his chambers. Thomas carried the monk with tenderness and laid him down tenderly on the hermit's couch.

"I best be alone with him," said the hermit. "Go outside and wait 'till I come to you. I think the brother is not wounded unto death."

Thomas went out obediently as the good monk faintly called his name. "Be not troubled," said the hermit. "He does not know that he calls you. He is delirious."

Alone with the monk, the hermit began to look at the wound. The hermit looked at the soft white flesh of the shoulder with surprise. Then on impulse, he removed the hood and confirmed his thought. Long hair cascaded over the monk's delicate face. The hermit paused in dismay.

6.   What is the setting?

   A.   a tiny chapel   C.   a doctor's quarters
   B.   a cabin   D.   a house

7.   The mood of this story is

   A.   humorous.   C.   relaxed.
   B.   dramatic.   D.   suspenseful.

8.   Who is **not** involved in the dialogue of this story?

   A.   the hermit   C.   Sir Lancelot
   B.   the enemy   D.   the monk

9.   What is the theme of this story?

   A.   the joy of life   C.   unexpected surprise
   B.   death is coming   D.   falling in love

The Case of the Missing Video Game

Brian, Jeremy, Katie, and Allison were taking turns playing Brian's video game, *Sewer Monsters*. Allison told Katie, "You know, Katie, what's so great about us is that we share everything in common."

"Will you girls please play instead of talk?" Brian asked. The girls kept talking, so Brian and Jeremy went outside to shoot hoops. When they returned from the basketball game, Katie was doing her nails in her bedroom, and Allison was playing the video game. Allison went into the kitchen to grab a snack. Brian and Jeremy took this as an opportunity to go in the living room and play *Sewer Monsters*.

However, the cartridge was missing from the game system.

"Girls!" they shouted. "The game is missing."

"Don't look at me," Allison said. "I just went into the kitchen." Allison's small purse, however, had a suspicious bulge in it.

"You know I couldn't have taken it," Katie said. "My nails are still wet, and I wasn't in this room when you two started shouting."

"I just don't like being accused," Allison said. "Come on, Katie, let's go outside." Slinging their purses on their shoulders, the two girls went outside together.

When the girls came back in, Jeremy and Brian both looked upset. Brian said, "OK, Allison, empty your purse."

Looking very mad, Allison said, "Fine then!" She turned her purse upside down, and there was no cartridge in the mess on the table.

Jeremy and Brian looked at each other and said, "Then who has the game cartridge?"

10. What is the best statement of the plot in this passage?

   A. Four siblings decide to play video games, basketball, and do their nails.
   B. The four siblings try to decide who took the video game *Sewer Monsters*.
   C. Brian and Jeremy play *Sewer Monsters* and basketball well.
   D. Allison and Katie agree to share everything in common, including video games.

11. What is the setting of this story?

   A. a school lunchroom   C. a home
   B. a computer store   D. a video arcade

A Fishing Trip

The traffic began moving again. Josh was glad to be finished building houses in Spartanburg. Now he was ready to relax for a couple of weeks in the Blue Ridge Mountains. The drive home would take about two hours on Interstate 26.

When Josh got home, he'd pack the tent, sleeping bags, food, and cooking gear in the truck. Then he'd pick up his son, David. They'd be together for the whole weekend in a secluded mountain woodland with no one around for miles. They'd fish the streams and rivers with fly rods. The cool air and water would refresh his mind and spirit. Josh could already smell the freshly caught trout sizzling over an open fire.

12. From which point of view is the story told?

   A. first person   C. David
   B. second person   D. third person

13. Who is the protagonist in the story?

   A. David   C. narrator
   B. Josh   D. the mountains

206

14. The mood in this story is

    A. humorous.   C. suspenseful.
    B. sad.   D. relaxed.

15. Which statement best expresses the theme of the story?

    A. The best fishing is trout fishing.
    B. Josh builds houses for a living.
    C. Josh and David are going for a fishing trip this weekend.
    D. Everyone needs time to relax away from home.

PRACTICE 7: STRUCTURAL DEVICES

A. **Passage Practice.** Read this passage from *The Red Badge of Courage*. Identify the **plot, character (s), setting, point of view, mood, and theme** in the passage. Then compare your answers with your classmates.

> Upon his fellows he beamed tenderness and good will. "Gee! ain't it hot, hey?" he said affably to a man who was polishing his streaming face with his coat sleeves.
> "You bet!" said the other, grinning sociably. "I never seen such dumb hotness." He sprawled out luxuriously on the ground. "Gee, yes! An' I hope we don't have more fightin' till a week from Monday."
> There were some handshakings and deep speeches with men whose features were familiar, but with whom the youth now felt the bonds of tired hearts. He helped a cursing comrade to bind up a wound of the shin.
> But, of a sudden, cries of amazement broke out along the ranks of the new regiment. "Here they come ag'in! Here they come ag'in!" The man who had sprawled upon the ground started up and said, "Gosh!"
> The youth turned quick eyes upon the field. He discerned forms begin to swell in masses out of a distant wood. He again saw the tilted flag speeding forward.
> The shells, which had ceased to trouble the regiment for a time, came swirling again, and exploded in the grass or among the leaves of the trees. They looked to be strange war flowers bursting into fierce bloom.

B. **Team Activity.** Review 1 or 2 stories or plays you have read in class. Each team writes a **structural device** on the front of 5 × 8 cards and an **example** of the device from the literature selection on the back of the cards. The leader flashes either side of the card to the opposing team, and team members must identify the other side. For instance, if the leader flashed an example, the team members would have to identify the structural device.

C. **Mood.** Review the types of moods learned in this chapter. Which ones would accurately describe the mood in the short stories and poems in your literature book. Which types of moods would apply to these selections?

D. **Theme.** Divide your class into teams. Then focus on 3 or 4 stories or poems that all your classmates have read. On 5 × 8 cards, write both valid and invalid themes. Then shuffle the cards. A quizmaster flashes a card before each team. The team decides whether it will support or reject the theme, giving reasons for the answer. The team with the most points is the winner.

E. **Literature Practice.** Read or listen to several of your favorite short stories or poems or some from the list below. Then answer the accompanying questions about structural devices.

Short Stories

Poe's "Masque of the Red Death"
London's "To Build a Fire"
Thurber's "Secret Life of Walter Mitty"
Henry's "The Gift of the Magi"

Poems

Poe's "The Raven"
Brooks "The Bean Eaters"
Orteiz "My Father's Song"
Shakespeare's "All the World is a Stage"

Questions

1. What is the plot? What are the conflicts? What is the climax? Do any events foreshadow the outcome or build suspense?

2. Who are the characters? Who is the protagonist? Who is the antagonist? Is there a narrator? Is there dialogue? Why is it important?

3. How do the setting and mood affect the plot and characters?

4. What is the theme of the story or poem? Would you change the ending? Why? Why not?

RHETORICAL DEVICES

Rhetorical devices are ways of expressing ideas that are unusual. Writers create rhetorical devices to achieve special effects in a passage. Authors achieve these effects by the way they arrange their words.

In this part of the chapter, you'll be learning about rhetorical devices. These devices can be found in **poetry, stories, essays, speeches, editorials, and advertisements.** Here are some important rhetorical devices used in literature.

alliteration	**onomatopoeia**
analogy	**personification**
euphemisms	**rhyme**
hyperbole	**simile**
metaphor	

Take some time now to learn about these rhetorical devices. Study these devices. Then you'll apply what you've learned to some sample passages.

Rhetorical Devices

alliteration - the repetition of the same consonants in lines of poetry or prose. Examples: 1) "Droning a drowsy syncopated tune,"– Langston Hughes (repetition of d and o sounds). 2) "I like to see it lap the miles. / And lick the valleys up," – Emily Dickinson (repetition of l sounds)

---

analogy	- a comparison between two things or ideas. Examples: comparing life to a journey, comparing students in a school to the members of a family
euphemisms	- using mild words to describe something instead of offensive ones. Examples: 1) **passed away** for died 2) **perspire** for sweat 3) **restroom** for bathroom 4) **sanitation engineer** for trash man
hyperbole	- exaggeration to create an effect. Examples: 1) "I can outrun, outjump, outshoot, outbrag, and outfight any man..." *Mike Fink's Brag.* 2) It was raining cats and dogs.
metaphor	- direct comparison between two unlike things without using the words "like" or "as." Examples: 1) The sun was a ball of fire. 2) "Life is but an empty dream!" Longfellow
onomatopoeia	- words whose sound suggests their meaning. Examples: 1) **splash, buzz, hiss, boom** 2) "The moan of doves in immemorial elms; / And murmuring of innumerable bees," Tennyson
personification	- giving human qualities to something not human. Examples: 1) "As she sang softly at the evil face of the full moon." Jean Toomer 2) "The oak trees whispered softly in the night breeze." John Steinbeck
rhyme	- occurs when the last words in lines of poetry have the same sounds. Examples: 1) "The old horse thrust his long head out, / And grave with wonder gazed about:" Whittier (**out** and **about** rhyme.) 2) "Happy the man who, safe on shore, / Now trims, at home, his evening fire; / Unmov'd, he hears the tempests roar, / That on the tufted groves expire:" "The Hurricane" by Philip Freneau (rhymes are on **shore/roar** and **fire/expire**)
simile	- comparison between two things using "**like**" or "**as**." Examples: 1) "Sometimes I feel **like** a motherless child" - African-American Spiritual 2) "My love is **like** a red, red rose" Robert Burns 3) Free **as** a bird

Tips for Understanding Rhetorical Devices

1. **Study the definitions and examples of:**

    alliteration, analogy, euphemisms, hyperbole, metaphor, onomatopoeia, personification, rhyme, and simile.

2. **Complete the following practice passages.**

3. **Apply them to the exercises at the end of this chapter.**

PRACTICE 8: RHETORICAL DEVICES

For practice, read each of the following passages. Then answer the questions about rhetorical devices.

1   You ought to see my Cindy
2   She lives way down south;
3   She's so sweet the honey bees
4   Swarm around her mouth.
5   Oh, Cindy is a pretty girl.
6   Cindy is a peach;
7   She threw her arms around my neck.
8   And hung on like a leech.
9   And if I were a sugar tree
10 Standing in the town
11 Every time my Cindy passed
12 I'd shake some sugar down.

– Traditional Folk Song

1.   Write down the words that **rhyme** in this song. _____

_____

2.   Which of the following lines from the song contain a **hyperbole?**

  A.   lines 1-2   C.   lines 5-6
  B.   lines 3-4   D.   lines 9-10

3.   Which of the following lines are an example of a **metaphor?**

  A.   line 5   C.   line 7
  B.   line 6   D.   line 8

4.   Which of the following lines are an example of a **simile?**

  A.   line 5   C.   line 7
  B.   line 6   D.   line 8

5.   Cite some examples of **alliteration** in the song. _____

_____

Common Sense

(In 1776, Thomas Paine wrote this paragraph urging Americans to fight for independence from England.)

1   "The heart that feels not now is dead; the blood of his children will curse his cowardice
2   who shrinks back at a time when a little might have saved the whole, and made them
3   happy. I love the man that can smile in trouble, that can gather strength from distress, and

4   grow brave by reflection. 'Tis the business of little minds to shrink; but he whose heart is
5   firm, and whose conscience approves his conduct, will pursue his principles unto death.
6   My own line of reasoning is to myself as straight and clear as a ray of light. Not all the
7   treasures of the world, so far as I believe, could have induced me to support an offensive
8   war, for I think it murder; but if a thief breaks into my house, burns and destroys my
9   property, and kills or threatens to kill me, or those that are in it, and to "bind me in all
10   cases whatsoever" to his absolute will, am I to suffer it?

– Thomas Paine *Common Sense*

6.   List examples of **alliteration** in the passage. _____

_____

_____

7.   Which lines in the passage contain an **analogy?**

    A.   1-2   C.   5-7
    B.   3-4   D.   8-10

8.   In your own words, describe the analogy. _____

_____

9.   Which line in the passage is an example of **personification?**

    A.   1   C.   3
    B.   2   D.   6

10.   Explain why your choice is a personification. _____

_____

11.   Which line in the passage is an example of a **simile?**

    A.   5   C.   7
    B.   6   D.   8

We Wear the Mask

1   We wear the mask that grins and lies,
2   It hides our cheeks and shades our eyes, –
3   This debt we pay to human guile;
4   With torn and bleeding hearts we smile,
5   And mouth with myriad subtleties.

6   Why should the world be over-wise,
7   In counting all our tears and sighs?
8   Nay, let them only see us, while
9   We wear the mask.

```
10    We smile, but O great Christ, our cries
11    To thee from tortured souls arise.
12    We sing, but oh the clay is vile
13    Beneath our feet, and long the mile;
14 .  But let the world dream otherwise,
15         We wear the mask!
```

– Paul Laurence Dunbar

12.   Line 4 of this poem is an example of _____.

13.   What does the author personify in line 14? _____

14.   Cite two examples of alliteration in the first stanza. _____

_____

15.   Why are "sighs" (line 7) and "cries" (line 10) examples of onomatopoeia? _____

_____

_____

Tips for Answering Questions About Structural and Rhetorical Devices

1.   **Read the literary selection at least twice.**

2.   **Try to summarize the selection in your own words.**

3.   **Decide which answer best describes the structural or rhetorical device you are asked to find.**

4.   **Choose your answer, and then confirm it by going back to the selection.**

PRACTICE 9:   RHETORICAL DEVICES

A.   **Passage Practice.** Locate rhetorical devices in poems or stories from your literature book. Identify **alliteration, analogy, euphemism, hyperbole, metaphor, onomatopoeia, personification, rhyme,** and **simile** in any passage. Then compare your answers with your classmates.

B.   **Media Search.** Find examples of rhetorical devices in magazines, newspapers, ads, poetry, stories, speeches, or editorials. Clip them out and attach them to a paper summarizing the use of each device in 1-2 sentences. Exchange your examples with a partner or in a group. Then see if they can find the rhetorical device without looking at your answers.

C. Creative Writing. Write a poem based on your reflections of photos or paintings. Then create metaphors, similes, onomatopoeia, hyperbole, etc. from your reflections. For example, if you write a poem about life, you might begin "Life is a roller coaster." Or using alliteration, you could describe a photo of a donut as "Donuts are delightfully delicious."

D. Team Activity. Do an activity like Practice 7B with rhetorical devices from poetry.

E. Collage. Create a collage based on the statement: _____ is like _____. (Examples: Life is like _____; Friday is like _____; etc.) Cut out pictures that reflect your feelings on the subject. Then paste them on a posterboard and describe your poem collage to the class.

TYPES OF LITERATURE

Writers use many different forms of writing to communicate their messages. Some of these forms have been used for centuries, while others are more recent inventions.

Fiction — Narrative writing drawn from the imagination rather than from history or fact. The term is most frequently associated with novels and short stories. Examples are many. They vary from "The Lady or the Tiger?" to *Gulliver's Travels*.

Nonfiction — factual writing which is meant to inform the reader. Examples include newspaper or magazine articles and speeches.

Biography — a written account of a person's life; a life history. Examples include William Roper's *Life of Sir Thomas Moore* and Kroeber's *Ishi, Last of His Tribe*.

Autobiography — The story of a person's life as written by that person. One famous example is Helen Keller's *The Story of My Life*.

Fantasy — a written work that takes place in an exaggerated world with bizarre characters in it. Example: J.R.R. Tolkien's *Lord of the Rings* trilogy

Science Fiction — a written work in which scientific facts, assumptions, or hypotheses form the basis of adventures in the future, on other planets, or in different dimensions of time and space. Example: Ray Bradbury's *Fareinheit 451*

Mystery — A term used to designate a work in which mystery or terror plays a controlling part. Example: Sherlock Holmes's *Hound of the Baskervilles*

Romance — written works describing extravagant places, remote locations, heroic events, and passionate love. Examples: Hawthorne's *The Scarlet Letter*, Fitzgerald's *The Great Gatsby*

Allegory — a device used to convey a deeper meaning based on the actions of the characters. It is considered an extended metaphor comparing a story with another meaning outside of the story. Examples include the parables of Jesus, John Bunyan's *Pilgrim's Progress*, and Orwell's *Animal Farm*.

Novel — any extended fictional narrative almost always written in prose. Examples: James F. Cooper's *The Last of the Mohicans* and Stephen King's *It*

Short Story	- A story varying in length from 500 to 15,000 words. Generally, these stories contain a plot and reveal the characters in the story through actions and thoughts. Examples of these include Chaucer's *Canterbury Tales*, Mark Twain's "The Celebrated Jumping Frog of Calaveras County," and Richard Connel's "The Most Dangerous Game."
Epic	- a long narrative poem in elevated style presenting characters of high position in adventures, always including a central heroic figure. Examples include Homer's *The Odyssey*, and the Old English *Beowulf*.
Fable	- a brief tale told to point a moral. The characters are frequently animals, but people and inanimate objects can also be central. Examples include George Orwell's *Animal Farm* and Joel C. Harris's *Uncle Remus* stories.
Tall Tale	- a humorous tale common on the North American frontier. Tall tales use realistic detail and a literal manner to explain seemingly impossible deeds and events. Usually, these events are accomplished by a superhuman character. Examples include the legends of Paul Bunyan and Davy Crockett.
Poem	- concentrated words expressing strong feeling. A *poem* can also be spoken. It contains significant meaning, sense impressions, and figurative language. Poets write poems for emotional pleasure in stanzas and for the beauty of the word combinations. Examples include "Psalm 51" and Robert Frost's "The Road Less Traveled."
Folk Tale	- a simple story set in the past. These stories contain animal, human, or superhuman characters. Supernatural events are included which resolve conflicts. Often, events in folk tales happen in threes. A good selection of folk tales can be found in *Grimm's Fairy Tales*.
Myth	- a story with supernatural characters and events used to explain religious beliefs or rituals. Myths are also written to explain certain natural phenomena. The journey of the Greek goddess Persephone to the underworld, for example, is used to explain the changing of the seasons.
Legend	- a story associated with some period in the history of a people or nation. The story is written to glorify a human hero or an object that has significance to a people. Examples include *The Iliad* and *The Odyssey*.

PRACTICE 10: TYPES OF LITERATURE

Read the following passages. Circle the type of literature you are reading, and then explain why you selected your answer.

Eight Cousins

Running down the long hall, she peeped out at both doors, but saw nothing feathered except a draggle-tailed chicken under a burdock leaf. She listened again, and the sound seemed to be in the house. Away she went, much excited by the chase, and following the changeful song, it led her to the china-closet door.

"In there? How funny!" she said. But when she entered, not a bird appeared except the everlastingly kissing swallows on the Canton china that lined the shelves. All of a sudden Rose's face brightened, and, softly opening the slide, she peered into the kitchen. But the music had stopped, and all she saw was a girl in a blue apron scrubbing the hearth. Rose stared about her for a minute, and then asked abruptly

"Did you hear that mocking-bird?"

"I should call it a phebe-bird," answered the girl, looking up with a twinkle in her black eyes.

"Where did it go?"

"It is here still."

"In my throat. Do you want to hear it?"

"Oh, yes! I'll come in." And Rose crept through the slide to the wide shelf on the other side, being too hurried and puzzled to go round by the door.

The girl wiped her hands, crossed her feet on the little island of carpet where she was stranded in a sea of soap-suds, and then, sure enough, out of her slender throat came the swallow's twitter, the robin's whistle, the blue-jay's call, the thrush's song, the wood-dove's coo, and many another familiar note, all ending as before with the musical ecstacy of a bobolink singing and swinging among the meadow grass on a bright June day.

Rose was so astonished that she nearly fell off her perch, and when the little concert was over clapped her hands delightedly.

"Oh, it was lovely! Who taught you?"   - Louisa Mae Alcott

1.   fantasy   fiction   poem

2.   Why did you select this answer? _____

_____

The crane's Reward

A great and fearsome lion went out hunting. It was not long before he caught and killed a zebra that was big enough for his lionesses and cubs to eat their fill, with plenty left over for himself. When he and his family were eating, a small bone got caught in the great lion's throat. He could barely squeak to his lionesses that a bone was caught in his throat.

One lioness tried to get the bone out with her paw, but she could not get her great paw far enough into the lion's mouth. The cubs could get to his throat with their little paws, but they were too clumsy to get the bone out. The lionesses tried to ask other animals to help, but they were all afraid of being eaten and ran away.

Soon the lion saw a crane sitting on a high branch watching him. "Crane," squeaked the lion. "Help your king. Your neck is long and thin and so is your beak. You can take this bone from my throat."

The crane was in no hurry. "Why would I do that? One bite and the bone and I will both be in your stomach."

"I shall reward you," said the lion.

The greedy crane could not resist the promise of a reward. He flew down to the lion and ordered, "Open your mouth as wide as you can." With the lionesses and cubs watching, the lion opened his mouth widely. The crane stuck its bill down the lion's throat until its whole head and part of its neck were in the lion's mouth. The bone was easily plucked out and dropped at the lion's feet.

"I'll have that reward now," said the crane.

"You already have it," said the lion. "Now you can tell the other animals that you gave an order to your king, and he obeyed. You can boast that you put your head into a lion's mouth and lived to tell of it."

3.   folktale   nonfiction   autobiography

4.   Why did you select this answer?

_____

Ancient Forest Rises from Italian Clay

Workers were digging for clay to supply a tile factory in Italy's Umbria region when they struck wood - old tree trunks, in fact. Upright but listing like Pisa's tower, they looked, felt, and even smelled like living trees.

But these relatives of modern sequoias and bald cypresses are about two million years old. Buried by an ancient earthquake, they were preserved by the moist clay. Sixty trees, some of them five feet in diameter and 26 feet high, have been exposed on a 25-acre site near Perugia; the tops of three dozen more break the surface. Nothing resembling them in the family called Taxodiaceae, live in Italy today, suggesting that the climate used to be far damper.

Exposure to air has led to some decay of the trees. "The primary object is to find some way to preserve them," says the site director, Sergio Vergoni of Umbria's archeological superintendency. His team has erected roofs over the trunks to provide protection from the elements and is monitoring their status.

Analysis of the trees revealed that some lived for a thousand years. "They are not petrified," Vergoni says, "They are wood; they still could be burned."

5.   allegory   biography   nonfiction

6.   Why did you select this answer? _____

My Bondage and My Freedom   - Frederick Douglass

"Make a noise," "make a noise," and "bear a hand," are the words usually addressed to the slaves when there is silence amongst them. This may account for the almost constant singing heard in the Southern states. There was, generally, more or less singing among the teamsters, as it was one means of letting the overseer know where they were, and that they were moving on with the work. But, on allowance day, those who visited the great house farm were peculiarly excited and noisy. While on their way, they would make the dense old woods, for miles around, reverberate with their wild notes. These were not always merry because they were wild. On the contrary, they were mostly of a plaintive cast, and told a tale of grief and sorrow. In the most boisterous outbursts of rapturous sentiment, there was ever a tinge of deep melancholy. I have never heard any songs like those anywhere since I left slavery, except when in Ireland.

7.   fable   autobiography   tall tale

8.   Why did you select this answer? _____

The Comeback of Rabies

Rabies, a deadly disease to both animals and humans, is on the increase in many areas of Florida. In fact, the number of reported human exposures to rabies has not been as high since the 1940s. This particular strain of rabies was brought to Florida by Texas coyotes. Truckloads of these coyotes are imported into the state by hunting clubs and are used in fox hunts. The disease has always been found among wild animals, but the real problem is that fewer than half of all dogs, cats, and farm animals have been vaccinated against it. In 1994, twenty cats, ten dogs, and three horses contracted rabies, an increase of 500% in the last five years. Domestic animals must be vaccinated, for they are the ones most likely to have contact with humans.

9. nonfiction   epic   novel

10. Why did you select this answer? _____

_____

Gorillas in the Mist

Fossey, Dian, an American zoologist, whose field studies of wild gorillas in the Virunga Mountains of Rwanda and the Congo served to dispel many misconceptions about the violent and aggressive nature of gorillas. Born in San Francisco, Fossey graduated from San Jose State College in 1954 with a degree in occupational therapy; she then worked at a children's hospital in Kentucky for several years. Inspired by the writings of American zoologist George B. Schaller, Fossey traveled to Africa in 1963. There she observed mountain gorillas in the wild and visited the anthropologist Louis Leakey; who believing that studies of great apes would shed light on the subject of human evolution, encouraged Fossey to undertake a long-term field study.

Fossey was an astute and patient observer of gorilla behavior. She knew each individual in her study area, and she came to regard the gorillas as gentle, social animals. Her study site, Karisoke, became an international center for gorilla research when she established the Karisoke Research Center in 1967. Fossey received a Ph.D. in zoology from the University of Cambridge in 1974. Her book, *Gorillas in the Mist* (1983), recounts observations from her years of field research.

Fossey spent 22 years studying the ecology and behavior of mountain gorillas. In 1985 she was found murdered at her campsite. Some authorities believe she was murdered in retaliation for her efforts to stop the poaching of gorillas and other animals in Africa. Due largely to Fossey's research and conservation work, mountain gorillas are now protected by the government of Rwanda and by the international conservation and scientific communities.

One thing is certain however. As it says on the marker at Dian Fossey's grave:

Dian Fossey   1932 - 1985   No one loved gorillas more…

11. biography   epic   novel

12. Why did you select this answer? _____

_____

Rags To Riches

One of the most inspiring "rags to riches" stories is absolutely true. Booker T. Washington was born a slave in 1856. After the Civil War, the one dream that the boy had was to get an education. In 1872, Booker Taliaferro Washington journeyed to the Hampton Institute, a school which trained black teachers, in Virginia. The young man had neither money nor references, but he had a clear desire to learn and to help others learn.

Booker T. Washington was a successful student and was quickly employed as a teacher. When a black college, the Tuskegee Institute, was built in Alabama, Washington became its first principal. Washington proved to be a true leader and a man of vision. He translated his vision for the college into words so that he was able to raise a great deal of money for the Institute's growth. Washington convinced many wealthy and powerful people, such as Andrew Carnegie, to help fund the expansion of the Institute.

Booker T. Washington was the first black man to dine at the White House; President Teddy Roosevelt invited him. The two men shared many views, including the need for healthy physical activity, the value of books and knowledge, and the power of morality.

In his time, Booker T. Washington was a great leader for his people—encouraging them to learn skills to become economically equal with the white race. He did, however, believe in the system or philosophy of the races being kept separate. He was called "The Great Accommodator." Other black leaders grew impatient seeing the slow change within the United States, and they urged stronger measures to gain equality. Washington was on a speaking tour in New York City when he fell ill. He asked to be taken home to the South to be buried. He made it back to Tuskegee where he died.

13.   fiction   biography   mystery

14.   Why did you select this answer? _____

Believe Me, If All Those Endearing Young Charms

Believe me, if all those endearing young charms,
    Which I gaze on so fondly to-day,
Were to change by tomorrow, and fleet in my arms,
    Like fairy gifts fading away!
Thou wouldst still be adored, at this moment thou art,
    Let thy loveliness fade as it will,
And around the dear ruin each wish of my heart
    Would entwine itself verdantly still.

It is not while beauty and youth are thine own,
    And thy cheeks unprofaned by a tear,
That the fervor and faith of a soul may be known,
    To which time will but make thee more dear!
Oh the heart that has truly loved never forgets,
    But as truly loved on tho the close,
As the sunflower turns to her god when he sets
    The same look which she turned when he rose!

15.   nonfiction   folk tale   poem

16.   Why did you select this answer? _____

Cherokee Wisdom

An old Cherokee was teaching his grandson about life. "A fight is going on inside each one of us," he said to the boy. "It is a fight to the death, and it is between two wolves.

"One is darkness -- he is anger, envy, sorrow, regret, greed, arrogance, self-pity, guilt, resentment, inferiority, lies, false pride, superiority, and ego."

"The other is enlighted -- he is joy, peace, love, hope, serenity, humility, kindness, benevolence, empathy, generosity, truth, compassion, and faith."

The grandson thought about it for a minute and then asked his grandfather, "Which wolf will win?"

The old Cherokee simply replied, "The one you feed."

17.   allegory   fantasy   autobiography

18.   Why did you select this answer? _____

_____

Finding the Precious Gift of Corn

A man wandering around found some kernels of corn colored red, blue and white. He knew right away these were of value, so he buried them in a dirt mound.

One day he thought it was time to check on his treasured kernels, but what he found instead were tall stalks with ears of corn bearing the colors of the kernels he had found. He took an ear of each color and gave the rest to his people for them to experiment with. They tried it as food and thought it was so good that it would become the root of life.

Knowing corn was good and served as life to the people, they took the shoulder bone of an elk to dig mounds and plant kernels like the ones that had provided the ears of corn. Soon the people had plenty of corn and were never hungry again.

19.   nonfiction   legend   folk tale

20.   Why did you select this answer? _____

_____

Read the following poem, and answer each question.

Sympathy

I know what the caged bird feels, alas!
When the sun is bright on the upland slopes;
When the wind stirs soft through the springing grass
And the river flows like a stream of glass;
When the first bird sings and the first bird opes,
And the faint perfume from its chalice steals-
I know what the caged bird feels!

–Paul Laurence Dunbar

1. Which point of view is used in this stanza? _____

2. In your own words, state the theme or message of this poem. _____

    _____

3. Write the line in this poem that is a simile. Then explain why it is a simile. _____

    _____

    _____

4. List two examples of alliteration in this poem. _____

    _____

Read the following story carefully, and then answer the questions.

The Cave

Traveling into northern Alabama, four high school seniors began their journey. Chad, a football player; Doug, an apprentice auto mechanic; Steve, a deer hunter; and Mike, a computer whiz all had one thing in common: they ate together at lunch. For weeks, they had planned this trip. Winter break had just begun, so they were ready for high adventure. They purchased exit markers, rope, helmets, and cave lights attached to their helmets so they could see. Steve's father owned about 600 acres of land near the Alabama - Tennessee border. About a month ago, Steve saw an old cave he'd heard stories about and was just waiting for the best time to explore it.

It was one of the coldest days of the winter when they left in Chad's Jeep Cherokee. They parked the vehicle and had to walk about 2 miles in the forest before they reached the entrance. Mike screamed, "There's smoke coming out of that hole!"

"Will you hush, you little book worm. Don't you know that caves are always warmer than the land in the wintertime? That's just mist!" Steve said. The cave entrance was slippery and muddy. Spiders crawled through the opening, and bats regularly flew in and out. Once they were past the entrance, however, there were no more bugs.

"It sure is a lot warmer in here than it is outside." Doug muttered.

They crawled, jumped, and sloshed their way through the cave. Everyone was taken away by the beauty of the cave. Crystal stalactites and stalagmites dotted the cave floor and ceiling. Chad reached his hand out to grab one of the pretty crystal formations. "Don't you touch that," Steve yelled. "I've heard talk from long ago that there's some sort of cave guardian here. The story is that the Guardian is supposed to be real mean and nasty, and it strikes whenever someone tries to steal part of the cave's formations." Chad dropped his hand, and the group continued crawling forward.

A few minutes later, the passage opened up into a huge cavern. The ceiling was about 100 feet high. Beautiful crystal formations resembling amethyst and topaz were everywhere. Mike screamed when he tripped on a bone on the cave floor. "Don't worry, Mike, it was probably some animal that crawled down here and died a long time ago," Steve said. While the rest were occupied comforting Mike, Chad was carefully examining a two foot long crystal shard. He couldn't resist any longer. Chad reached up and started breaking the shard with his hands. Suddenly, a low growl filled the cavern. "What was that?" everyone asked. Two yellow eyes appeared out from a ledge near the ceiling.

A voice was heard, saying "Get! Out!"

The group broke into a run. Steve was leading everyone else out of the cave. "Don't look back. Whatever you do, don't look back," he yelled. They could feel a presence behind them all the way to the cave's entrance. Then, stumbled through the forest. They were near exhaustion when they reached the jeep. Steve spoke, "Chad, get us out of here." Chad fumbled for his keys and jumped in. Steve heard something behind him. Then he saw the Guardian coming. Steve told everyone, "Mike and I are going to run in front of the jeep. When you see the Guardian, you'd better run it over."

Mike and Steve waited for the Guardian to catch up with them, scared out of their minds. Then, they dashed in front of the jeep. Chad waited until the spider creature was in front of him, pushed the gas pedal, and ran over the Guardian. A flash of blue light flared from beneath the jeep, and the guardian was nothing but a pile of big crab legs. "Let's get out of here for good," Steve said.

5. Who is the main character? _____

6. Is the author purpose to persuade, to cause doubt, or to relate an adventure? Explain your answer.

_____

_____

Cite examples of the following in this story.

7. foreshadowing _____

_____

8. conflict _____

_____

9. climax _____

_____

10. suspense _____

_____

11. What lesson do the characters learn from their experience? _____

_____

Read the following examples of propaganda. Then answer the questions.

Some people care about their smiles. Other people care about their teeth. Sparkle toothpaste cares about everyone's smiles and everyone's teeth. Its patented "Clean Smile" formula whitens teeth and brightens smiles. Bring some Sparkle into your life today!

12. What is the purpose of this advertisement? _____

_____

13. What makes this ad propaganda? _____

_____

Read the poem "Work," and answer the questions below.

WORK

Work, work, my boy, be not afraid;
  Look labor boldly in the face;
Take up the hammer or the spade,
  And blush not for your humble place.

There's glory in the shuttle's song;
  There's triumph in the anvil's stroke;
There's merit in the brave and strong,
  Who dig the mine or fell the oak.

– Eliza Cook, 1879

14. What types of propaganda does the author use in this poem? _____

_____

15. What makes this poem propaganda? _____

_____

_____

Read the poem below, and answer the questions.

No willing grave received the corpse
    of this poor lonely one; –
His bones, alas, were left to bleach
    and moulder 'neath the sun!

The night-wolf howl'd his requiem,–
    the rude winds danced his dirge;
And e'er anon, in mournful chime
    sigh's forth the mellow surge!

The spring shall teach the rising grass
    to twine from him a tomb;
And, o'er the spot where he doth lie,
    shall bid the wild flowers bloom.

But, far from friends, and far from home,
    ah, dismal thought, to die!
Ah, let me 'mid my friends expire,
    and with my fathers lie.

–Rufus B. Sage

16. What is the setting for this poem? _____

17. Why was the poem written? _____

    _____

18. Based on the first three stanzas, the point of view is _____ .

19. The point of view changes in the last stanza. This point of view is _____ .

20. Personification is the main rhetorical device used in this poem. List two examples of personification in the poem.

    _____

    _____

Read this passage. Then answer the questions that follow.

Christera

 Christera walked carefully between the yawning craters of Lovos. Moments before her bubble rocket had crash-landed on a ridge of soft volcanic sand. Little was left of the vast meteor shower that carried her off course, hurling the rocket into this strange place. All that remained of her misfortune were flaming bits of meteors that still fell occasionally from the sky.

She stared into the black void of space. Somewhere out there was a burning cinder or perhaps a swirl of smoky debris. That was all one would find of the planet Earth. Because of the great A-War, she and thousands like her had sought a way out of annihilation. The famous bubble rockets were the answer, but only a few people had been able to secure them. She was sure the rest had perished.

Where were the others, she wondered? Did they reach the earth-like planet Geos, or did they too lose their way?

Ahead of her, Christera saw rocks of many colors, and they glowed. She heard an odd sound like water rushing over rocks. She listened more closely for other sounds. Suddenly, there was a noise like a squeal, perhaps human but possibly an animal. She was not sure. She pulled out her laser gun, stopped, and listened again. Was she safe or was she about to confront an alien? Christera did not know, but she was not going to take any chances.

21. What type of literature is this passage? List two reasons for your choice.

_____

_____

22. What is the author's main purpose in the passage? _____

_____

23. Describe any conflicts in this story. _____

_____

_____

24. Where does the story take place? _____

25. What do you think will happen next in the story? In two to three paragraphs, write the rest of this story. Use your own paper.

CHAPTER 9 TEST

Read the following selections. Then choose the best answer for each question.

Offer Education

In reference to the article on ending prison education plans, I find these "get tough" measures shortsighted and lamentable. Rather than denying educational opportunity, the prison system should incorporate educational incentives with work requirements.

Illiteracy imprisons the mind and shackles human potential. While withdrawing funding for college classes, policy-makers should pledge to upgrade the GED program, even to make it obligatory for high school dropouts and to offer scholarship incentives.

Unfortunately, we are too ready to expend vast sums on incarceration but very little money on effective prevention and rehabilitation. The politics of vengeance is alive and well and self-destructive.

– Barbara Allen Kenney

1. Which of the following statements best describes the argument of the writer in the selection above?

   A. The writer constructs a valid argument.
   B. The writer explores only two sides of an issue.
   C. The writer attacks the person rather than the problem.
   D. The writer does not directly address the issue.

Attitude

This may shock you, but I believe the single most significant decision I can make on a day-to-day basis is my choice of attitude. It is more important than my past, my education, my bankroll, my successes or failures, fame or pain, what other people think of me or say about me, my circumstances, or my position. Attitude is that 'single string' that keeps me going or cripples my progress. It alone fuels my fire or assaults my hope. When my attitudes are right, there's no barrier too high, no valley too deep, no dream too extreme, no challenge too great for me.

– Charles R. Swindoll

2. Which of the following argument best describes the argument of the writer in the selection above?

   A. The writer describes a valid argument.
   B. The writer uses a famous person to endorse a product.
   C. The writer only explores two sides of an issue.
   D. The writer attacks a person rather than the idea.

Lawyers

It is a plain fact that lawyers, instead of being the preservers of the rights of the people, are the great disturbers of their rights. They make it their special business to counsel men to all kinds of quarrels and fusses, so they can charge an exorbitant fee for defending persons from a difficulty they have gotten them into by their advice.

It isn't safe nowadays for a man of property to make a will and die, or die without one, for as sure as he does, a lot of lawyers will buzz around some of his heirs and get them to bust up the will. They will gather around that estate like so many hungry buzzards around a carcass, and they'll linger around it until every dollar is consumed, and then the poverty-stricken heirs can go to the Devil, for all they care. They are grand preservers of the people's rights, ain't they? Show me a single right that some of them have not trampled upon. I will admit there are a good many things a lawyer can do that will benefit some, once in a while, and also there are some very honorable lawyers, but not many. The great run of them are figuring all the time how they can thrive upon the misfortunes and errors of others.

– excerpt from *Shams* by John S. Draper

3. Which of the following statements best describes the argument of the writer in the above selection?

    A. The writer believes most lawyers work for the people.
    B. The writer wants to portray lawyers as impartial searchers of the truth.
    C. The writer wants people to know that lawyers fight for your legal rights.
    D. The writer feels that lawyers are greedy and work for selfish reasons.

4. Which of the following fallacies does this argument contain?

    A. The writer attacks the personal life of lawyers.
    B. The writer attacks the person rather than a group.
    C. The writer jumps to conclusions.
    D. The argument does not contain any fallacies.

Try the new fragrance, Swan Song, just once and you won't believe the results! With exclusively patented pheromones, this fragrance will attract handsome men to you wherever you are. Try it today and receive a complimentary Swan Song umbrella.

5. The propaganda in this advertisement is to convince the reader to

    A. go out on a date.
    B. change her life.
    C. buy an umbrella.
    D. buy Swan Song perfume.

6. Which passage contains propaganda?

    A.   Grace Chisolm, a well-known psychic, had this to say about Batwing XR 71A. "It drives like a dream. I can definitely tell this car is going to redefine the future of the automotive industry." Like Ms. Chisolm, we at American Motors believe this sports car looks better, rides better, and feels better than anything else in its class.

    B.   Try all the other fine jewelry stores in the area. Then visit us. At Simpson & Hyde, we offer a selection of over 6,000 pieces of jewelry in every price range. Our staff undergoes two months of training before they are allowed to help customers like you. Compare and see the difference.

    C.   For overnight and 2-day deliveries of goods at the lowest price available, try Value Express. We promise to go 5% below the lowest quote for shipment in the Birmingham area. All packages are tracked with scanners to ensure accuracy in shipments.

    D.   When looking for the most knowledgeable travel agents, try Globe World Travel. Each of our travel agents has personally been on the tours we offer. They can tell you what to see and what to avoid on your trips overseas. For experienced travel agents, try Globe World Travel.

The Gift of the Magi

Della finished her cry and attended to her cheeks with the powder rag. She stood by the window and looked out dully at a gray cat walking a gray fence in a gray backyard. Tomorrow would be Christmas Day, and she had only $1.87 with which to buy Jim a present. She had been saving every penny she could for months, with this result. Twenty dollars a week doesn't go far. Expenses had been greater than she had calculated. They always are. Only $1.87 to buy a present for Jim. Her Jim. Many a happy hour she had spent planning for something nice for him. Something fine and rare and sterling – something just a little bit near to being worthy of the honor of being owned by Jim.

There was a pier-glass between the windows of the room. Perhaps you have seen a pier-glass in an $8 flat. A very thin and agile person may, by observing his reflection in a rapid sequence of longitudinal strips, obtain a fairly accurate conception of his looks. Della, being slender, had mastered the art.

Suddenly she whirled from the window and stood before the glass. Her eyes were shining brilliantly, but her face had lost its color within twenty seconds. Rapidly she pulled down her hair and let it fall to its full length.

                – From *Tales of O. Henry*

7. What is the mood of this passage?

    A. hysterical   C. expectant
    B. gloomy   D. fearful

8. What is the plot of the above passage?

    A.   Della is trying to do something new with her hair.
    B.   Della is trying to think of what to do for Christmas.
    C.   Jim wants to rent an apartment for $8 a week.
    D.   Della wants to give Jim a costly Christmas gift but cannot afford it.

A Warrior's Quest

"After so many years, what's another day," Vlad muttered to himself as he waited for the return of his long-lost daughter, Kyla. They had been separated by a tragic mishap five years ago. Vlad sat down and started pounding the dirt with his boot in exasperation. His thoughts kept returning to the way his daughter smiled and skipped around the woods at their home. She was so courteous and fragile - his eyes grew mistier by the minute.

Hearing the thunder of many horses, Vlad quit his thoughts, drew his broadsword, and stepped into the woods. Pale, ghost-like forms traveling on horses with red eyes slowly rode along the path close to his hiding place. "These evil, ugly freaks have been following me for too long," he muttered softly to himself. In a piece of bad luck, one of the horses looked directly in Vlad's direction and began stomping hysterically. Realizing he would be discovered, Vlad leapt up and attacked the first horseman, neatly impaling him through the chest. Meanwhile, the three remaining ghost riders encircled him. Throwing a net that neatly entangled him in a crushing heap, the ghost riders circled around Vlad clockwise and prepared themselves for a feast.

At this moment, a robed figure and a panther, Manx, jumped down on the horses from a ledge and attacked the ghost riders from behind. Strong, soft hands quickly cut one of the riders to pieces with a dagger while Manx finished off a ghost rider dinner on another horse. The remaining ghost rider galloped away faster than light.

By this time, Vlad had cut himself free of the net and stood up, saying, "Thank you, sir. You saved me just in the nick of time." "Actually, I thought I was a few years late," the figure said as the hood fell down. Recognizing the figure, Vlad fainted and fell to the ground with a thud.

9. In which time period could this most likely have occurred?

    A.   the Middle Ages   C.   The Civil War
    B.   the Age of Enlightenment   D.   the Modern Age

10. According to this passage, what is the climax of the story?

    A.   Vlad jumps into the woods to hide.
    B.   Vlad attacks the first horseman and impales him through the chest.
    C.   The ghost riders entangle Vlad in a net.
    D.   A robed figure and a panther come to Vlad's rescue.

11. Who is/are the antagonist (s) in this story?

    A.   Vlad   C.   the ghost riders
    B.   Kyla   D.   Manx

12. What is the mood of the first paragraph?

    A.   disgusting   C.   satirical
    B.   melancholy   D.   hysterical

13. What is the theme for this story?

    A.   Help can come at the most unexpected times.
    B.   We can never have enough friends.
    C.   Always go into forests alone.
    D.   Wild pets offer the best protection on the open road.

14. What kind of literature is this passage?

    A. science fiction   C. play
    B. poetry   D. fantasy

He was quick and alert in the things in life, but only in the things, and not in the significant things. Fifty degrees below zero meant eighty degrees of frost. Such fact impressed him as being cold and uncomfortable, and that was all. It did not lead him to meditate upon his frailty as a creature of temperature, and upon man's frailty in general, able only to live within certain narrow limits of heat and cold; and from there on it did not lead him to the conjectural field of immorality and man's place in the universe. Fifty degrees below zero was to him just precisely fifty degrees below. That there should be anything more to it than that was a thought that never entered his head.

As he turned to go on, he spat speculatively. There was a sharp explosive crackle that startled him. He spat again. And again, in the air, before it could fall to the snow, the spittle crackled. He knew that at fifty below spittle crackled on the snow, but this spittle had crackled in the air. Undoubtedly it was colder than fifty below – how much colder he did not know. But the temperature did not matter. He was bound for the old claim on the left fork of Henderson Creek, where the boys were already. They had come over across the divide from the Indian Creek country, while he had come the roundabout way to take a look at the possibilities of getting out logs in the spring from the islands in the Yukon. He would be in to camp by six o'clock; a bit after dark, it was true, but the boys would be there, a fire would be going, and a hot supper would be ready. As for lunch, he pressed his hand against the protruding bundle under his jacket. It was also under his shirt, wrapped up in a handkerchief and lying against the naked skin. It was the only way to keep the biscuits from freezing. He smiled agreeably to himself as he thought of those biscuits, each cut open and sopped in bacon grease, and each enclosing a generous slice of fried bacon.

He plunged in among the big spruce trees. The trail was faint. A foot of snow had fallen since the last sled had passed over, and he was glad he was without a sled, traveling light. In fact, he carried nothing but the lunch wrapped in the handkerchief. He was surprised, however, at the cold. It certainly was cold, he concluded, as he rubbed his numb nose and cheekbones with his mittened hand. He was a warm-whiskered man, but the hair on his face did not protect the high cheek-bones and the eager nose that thrust itself aggressively into the frosty air.

– Jack London

15. What is the conflict in this story?

    A. the campers against the loners   C. fire against ice
    B. man against nature   D. man against mountain

16. Where does this story take place?

    A. the tundra   C. the rain forest
    B. the desert   D. the mountains

17. What type of literature is this passage?

    A. poetry   C. autobiography
    B. fiction   D. mythology

Read the following poem, and answer the questions below.

With His Venom

With his venom

Irresistible
and bittersweet

the loosener
of limbs, Love

reptile-like
strikes me down
                    – Sappho

18. Which technique is Sappho using to describe love?

    A.   euphemism   C.   onomatopoeia
    B.   hyperbole   D.   personification

19. What is love compared to in the poem above?

    A.   a poison   C.   a tranquilizer
    B.   a serpent   D.   a handsome man

A Beautiful Girl Combs Her Hair

Awake at dawn
she's dreaming
by cool silk curtains

fragrance of spilling hair
half sandalwood, half aloes
windlass creaking at the well
singing jade

the lotus blossom awakes, refreshed
her mirror
two phoenixes
a pool of autumn light

– Stanzas I-III by Li Ho (about 810 A.D.)

20. What is the woman being compared to in this poem?

    A.   a mirror   C.   a windlass
    B.   a lotus blossom   D.   a phoenix

21. What type of figurative language does Li Ho use in this poem?

    A. dialogue   C. metaphor
    B. rhyme   D. simile

During the 1880s and 1890s, Andrew Carnegie was a prominent leader in the steel industry and one of the richest men in the world. With his money, he established 1,681 libraries in urban centers across the United States. In 1956, the Library Services Act gave libraries strong federal support.

22. The author's purpose in writing this selection is

    A. to motivate.   C. to inform.
    B. to persuade.   D. to teach a lesson.

He thought he could hear the whistle of the bombs as they dropped through the air. And then, they were dropping all around him. Fires started to light up the sky. He must get home to his Marlene. He must get home. Only two more blocks now.

23. The author's purpose in writing this passage is

    A. to relate an adventure.   C. to cause doubt.
    B. to entertain.   D. to create suspense.

The Fox and the Grapes

A hungry fox came into a vineyard where there hung delicious clusters of ripe grapes. His mouth watered to be at them; but they were nailed up to a trellis so high, that with all his springing and leaping he could not reach a single bunch. At last, growing tired and disappointed, the fox said, "Let someone else take them! They are but green and sour; so I'll leave them alone."

– Aesop (ca. 6th century B.C.)

24. What is the message of this story?

    A. Never give up on reaching your goal.
    B. If an obstacle seems difficult, we sometimes convince ourselves that the prize is worthless.
    C. It is very important to share what you have with those around you.
    D. If you have people to help you, you can accomplish many things that you could not do alone.

25. This story is an example of a

    A. myth.   C. mystery.
    B. tall tale.   D. fable.

APPENDIX A: ELECTRONIC AND PRINT RESOURCES

WEB SITES

These Web sites include a variety of information with links to still more sites designed as supplemental aids for students. We visited these sites and devised a rating system for them.

Ratings:

Excellent	☺ ☺ ☺ ☺
Good	☺ ☺ ☺
Nearly Good	☺ ☺ ☺
Fair	☺ ☹
Poor	☹

1.0 Vocabulary and Concept Development:
Key concepts:
a. Literal and figurative meanings of words.   b. Denotative and connotative meanings

---

The UVic Writer's Guide: A Dictionary Of Usage

The site has a listing of words that are commonly confused or misused (for example: effect/affect). The site is simply formatted and easy to use.

Web address   http://web.uvic.ca/wguide/
                   Pages/DictionUsageToc.html   **Rating -** ☺ ☺ ☺

Vocabulary Quizzes: (Part of The Internet TESL Journal's Activities for ESL Students)

This site deserves at least a page full of ☺'s. However, since we don't have the space, I will simply say that the site has a great deal of information and games to make the learning almost easy. The section on English idioms, figures of speech, is varied and has translations for common slang phrases. There are trivia games, crossword puzzles, and a page called "Interesting Things" that is worth checking out.

Web address   http://www.aitech.ac.jp/~iteslj/
                   quizzes/vocabulary.html   **Rating -** ☺ ☺ ☺ ☺
                                                            ☺ ☺ ☺ ☺

Your Dictionary. Com

Ignore the lined background; this site is way better than the common paper-look. Besides having different language dictionaries linked to the site, there are several unusual features: a synthesizing page (It reads aloud what you write and gives you a choice of six voices. This will help with pronunciation fluency.), a Dr. Language page (for questions) , an ancient writing systems link (for people who like to write like an Egyptian), and a "Games room." Easy to move around, but with so much stuff it's hard to decide where to go first!

Web address   http://www.yourdictionary.com   **Rating -** ☺ ☺ ☺ ☺

Your Dictionary.Com: Diction 3

Same source and same background. This is a solid reference for dictionaries and thesauruses.

Web address   http://www.yourdictionary.com/   **Rating -** ☺ ☺ ☺
                   languages/germanic.html#english

2.0 Reading Comprehension

Key concepts:
a. Consumer materials   b. Workplace documents   c. Bibliography
d. Comprehension   e. Analysis   f. Critique

First Gov for Consumers

A brightly decorated and sectioned site. This site has consumer information, forms, and links to more forms of all kinds: school loans, housing, childcare loans, etc. There are both federal and individual state government forms. Some of the features include a Consumer Action Handbook, Fraud information, and current consumer news alerts.

Web address   http://www.consumer.gov/   **Rating -** ☺ ☺ ☺☺

Free Consumer Information

Interesting look to this site. Careful though. It does have several ways for you to get into a "buying on line" situation. The features include links to federal, state, and private consumer agencies and Web sites. There is consumer information on cars, travel, education, etc.

Web address   http://www.ifg-inc.com/   **Rating -** ☺ ☺

LawInfo.Com: Legal Research Center

This site definitely has a tremendous amount of legal forms and information. However, it can be difficult to pin down what you want to see and/or print. I worked steadily for almost an hour to download a promissory note from the HUD page. There is legal information on this site for both federal and state law.

Web address   http://www.lawsmart.com/   **Rating -** ☺ ☺ ☺

University Libraries: Citation Format Guides

The site has a peach color background that is easy to look at. Otherwise it is a straight-forward, no-frills site. The information seems accurate, and it features not only the MLA (Modern Language Association) style, but also three other styles. There is a page for examples of **online** citations, "Citing Electronic Sources." This feature alone is worth a visit to this Web site. There is one concern; however, the site has not been updated since January 11, 1999. If that is as troubling to you as it is to us, you can browse through the links on the site to find updated information on the Web.

Web address   http://www-libraries.colorado.edu/about/citing.htm

Rating - ☺ ☺☺

3.0 Literary Response and Analysis

Key concepts:
a. Forms of dramatic literature   b. Narrative analysis
c. Character   d. Theme
e. Figurative language: imagery, allegory, symbolism, irony
f. Literary criticism: style, historic theme, tradition

Annenberg / CPB: Learner.org: Theme

A very well-presented site. It contains valuable information about the five major topics for reading analysis: theme, plot, point-of-view, setting, and characters.

Web address   http://www.learner.org/exhibits/literature/read/theme1.html

Rating - ☺ ☺ ☺☺

Literary Resources -- Theatre and Drama: Part of Rutger's Collection

This site is simply a long list of Web sites: some excellent, some serviceable, and some no longer existing. Still, if you have the time and curiosity for drama, there is a wide variety of topics and elements of drama explored in the sites.

Web address   http://andromeda.rutgers.edu/~jlynch/Lit/theatre.html

Rating - ☺☺☺

Mr. William Shakespeare and the Internet

An award winning site that has too many features to list. The most important feature for reading standards is titled "Tales from Shakespeare." It has different plays formed into stories with the language being modified for easy understanding. The tales basically give a short retelling of the plays: many but not all of Shakespeare's works, including *King Lear*, are on the site.

Web address   http://shakespeare.palomar.edu   **Rating -** ☺ ☺ ☺☺

Planet Papers

WARNING: This has been set out as a <u>supposedly</u> good source of critical analysis. It is composed of papers written by other students and described as "free essays." Do not be mislead into thinking that "free" means free use. There is some information about plagiarism buried under other topic headings. The information mentions that <u>none</u> of the text should be used without citing the Web site as a source. Please understand that you may use the site **only** for examples of papers and as a documented source.

Web address   http://www.planetpapers.com/Literature/   **Rating -** ☺

A-4

Copyright © American Book Company

Theatre History on the Web

The site is very structured but still can be confusing to move through. The time spent searching is rewarding, however, particularly if you are searching for fables or mythology. The site includes studies of different eras, cultures, and links to some impressive cultural sites, such as the British Museum.

Web address   http://www.videoccasions-nw.com/history/jack.html

Rating - ☺ ☺ ☺

Telectronic Text Center: University Of Virginia's E-book Library

This site is linked to thousands of complete texts that readers can view with Microsoft and hundreds of other texts that can be read with a palm device. There are also some journals linked to the site, such as a journal of essays about history. The site is fairly easy to move through and, in many examples, has illustrations to break up the text.

Web address   http://etext.lib.virginia.edu/ebooks/ebooklist.html

Rating - ☺ ☺ ☺ ☺

UM Fantasy and Science Fiction: Dictionary of Symbols

This is a visually interesting site. Not only is it fun to find "hidden meanings," the value of the information is in the clues that you can find for theme in literature. The symbols are arranged in alphabetical listings for easy access. The only suggestion for improvement would be to add even more symbols. The site also has pages about Monsters and Visual Symbolism—view at your own risk . . .

Web address   http://www.umich.edu/~umfandsf/
symbolismproject/symbolism.html/index.html   **Rating -** ☺ ☺ ☺

BOOKS

When the Web is not enough, think "Library Card." On the next few pages, you will find a partial list of books and stories that are recommended for student reading. If there is a book that you would prefer to read, speak to the librarian about it. You could also see if your local library has school reading lists with more book choices that are approved by the schools. **Anthologies** (collections of literature) are good sources for different types of literature gathered in one book. There are also collections of poetry, short stories, and collections of a particular author's works. There is also a list of teacher resource books at the end of this section.

AMERICAN LITERATURE

Fiction

<u>Early Authors</u>

Cather, Willa	*My Antonia*	*O Pioneers!*
Crane, Stephen	*Red Badge of Courage*	
Emerson, Ralph Waldo	*Civil Disobedience*	
Harte, Bret	"The Outcasts of Poker Flat"	
Hawthorne, Nathaniel	"Young Goodman Brown"	*The Scarlet Letter*
London, Jack	*Call of the Wild*	
Poe, Edgar Allan	"Fall of the House of Usher"	
Twain, Mark	*Huckleberry Finn*	
Wharton, Edith	*Ethan Frome*	

<u>Modern Authors</u>

Bradbury, Ray	*Fahrenheit 451*	*The Martian Chronicle*
Buck, Pearl	*The Good Earth*	
Cisneros, Sandra	*The House on Mango Street*	
Hurston, Zora Neale	*Their Eyes Were Watching God*	"Sweat"
Keyes, Daniel	*Flowers for Algernon*	
Okada, John	*No-No Boy*	
Morrison, Toni	*Jazz*	*Beloved*
Momaday, N. Scott	*House Made of Dawn*	
Newton, Robert	*A Day No Pigs Would Die*	
Rivera, Thomas	*And the Earth Did Not Part*	
Steinbeck, John	*Of Mice and Men*	*The Grapes of Wrath*
Uchida, Yoshiko	*Picture Bride*	
Wiesel, Elie	*Night*	

Poetry

<u>Early Poets</u>

Dickinson, Emily	
Longfellow, Henry Wadsworth	"Paul Revere's Ride"

<u>Modern Poets</u>

Frost, Robert	"The Road Not Taken"	"The Hired Man"
Hughes, Langston		

Drama

Fugard, Athol	*Master Harold and the Boys*	
Lum, Wing Tek	*Oranges Are Lucky*	
Medoff, Mark	*Children of a Lesser God*	
O'Neill, Eugene	*Anna Christie*	*The Iceman Cometh*
Sakamoto, Edward	*In the Alley*	
Valdez, Luis	*Zoot Suit*	

Non-Fiction

<u>Early Authors</u>

Jefferson, et al	*Declaration Of Independence*
Lincoln, Abraham	*With malice toward none . . .*
Thoreau, Henry D.	*Walden*

<u>Modern Authors</u>

Angelou, Maya	*I Know Why the Caged Bird Sings*
Martin L King	*I Have a Dream*
Roosevelt, Franklin	"The only thing we have to fear is fear itself"
	"Yesterday, Dec. 7, 1941. . . a date which will live in infamy"

BRITISH LITERATURE

Fiction

Austen, Jane	*Pride and Prejudice*	*Emma*
Bronte, Charlotte	*Jane Erye*	
Conrad, Joseph	*The Heart of Darkness*	*Lord Jim*
Forester, E. M.	*Passage to India*	
Greene, Graham	*The Power and the Glory*	
Huxley, Aldous	*Brave New World*	

<u>**Poetry**</u>

Eliot, T. S.	"The Love Song of J. Alfred Prufrock"
	The Wasteland
Keats, John	"Ode on a Grecian Urn"
Milton, John	*Paradise Lost*
Shakespeare, William	*Sonnets*
Thomas, Dylan	*The Poems of Dylan Thomas*

Drama

Bolt, Robert	*A Man for All Seasons*		
Marlow, Christopher	*Doctor Faustus*		
Shakespeare, William	*King Lear*	*Hamlet*	*Romeo and Juliet*
Shaw, Bernard	*Arms and the Man*	*Pygmalian*	

Non-Fiction

Churchill, Winston   "Blood, toil, tears, and sweat" speech

WORLD LITERATURE

Ancient Literature

Aeschylus	*Oresteian Trilogy*		
Euripedes	*Medea*		
Sophocles	*Oedipus Rex*	*Antigone*	*Oedipus at Colonus*

Fiction:

Achebe, Chinua	*Things Fall Apart*	
Confucius		
Dante	*The Divine Comedy*	
Dickens, Charles	*David Copperfield,*	*Oliver Twist*
	A Tale of Two Cities	*A Christmas Carol*
Eliot, George	*The Mill on the Floss*	*Silas Marner*
Flaubert, Gustave	*Madam Bovery*	
Garcia Lorca, Federico	*Blood Wedding*	
Garcia Marquez, Gabriel	*Love In the Time of Cholera*	
Hesse, Herman	*Siddhartha*	
Ibsen, Henrik	*A Doll's House*	*An Enemy of the People*
	The Wild Duck	*The Master Builder*
Mishima, Yukio	*The Sound of Waves*	
Moliere, Jean	*The Misanthrope and Other Plays*	
Paton, Alan	*Cry, the Beloved Country*	
Saint-Exupery, Antoine de	*The Little Prince*	
Shelley, Mary W.	*Frankenstein*	
Tolstoy, A.	*Anna Karenina*	*War and Peace*

Basics Made Easy: Reading Review

This workbook provides clear explanations and plentiful practice exercises on reading and literature. Chapter reviews reinforce concepts taught in each lesson. The book is a thorough and excellent support for readers.

Pintozzi, Frank, and Devin Pintozzi. *Basics Made Easy: Reading Review.* Woodstock, GA: American Book Co., 1998.
Web Address: www.americanbookcompany.com

TEACHER RESOURCES

WEB SITES

The Educator's Reference Desk: Resource Guides

Previously "AskERIC.com," this site is the "alpha and the omega" of educational resources. Below is a quote from the Educator's Reference Desk Home Web page:

> "Through The Educator's Reference Desk you can access AskERIC's 2,000+ lesson plans, 3,000+ links to online education information, and 200+ question archive responses."

Plus, the site is easy to search and use. Note that information for ESL students is under the topic heading of "Subject," then "Foreign Language," and then "English Second Language" or in the site search under "English as Second Language."

Web Address   http://www.eduref.org/

EDSITEment

This Web site is linked with the California Department of Education site through Marco Polo (see next page). It has grade appropriate lesson plans for literature and drama along with the other areas of a curriculum. The site has several features, including "Teachers' Lounge," more "Web Sites,"and a "Reference Shelf."

Web Address   http://edsitement.neh.gov/

Marco Polo

A jumping-off point for teacher resources. It focuses its materials and links on how to use the Internet in the classroom.

Web Address   http://www.marcopolo-education.org/

MegaEd

The name says it all—truly a mega-site for educational resources. There is a link to ERIC here as well as a link to Lesson PlanZ.com. Easy to move through and a lot to explore.

Web Address   http://www.megaed.com/

BOOKS AND SOFTWARE

American Book Company: TestCreator Software

A software program set (2) offered to teachers allowing them to custom design tests for any subject and any grade level. The software consists of two programs. The first program, TestCreator, the teacher uses to design tests with or without hints, with or without a clock for timing, and with a scoring feature. The second program, TestTaker, the students use to take the tests designed by their teacher. The program material for this software was developed in conjunction with the software company, Aubrey Daniels Inc.

TestCreator. Woodstock: American Book Company, 2001.
Web Address: www.americanbookcompany.com

Content Knowledge: A Compendium of Standards and Benchmarks for K-12 Education.

This text has taken seven years of research into state and national standards and it is set into a tabbed reference that is easy to use. It is tabbed in the different study areas and internally broken down further into grade standards. There is also a Resources section.

Kendall, John S. and Robert J. Marzano. *Content Knowledge: A Compendium of Standards and Benchmarks for K-12 Education.* Aurora: McREL, 1997.

Holt, Rinehart, Winston: Elements of Literature

This is a text widely used in the school systems. The anthologies are arranged and selected to meet the needs of the different levels in secondary schools. For example, *Elements of Literature: Fourth Course* is designed for use in tenth grade, and the focus is on World Literature. The publishers have a well-designed Web site that includes an online textbook and online essay scoring.

Holt, Rinehart, Winston. *Elements of Literature*. Dallas: Holt, Rinehart, Winston, 1997.
Web Address: http://www.hrw.com/

Prentice Hall Literature: Timeless Voices, Timeless Themes

A time-tested and true publisher of literature in its many classifications. We recommend supplementing you class texts with one or more of these anthologies. The **Timeless Voices, Timeless Themes** title series, 6th edition (2000) includes 5 different levels: Copper, Bronze, Silver, Gold, and Platinum. The **Timeless Voices, Timeless Themes** title series, 7th edition (2002) includes 3 different levels: Copper, Bronze, Silver.

Prentice-Hall, Inc. *Timeless Voices, Timeless Themes*. 6th ed. Englewood Cliffs: Prentice Hall, 2000.

Prentice-Hall, Inc. *Timeless Voices, Timeless Themes*. 7th ed. Englewood Cliffs: Prentice Hall, 2002.
Web Address: http://www.phschool.com/language_arts/index.html

Recommended Literature: Grades Nine Through Twelve.

This is a book compiled and printed by the California State Department of Education. It has a well-organized listing of the core and extended reading recommended by California educators. There are the classic books and a good collection of titles for a multi-cultural approach to literature. The text also offers an appendix about story-telling, and it offers a page of other books published by the California Department of Education.

California State. Dept. of Ed. *Recommended Literature: Grades Nine Through Twelve*. Sacramento: CA St. Dept. of Ed., 1989.
Web Address: http://www.mcrel.org/

APPENDIX B: GAMES AND ACTIVITIES

VOCABULARY (WORD MEANING)

Here are some suggestions for vocabulary games and activities:

1. **Pop Poetry.** Cut out new words, phrases, and accompanying pictures from newspaper and magazine ads, articles, or catalogues. Enlarge the words if they are too small. Make poems or collages by gluing them together on construction paper or poster board. Explain the meanings of the new words and the theme or message of the poem or collage.

2. **Crossword Puzzles.** Locate crossword puzzles in magazines, newspapers, or books. Working in pairs, students guess at the letters that fit the horizontal and vertical boxes. Looking up some words in the dictionary may be necessary and encourages vocabulary development.

   If you want to learn content-specific vocabulary words, *Crossword Magic*, (HLS Duplication, Inc.), a computer software program, takes lists of words and clues and automatically creates a crossword puzzle. For other crossword puzzle activities, look up crossword puzzle sites on the Internet.

3. **Test Creator Software.** Teachers and students can create their own vocabulary or comprehension tests. This program creates multiple-choice and true/false questions for any subject. Hints and feedback can also be included with the tests. In addition, tests show student scores and track time on tasks. *Test Creator Software* can also be used for classroom presentations and demonstrations with such added features as spotlight, magnify, zoom, underline, edit, create sounds, and more. You can download a free demo disk at www.americanbookcompany.com. To place an order, contact American Book Company toll free at 1-888-264-5877.

4. **Shopping Trip.** Students sit in a circle of 5-6 persons. In a class, several circles would be formed. The leader starts the chain by saying, "Today, I'm shopping for a short story for dinner. I'll need some ingredients like a plot. A plot is a series of events leading to a climax and resolution." The next student says, "The leader is going to buy a plot, and I am going to buy a character. A character is etc." Continue around the circle until all of the ingredients are identified and defined. Then the leader can ask, "Who remembers what anyone bought?" Students can volunteer answers such as, "remember that Ben bought some conflicts."

   Variation. For variation, students can shop for types of clothing, parts of a car, house, etc. For example, the leader could say, "I'm dressing up for my play, so I'm going shopping for a scene. A scene is...etc."

5. **Word Game.** Each week students bring two words and their definitions to class. Students can choose these words from newspapers, magazines, books, television, etc. Weed out duplicate words. In the following week, students can either take a quiz by defining the words, using them in sentences, or taking a multiple-choice test. Students can also form teams with the teacher asking questions and providing prizes for the best scores.

6. **Semantic Map.** A semantic map is a visual aid that helps you understand how words are related to each other. You write a word or concept in a circle in the center of a page. Then you draw branches out of the center of the circle with related words in circles at the end of these branches. You can work in pairs or in groups to develop these maps. For example, the word *collaborate* relates to the words *cooperate, team, communicate,* etc. The root word *super* relates to such words as *superior, supersede, superstar,* etc.

READING COMPREHENSION

Here are some suggested games and activities:

1. **Prereading.** Before reading an article or story, preview the title, the first paragraph, first sentences of each of the other paragraphs, the last paragraph, and any illustrations. You then write down and, if possible, discuss what you already know about the article or story. This prereading activity helps you improve your comprehension.

2. **5 W's and H.** After you preread or skim a selection, you can increase your comprehension by developing questions based on the 5W's and H. News reporters often use these questions for their news articles. The 5 W's stand for *who, what, when, where, and why.* The H refers to *how* something happened or was done. After prereading, you should write down questions about the selection based on the 5 W's and H. After reading the selection, you then answer these questions, rereading the text as needed to confirm your answers.

3. **K-W-L.** With K-W-L , you can improve your comprehension of many types of literature. It involves activities you can do *before* and *after* you read. **K** stands for what you already know about the article. **W** refers to what you want to know about the article. **L** stands for what you learned from the article. Discussing and writing down your K-W-L thoughts will help you remember what you read.

4. **Think-Alouds.** With think-alouds, you talk to yourself and ask questions while you are reading a selection. In this way, you can think about and understand the ideas better. You can also form thoughts and questions and write them down as you are reading. As a result, you are starting to learn and retain what you are reading.

5. **Semantic Map.** In format, a semantic map for comprehension is similar to the one you learned about under *Vocabulary (Word Meaning)*. Since it represents ideas visually, it can help you remember what you have read. To summarize what you have learned in a reading selection, create a semantic map of the main ideas and supporting details in the article. Then use it for recalling and reviewing what you have read.

6. **Split-Half Sheets.** With a split-half sheet, you can review the main ideas and facts in a reading selection. Fold a sheet of paper in half lengthwise. On the left side of the sheet, write the questions you wrote based on the 5 W's and H and K-W-L. On the right side of the sheet, write the answers to each question in your own words. Review the reading selection to check your answers. Then fold back the answer side of the sheet so you cannot see the answers. Then read the questions only and answer as many you can. Place a check besides the questions you got right, and review the ones you missed until you can answer them correctly.

7. **Make Your Own Tests.** You will read more effectively if you make your own tests. After you complete a reading selection, work in a small group to develop practice tests based on the reading. You can develop true/false statements, multiple-choice questions, short answer, or essay questions. The teacher will collect the best test questions and include them in a comprehensive test on the reading selection.

ANALYSIS OF LITERATURE

Here are some suggested games and activities:

1. **A Book a Day.** Reading books often is one of the best ways to develop an understanding and appreciation for literature. The teacher and/or the students choose a book to read in one day. They rip the book apart into sections of 1-2 chapters. Students then divide into groups of two or four. They read their section, take notes on the key ideas, and discuss what they read. Then each group draws pictures and words based on the characters, setting, and events in the section. Finally, the teacher reviews the entire book with the class with each group explaining their section of the book.

2. **Poetry Gallery.** The teacher posts 10-20 short to medium-length poems around the room. As the students enter the classroom, they are told to take out their notebooks and walk through the poetry gallery. As they read each poem, they would decide on the one they like the best and the one they dislike the most. They would copy these poems into their notebooks and answer these questions: *What did you like or dislike about the poem? Describe what is happening in the poem. List a few examples of figurative language. Is there a theme or message the poem is trying to convey? Does this poem have any special meaning for your life? Why? With whom would you share this poem? Why?*

3. **Anticipation Guide.** The teacher distributes a handout with a short excerpt from a work of literature. The author's name and the title of the work are omitted. The teacher or a student reads the selection aloud while the students follow along from the handout. For 10-15 minutes, the students then write their impressions of the author and the work. They should include what we can learn about the author's values and beliefs from the selection. Students then share their impressions with the class. The teacher then shares the name of the author and his/her background and the title of the work with the class. Students reread the selection and discuss if their impressions changed as a result of the additional information.

    Variation. Students can read the same selection or a new selection and write their impressions of the aesthetic qualities of the work. These qualities include style, diction, figurative language, plot, character, tone, theme, and impact on the reader. They share their impressions and the teacher then provides additional information about the aesthetic qualities of the work.

4. **Class Newspaper.** This project can help you understand the setting, historical background, author's values and beliefs, and the various cultural influences on a work of literature. For example, after reading *The Outsiders*, students would create a daily city newspaper from the early 1960's. The articles would contain eyewitness accounts of events in the book as well as ads, town announcements, editorials, and other parts of a newspaper from that time. Students work together in groups to revise their articles and create a compete newspaper edition.

Variation: Instead of a newspaper, students can create an early 1960's radio or television news show and include similar features as well as television commercials from that time. Students could also try a talk show format from the early 1960's. The teacher and students can choose other works of literature for these types of projects as well.

5. **Point of View.** After reading a work of literature, students write a brief description of the narrator and explain how the story reflects his/her perspective of the characters and events. Identify also the point of view. Then students retell the story from another character's point of view. How does this new perspective change the story? Is it an advantage or disadvantage?

6. **Concept Cards.** You can use concept cards to help you retain key ideas, facts, and definitions about literature. Concept cards are usually 3 x 5 or 5 x 8 index cards. On the front of the card, you write the concept or term you are learning. On the back of the card, you write a definition with an example from literature. Review these cards to reinforce your understanding of literary analysis.

APPENDIX C: STRATEGIES FOR ENGLISH LANGUAGE DEVELOPMENT STUDENTS

1. **Literature Diagrams.** To simplify understanding of a work of literature, create a summary of a literary work on a sheet of paper. Use various sizes of boxes for the basic diagram. In the middle of the sheet, write the title and author of the selection. In the upper left corner of the sheet, list the main characters. In the upper right corner of the paper, include the **setting** (where and when the story takes place). Underneath the title of the selection, explain the main conflicts in the literary work. On the bottom third of the paper, draw three boxes labeled Beginning, Middle, and End. Then list the key events in the literary work in each box. Draw lines connecting the boxes together.

2. **Plot Timeline.** The purpose of a plot timeline is to create a visual sequence and display of the important events in a literary work. Draw a horizontal line across a sheet of paper. Then add equidistant intersecting vertical lines across the horizontal line. Starting from the beginning of the story on the left side of the page, use words below the horizontal line and pictures above the horizontal line to describe the sequence of events in the story. The sequence of events would end on the right side of the paper. Students can then explain the sequence of events to the class or teacher.

3. **Question Journal.** Journals can be helpful tools for learning about literature. To improve your understanding of a work of literature, keep a daily journal of questions and comments you write as you are reading. Share those questions and comments in class with your teacher or with other students. Seek their feedback for better understanding of what you are reading.

4. **Character Portrait.** The purpose of a character portrait is to think more deeply about a character and the events that affect this character. Students do not have to be great artists to do this activity. They are simply trying to explain what they know in a more visual way. On a sheet of paper, students draw and can color a portrait of the head and neck of a character in a story they are reading. They cut out the portrait and then attach it with a staple to the top of another sheet of paper. Students then lift the portrait. On the other side of the portrait, they draw and write about the main thoughts of the character in significant parts of the story. Finally, they share their portraits with the class or teacher.

5. **Word Boards.** You can create word boards from poster board or long sheets of butcher paper. On these boards, the teacher and the students write down words that are important or confusing from an article or work of literature they are reading. While they are reading a section of their assignment, the students and teacher can discuss and clarify the meanings of these words and how they relate to their reading assignment. New words can be added and explained as the reading assignment progresses.

6. **Graphic Organizers.** Graphic organizers offer a very visual and concrete way to analyze what you are reading. You can use them to summarize and explain fiction and nonfiction. Basically, you connect boxes or circles on a sheet of paper. Inside these boxes or circles, you write the key words and ideas with the supporting facts and details. Ask your teacher to demonstrate these helpful learning tools.

7. **Brown Bag Review.** After reading an article or other work of literature, students divide into small groups. Each group receives a paper bag with several objects from the reading assignment in it. For example, after reading *House on Mango Street*, students would find a red balloon, a paper lunch sack, and a miniature yellow sports car. Within each group, the students discuss the significance of each object. Each group has different objects from the reading selection. The teacher then writes the name of each object on the board. The leader of each group would then write the explanation for each object on the board. Students then choose the one object that represents them the best. They should also explain why it is important to them.

8. **Nerf Ball Quiz.** To review elements of literature, the student tosses a nerf ball to one student who will then have to define the vocabulary word. If the word is defined correctly, the student can toss the ball to another student who is asked to explain another vocabulary word. If a student misses a word, he/she loses a turn. The game continues until all the words are reviewed.

   Variation: The Nerf BallQuiz can also be used for true/false and multiple-choice questions. The teacher can also present a short quotation from a literary work, and the student must name the literary device.

9. **Videos.** Viewing a video of a work of literature can increase understanding, particularly when the characters and setting are unfamiliar to most students. Even viewing scenes from a video can be helpful. The pictures, sounds, and words work well together to clarify literary elements and the sequence of events.

COMPUTER RESEARCH

As you read in Chapter 8, "Using and Choosing Reference Sources," both software programs and the Internet have become vital sources for research. One drawback to using the Internet is that there is a overwhelming amount of information available on almost any subject imaginable. It takes some practice and a new set of research skills to find accurate and reliable information on the Web.

Software programs are in some ways a better tool for the beginning researcher. The programs are usually specific to a certain field of study, such as history, arts, or science. There are also general knowledge software products which have information on them like you would find in an encyclopedia.

The Internet offers not only text, but also images and sounds to complement the written materials. The following repeats information used in Chapter 8 to introduce some of the concepts needed in research on the Internet.

Using the Internet can challenge your research skills. First, you must decide which **key words** to use and how to frame them in the search mode to find the material you want, instead of a lot of marketing sites or opinion based information. In addition, you must access various **search engines** such as Google, Yahoo, or Lycos to find the best Web sites about your topic. Then, you must **validate** the material, checking the site for its credibility or the material for accuracy. Next, you must decide how best to use the material and if it is the **appropriate** source for your particular topic. Read at least the first two paragraphs of a passage before printing. This should give you an idea of its tone, its supporting research, and often an overview of its contents. Last, but perhaps most important, is the skill of **safe research** on the information highway.

There are some basic guidelines to follow that you may have heard before. These guidelines will be briefly noted at the end of the Internet material. This Internet research section will consist of Web page examples.

Research Keywords

Keywords are tools for searching to find the most useful sites in the shortest amount of time in a database. These key words are arranged with different directional words for broadening a search that is too narrow or narrowing one that is too broad.

1) Make a list of words that best describe what you are looking for in a site. The beginning list should include words that you would use in describing the topic to a friend. Use those words for a first search.

2) Next, make a list of synonyms for the words you have. This will give you ways to narrow your topic later.

3) Try using both the singular and plural forms of the search words for your topic.

4) Be careful how you use abbreviations and numerals, such as in WWII. Also, check the spelling, hyphens, and spacing of your keywords before you click on the search button.

5) Use methods of searching, like the Boolean Method, using the words "**AND, OR, NOT**" to either expand or restrict your search. You may also use quotation marks or the plus sign to refine a search. Many search engines such as Google do not need for you to use the Boolean Method, but smaller inter-site searches may still benefit from your using this method of keyword listing.

Validation: Checking Sources

Why should you bother with validating sources? After all, if you can find material on a Web site it must be OK, right? No, not always. Many Web sites are created by students and ordinary citizens, who may believe what they have posted is true, but are mistaken in that belief: "Let the searcher beware!" Researchers protect their work by screening the material they find for quality and accuracy.

• Find two or more sources that agree with the information that you wish to use.

• Read material carefully, watching for any bias or particularly strong opinion expressed in it.

• Look at the URL for the source of the material. It should name an organization or individual. If the organization is an educational, government, or professional center the material is probably valid.

• Look for "links" within the text of a Web site; these are an indication of a serious, validated work (they're like footnotes in a book). Go to some of the linked sites to check the accuracy of the source, as well as to find additional material.

• Look at the homepage of the source for other related works by the author of the site. The more the author has published on a topic, the more trustworthy the material.

• Check the date on the material. Obviously if your topic is on a current event, the more recent the date, the better the information. Less urgent, but still valid, is the point that recent data and theories are valuable for any topic.

• If you are using informal sources, such as chat rooms, for clustering or sharing ideas, again, the information needs to be confirmed by two or more other sources before it is validated.

Some sites on the Internet have been validated already. These are **database sites**. The organization which creates the database checks the material it offers to ensure both accuracy and relevancy. Information is generally found quickly in a database. Many databases are offered through educational organizations and are free to all. Using databases is not only a quick way to find information but it's also a way to make sure that material you find is appropriate and credible. One word of caution, **plagiarism** or copying directly from a source is a serious offense; be sure to always cite your Internet sources. If you want to use a reproduction of material, as on this page, get written permission from the Web site owner to use it.

On the following pages, you will find three examples of Web pages, each showing a different structure and focus for a Web search of "fossils." Notice the focus of the pages, and decide which would be the most appropriate source of information in a Web search for fossils.

Notice the name of the organization that has established this Web site. If you scan the page, you see that this is an advertisement. While it is an attractive and well-formatted site, you see there is no educational material here. That is part of the drawback in using the Internet; it serves so many purposes, and they are not always clear at first glance. Validation for this example is simple; it is not an appropriate or relevant source for scholarly research.

The Web site on the next page is an example of a site that has relevant information but lacks the background of serious educational focus. It is well-written and attractive in structure. The facts may be accurate but should be double-checked against other sources before being used.

Page 1 of 3 in this site has name of topic and information for topic.

Middle pages of this Web site have <u>scientific information</u>, linking to an essay about the history of the Jurassic era. There is also a photo gallery of the dinosaur's discovery.

Last page has update information and contact information for the <u>commercial use</u> of the site.

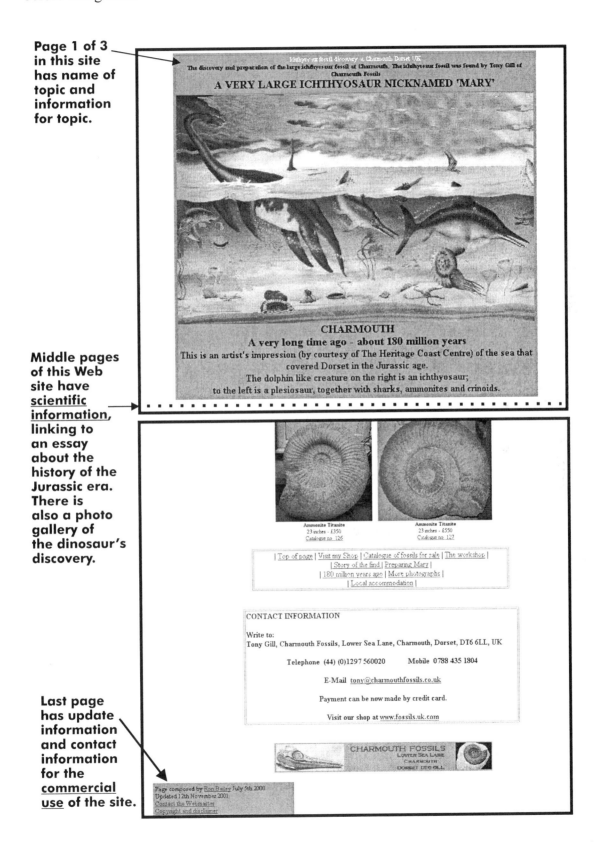

The next example is of a printed Web page. The information that is needed to validate the material is labeled.

Name of organization creating the Web site and the topic

Page count

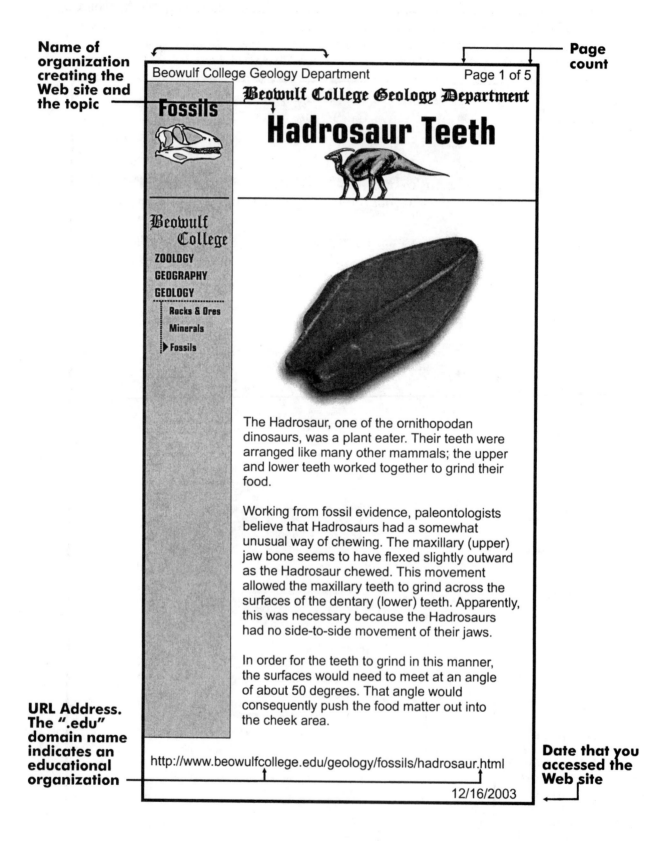

Beowulf College Geology Department   Page 1 of 5

Beowulf College Geology Department

Hadrosaur Teeth

Fossils

Beowulf College

ZOOLOGY
GEOGRAPHY
GEOLOGY
  Rocks & Ores
  Minerals
  Fossils

The Hadrosaur, one of the ornithopodan dinosaurs, was a plant eater. Their teeth were arranged like many other mammals; the upper and lower teeth worked together to grind their food.

Working from fossil evidence, paleontologists believe that Hadrosaurs had a somewhat unusual way of chewing. The maxillary (upper) jaw bone seems to have flexed slightly outward as the Hadrosaur chewed. This movement allowed the maxillary teeth to grind across the surfaces of the dentary (lower) teeth. Apparently, this was necessary because the Hadrosaurs had no side-to-side movement of their jaws.

In order for the teeth to grind in this manner, the surfaces would need to meet at an angle of about 50 degrees. That angle would consequently push the food matter out into the cheek area.

http://www.beowulfcollege.edu/geology/fossils/hadrosaur.html

12/16/2003

URL Address. The ".edu" domain name indicates an educational organization

Date that you accessed the Web site

A-22

The name of the author or organization and the date when the site was updated (modified) can usually be found on the last page of the material:

> ABOUT // CALENDAR // PLACES // RESOURCES // MARKETPLACE // LINKS //
> <http://www.ohiohistory.org/about/index.html> Last modified Friday, 10-Nov-2000 15:43 EST
> **Ohio Historical Society** - 1982 Velma Ave. - Columbus, OH 43211© 1996-2001 All Rights Reserved

Safety

The use of the Internet, without special "safe" servers is basically unregulated and unguarded. This situation brings up concerns over credibility, safety, and privacy issues. The following is an informal listing of ways to make your Internet use as safe and as positive as possible.

- Develop a <u>healthy distrust</u> of much of what you read on the Web. Databases are usually OK, but chat rooms and personal Web sites are open to all sorts of deceptions and second class information, causing frustrating detours for you.

- Always use a very different name on the Internet and understand that others are doing the same as a safeguard or as a false identity.

- Make sure that you understand and follow the expectations that your school, library, or home has about the way the Internet is to be used.

- Understand that some sites have built-in roadblocks; there is no way for you to exit the site. Should you run into this trap, disconnect from your Internet server, then sign on again. You will also want to alert your teacher or the webmaster to the problem.

- Watch out for anyone on-line asking you personal questions. This is a flashing red stoplight. Do not respond to those questions and exit that site.